BBC

DOCTOR WHO

THE TENTH DOCTOR

VOL 5: ARENA OF FEAR

"Abadzis is firing on some heavy-duty imaginative cylinders!"
WARPED FACTOR

"One of the best stories to be told via the comic book medium."
SNAP POW

"The artwork remains the high quality stuff we've come to expect. The characters come to life wonderfully. Titan Comics has taken the Doctor to places we've not seen from anyone else."
READING WITH A FLIGHT RING

"Go buy this!"
COMICS VERSE

"The best of Titan Comics' slate of *Doctor Who* comics."
GIANT FREAKING ROBOT

"Has it all: great character work, an intriguing mystery, and a
THE FANDOM POST

"Perfectly captures the spirit of *Doctor Who!*"
KABOOOOOM!

"Fully embracing the spirit of the series, all Whovians will find themselves shouting, 'Allons-y!'"
NEWSARAMA

"A neat mystery with some fun visuals."
SCIFI PULSE

"This book is well done to the point that it feels like an episode that was misplaced. 5/5"
OUTRIGHT GEEKERY

"Injects a massive jolt of excitement and nostalgia. A blockbuster epic."
POP CULTURE BANDIT

"*Doctor Who* fans are well-served."
SOUNDS ON SIGHT

"The *Doctor Who* comic fans have always deserved."
BLOODY DISGUSTING

"If you've missed the skinny one with the sandshoes, then you'll enjoy this."
SCIFI BULLETIN

TITAN COMICS

SENIOR COMICS EDITOR
Andrew James

ASSISTANT EDITORS
Jessica Burton, Amoona Saohin

COLLECTION DESIGNER
Rob Farmer

TITAN COMICS EDITORIAL
Lizzie Kaye, Tom Williams

PRODUCTION SUPERVISORS
Maria Pearson, Jackie Flook

PRODUCTION MANAGER
Obi Onuora

STUDIO MANAGER
Emma Smith

SENIOR SALES MANAGER
Steve Tothill

SENIOR MARKETING & PRESS OFFICER
Owen Johnson

DIRECT SALES & MARKETING MANAGER
Ricky Claydon

COMMERCIAL MANAGER
Michelle Fairlamb

PUBLISHING MANAGER
Darryl Tothill

PUBLISHING DIRECTOR
Chris Teather

OPERATIONS DIRECTOR
Leigh Baulch

EXECUTIVE DIRECTOR
Vivian Cheung

PUBLISHER
Nick Landau

Special thanks to Steven Moffat, Brian Minchin, Mandy Thwaites, Matt Nicholls, James Dudley, Edward Russell, Derek Ritchie, Scott Handcock, Kirsty Mullan, Kate Bush, Julia Nocciolino and Ed Casey for their invaluable assistance.

BBC WORLDWIDE

DIRECTOR OF EDITORIAL GOVERNANCE
Nicholas Brett

DIRECTOR OF CONSUMER PRODUCTS AND PUBLISHING
Andrew Moultrie

HEAD OF UK PUBLISHING
Chris Kerwin

PUBLISHER
Mandy Thwaites

PUBLISHING CO-ORDINATOR
Eva Abramik

DOCTOR WHO: THE TENTH DOCTOR VOL 5: ARENA OF FEAR
HB ISBN: 9781785854286 SB ISBN: 9781785853227
Published by Titan Comics, a division of Titan Publishing Group, Ltd. 144 Southwark Street, London, SE1 0UP.

A CIP catalogue record for this title is available from the British Library.
First edition: August 2016.

10 9 8 7 6 5 4 3 2 1

Printed in China. TC1747

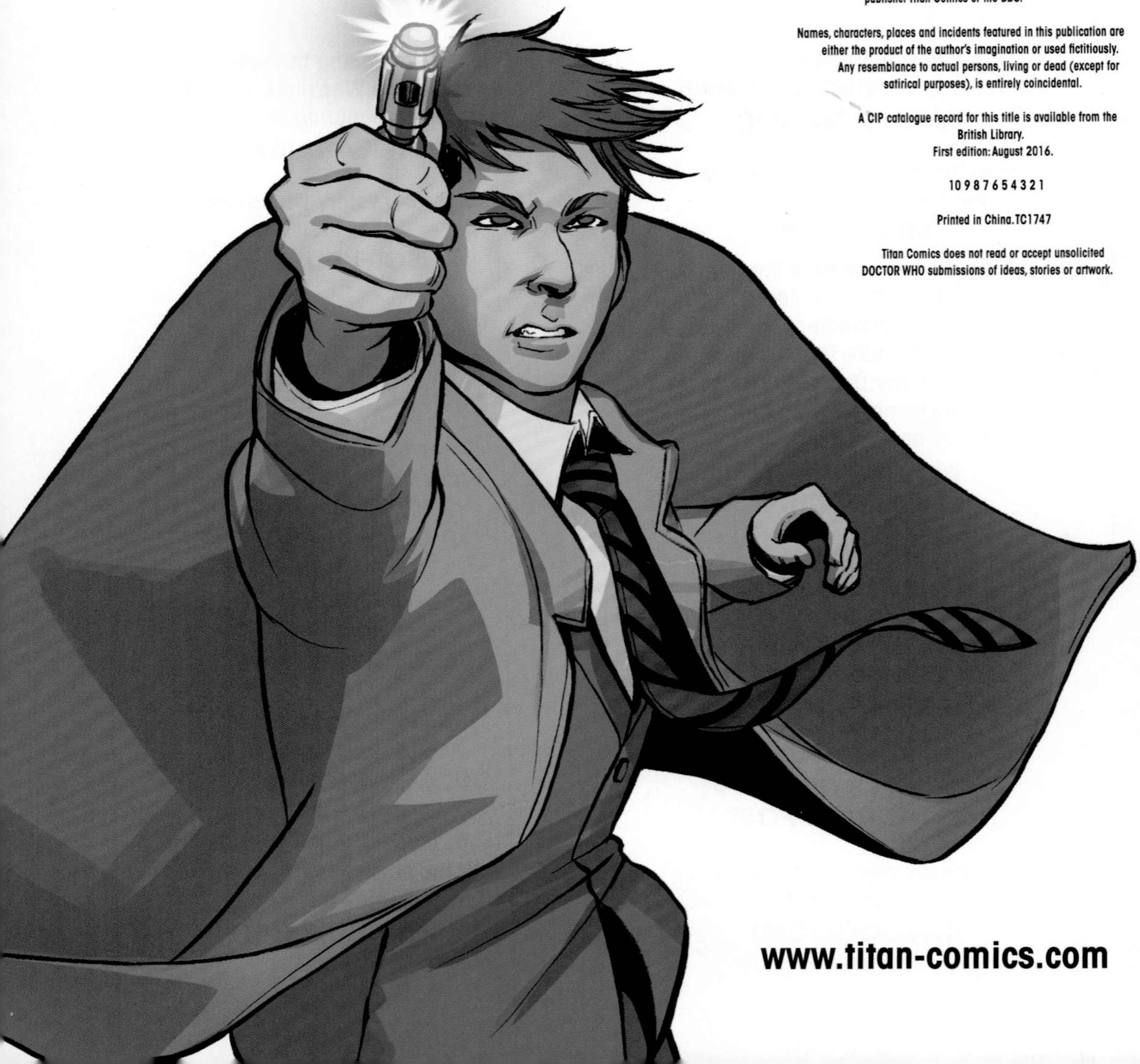

www.titan-comics.com

DOCTOR WHO
THE TENTH DOCTOR

VOL 5: ARENA OF FEAR

WRITER: NICK ABADZIS

**ARTISTS: ELEONORA CARLINI,
ELENA CASAGRANDE, IOLANDA ZANFARDINO**
WITH SIMONE DE MEO & LUCA MARESCA

**COLORISTS: ARIANNA FLOREAN,
ROD FERNANDES, & HI-FI**
WITH AZZURRA FLOREAN

**LETTERS: RICHARD STARKINGS AND
COMICRAFT'S JIMMY BETANCOURT**

BBC
DOCTOR WHO
THE TENTH DOCTOR

THE DOCTOR

An alien who walks like a man. Last of the Time Lords of Gallifrey. Never cruel or cowardly, he champions the oppressed across time and space. Forever traveling, the Doctor lives to see the universe anew through the eyes of his human companions!

GABBY GONZALEZ

Gabriella Gonzalez is a would-be artist, stuck working in her father's laundromat until she met the Doctor. Having impressed him with her courage and creativity during her first voyage through time and space, Gabby's very essence is about to be put in jeopardy!

CINDY WU

Gabby's fiercely loyal best friend, Cindy's biggest regret was declining the offer to travel in the TARDIS with the Doctor and Gabby. Now she has a second chance. She just wishes alien threats would stop ruining her vacation through time and space!

PREVIOUSLY...

The Doctor and Gabby arrived in ancient prehistory, only to be attacked by giant, sentient, flying metal discs, the Monaxi, which had been kidnapping groups of humans – Neanderthal and Sapiens alike – and pitting them against one another in a gladiatorial arena! With the help of a gang of intergalactic bounty hunters, the Doctor and Gabby attempted to put a stop to this cruel sport...But only succeeded in angering the enemy into creating a temporal tornado! What on (or off) Earth could be waiting for them on the other side?!

When you've finished reading this collection, please email your thoughts to doctorwhocomic@titanemail.com

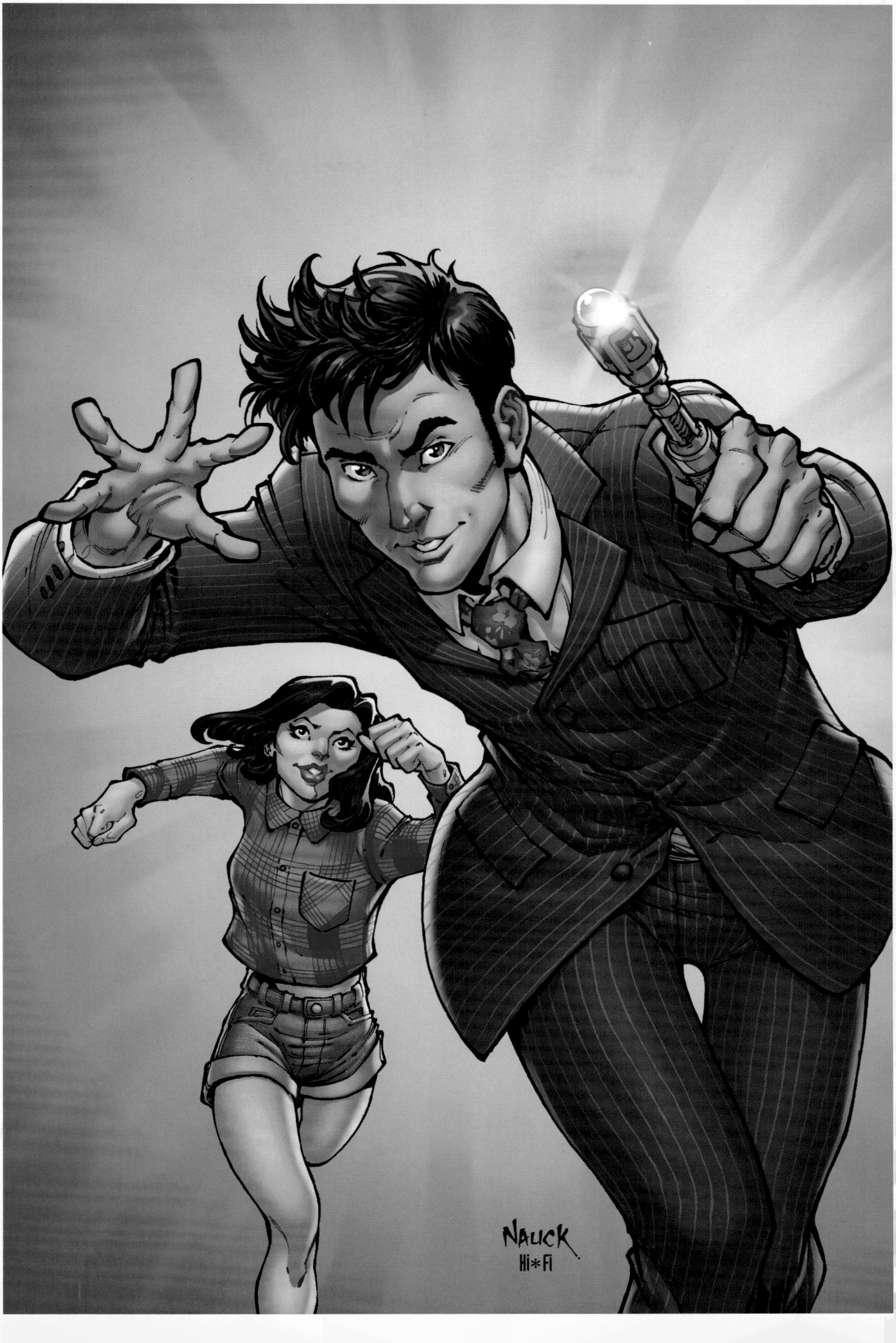
NAUCK
Hi*Fi

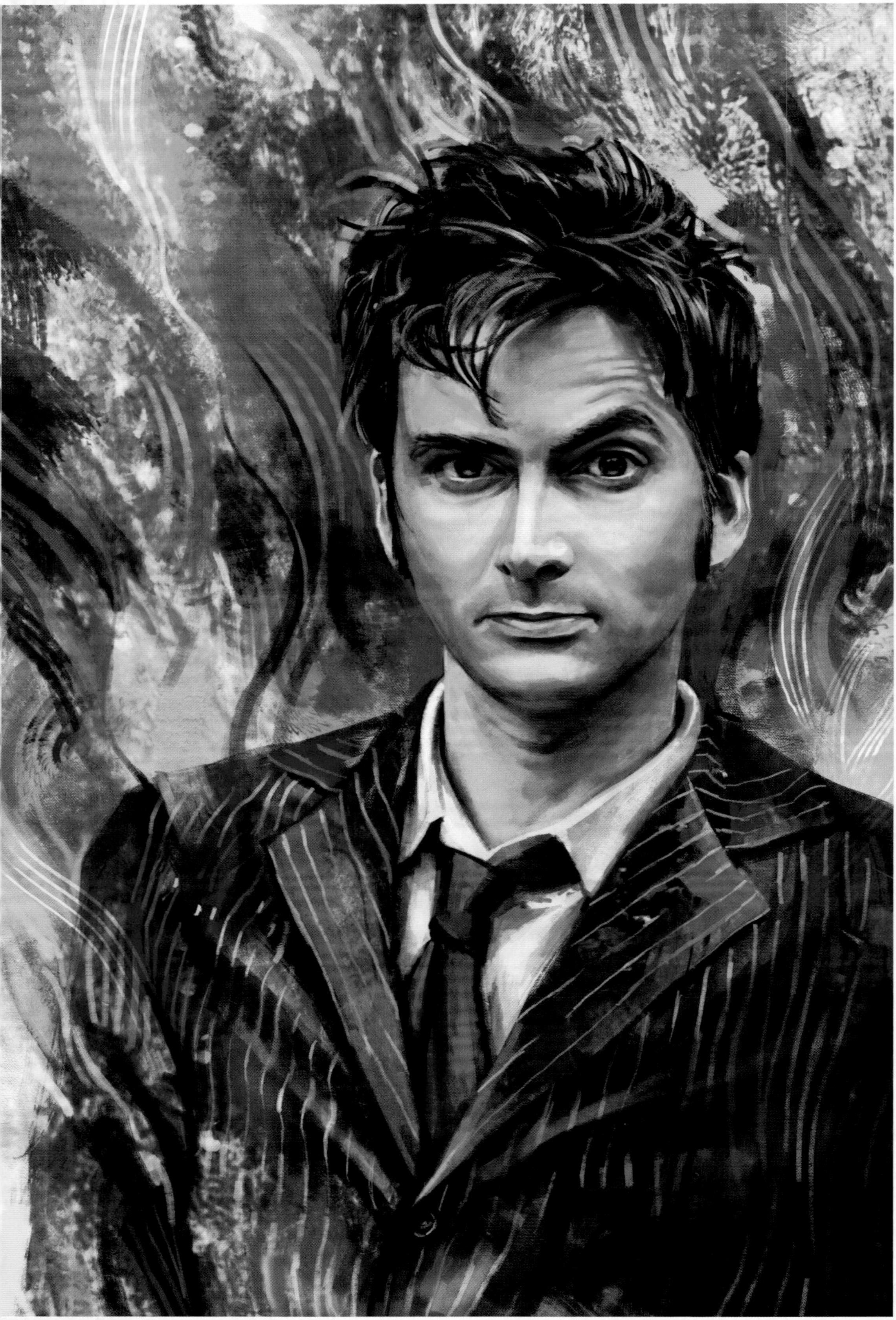

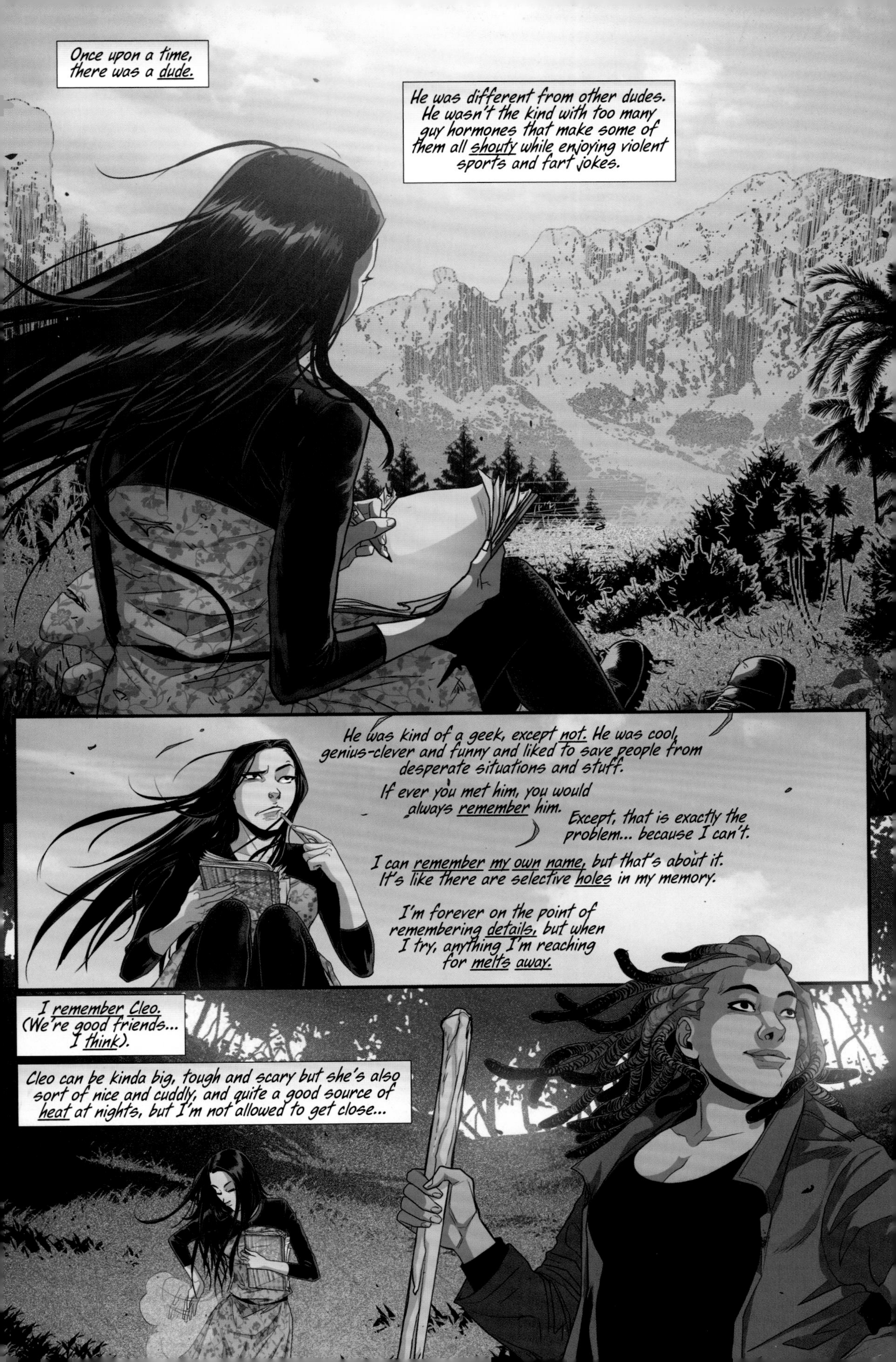
Once upon a time, there was a dude.
He was different from other dudes. He wasn't the kind with too many guy hormones that make some of them all shouty while enjoying violent sports and fart jokes.
He was kind of a geek, except not. He was cool, genius-clever and funny and liked to save people from desperate situations and stuff.
If ever you met him, you would always remember him.
Except, that is exactly the problem... because I can't.
I can remember my own name, but that's about it. It's like there are selective holes in my memory.
I'm forever on the point of remembering details, but when I try, anything I'm reaching for melts away.
I remember Cleo. (We're good friends... I think).
Cleo can be kinda big, tough and scary but she's also sort of nice and cuddly, and quite a good source of heat at nights, but I'm not allowed to get close...

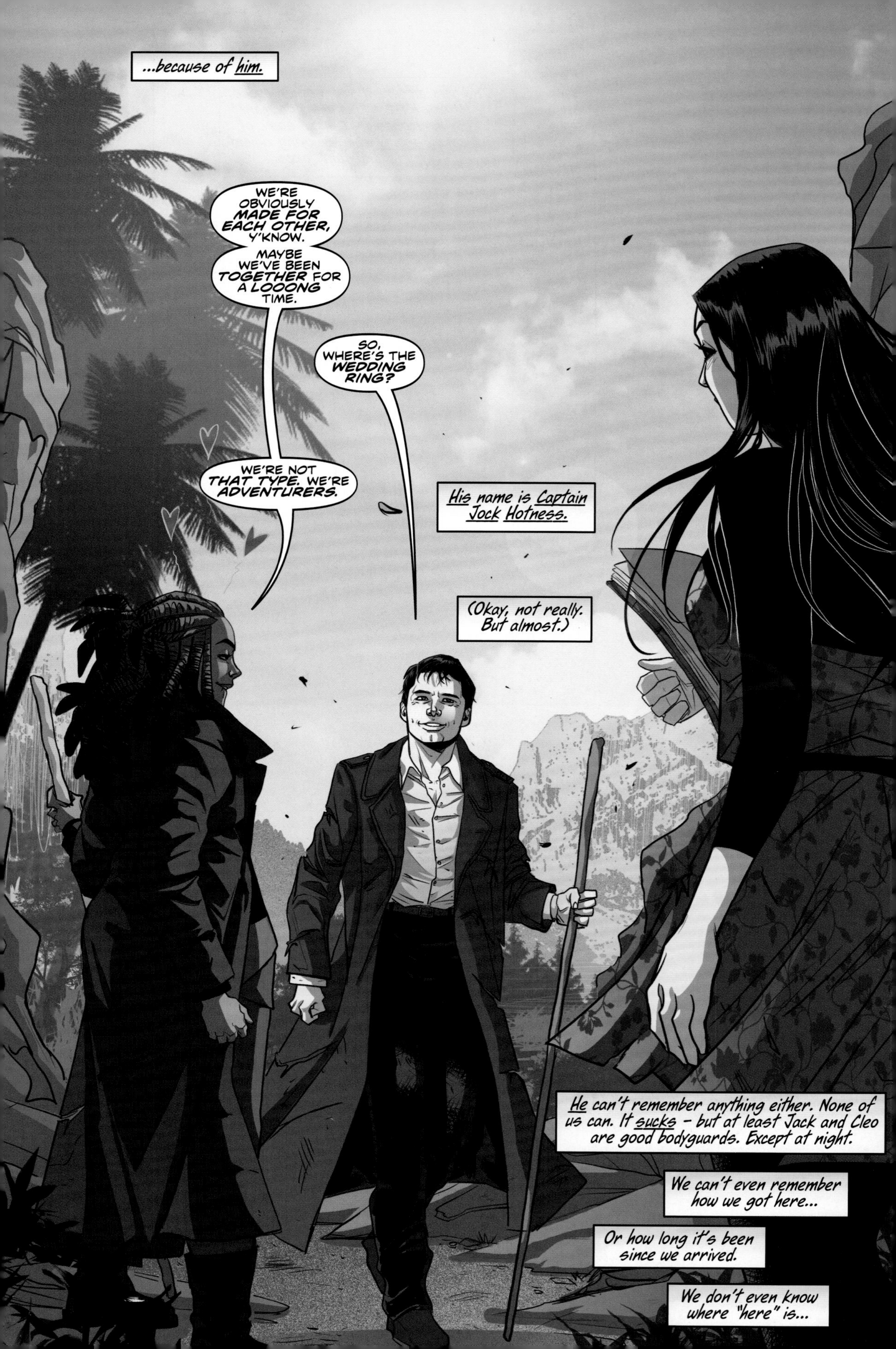
...because of him.
WE'RE OBVIOUSLY MADE FOR EACH OTHER, Y'KNOW.
MAYBE WE'VE BEEN TOGETHER FOR A LOOONG TIME.
SO, WHERE'S THE WEDDING RING?
WE'RE NOT THAT TYPE. WE'RE ADVENTURERS.
His name is Captain Jock Hotness.
(Okay, not really. But almost.)
He can't remember anything either. None of us can. It sucks - but at least Jack and Cleo are good bodyguards. Except at night.
We can't even remember how we got here...
Or how long it's been since we arrived.
We don't even know where "here" is...

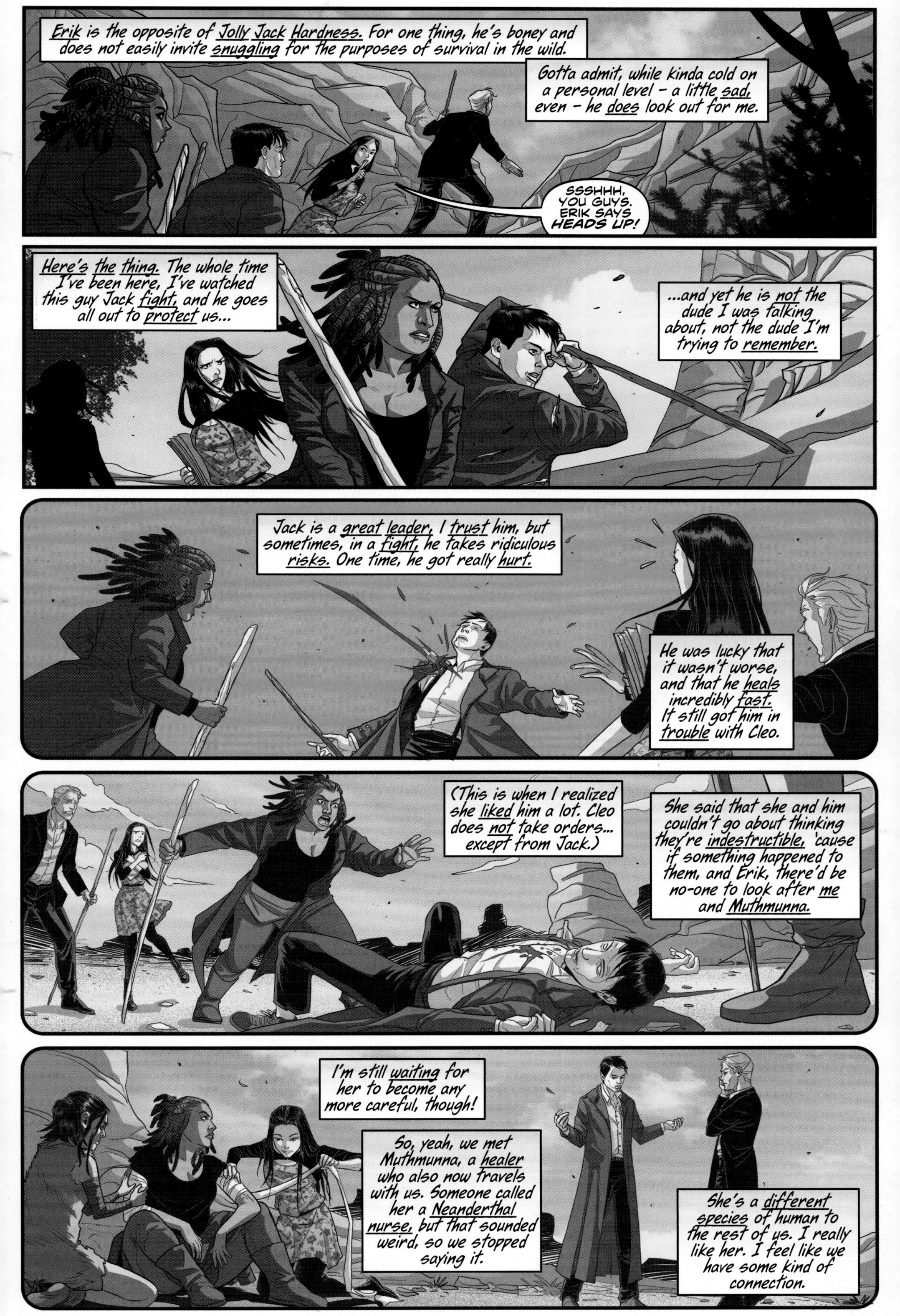
Erik is the opposite of Jolly Jack Hardness. For one thing, he's boney and does not easily invite snuggling for the purposes of survival in the wild.
Gotta admit, while kinda cold on a personal level – a little sad, even – he does look out for me.
SSSHHH, YOU GUYS. ERIK SAYS HEADS UP!
Here's the thing. The whole time I've been here, I've watched this guy Jack fight, and he goes all out to protect us...
...and yet he is not the dude I was talking about, not the dude I'm trying to remember.
Jack is a great leader, I trust him, but sometimes, in a fight, he takes ridiculous risks. One time, he got really hurt.
He was lucky that it wasn't worse, and that he heals incredibly fast. It still got him in trouble with Cleo.
(This is when I realized she liked him a lot. Cleo does not take orders... except from Jack.)
She said that she and him couldn't go about thinking they're indestructible, 'cause if something happened to them, and Erik, there'd be no-one to look after me and Muthmunna.
I'm still waiting for her to become any more careful, though!
So, yeah, we met Muthmunna, a healer who also now travels with us. Someone called her a Neanderthal nurse, but that sounded weird, so we stopped saying it.
She's a different species of human to the rest of us. I really like her. I feel like we have some kind of connection.

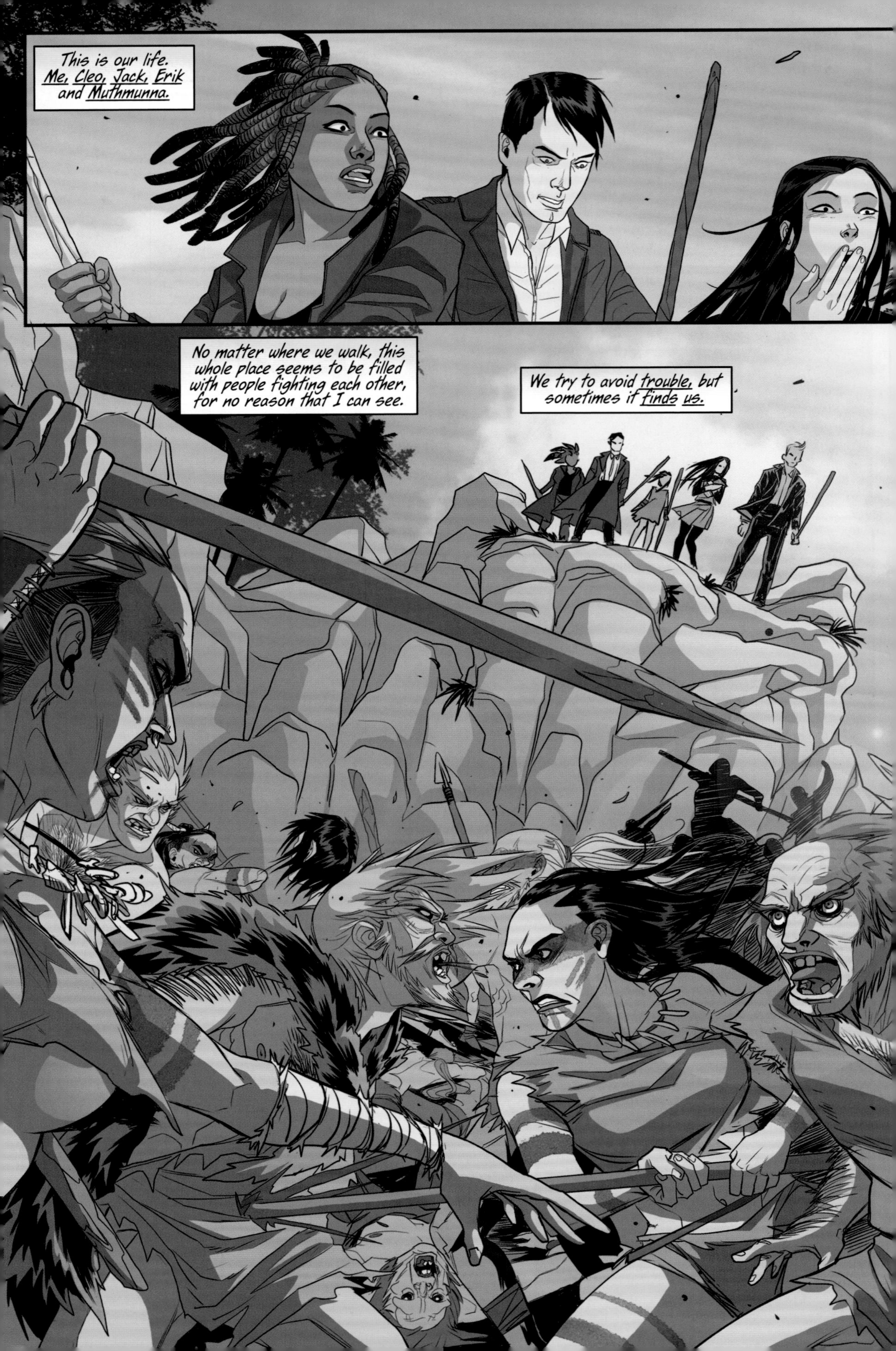

This is our life. Me, Cleo, Jack, Erik and Muthmunna.
No matter where we walk, this whole place seems to be filled with people fighting each other, for no reason that I can see.
We try to avoid trouble, but sometimes it finds us.

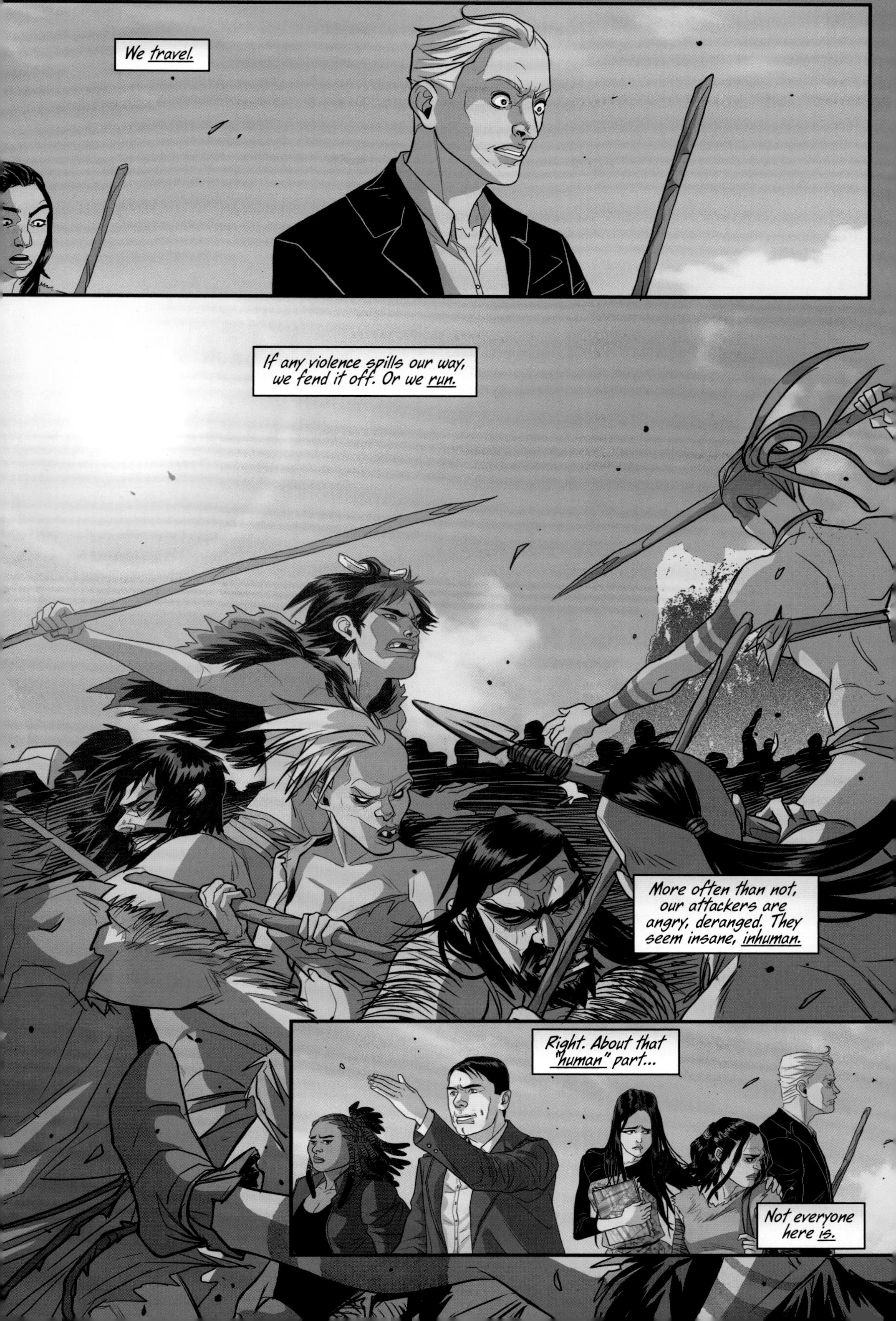
We travel.
If any violence spills our way, we fend it off. Or we run.
More often than not, our attackers are angry, deranged. They seem insane, inhuman.
Right. About that "human" part...
Not everyone here is.

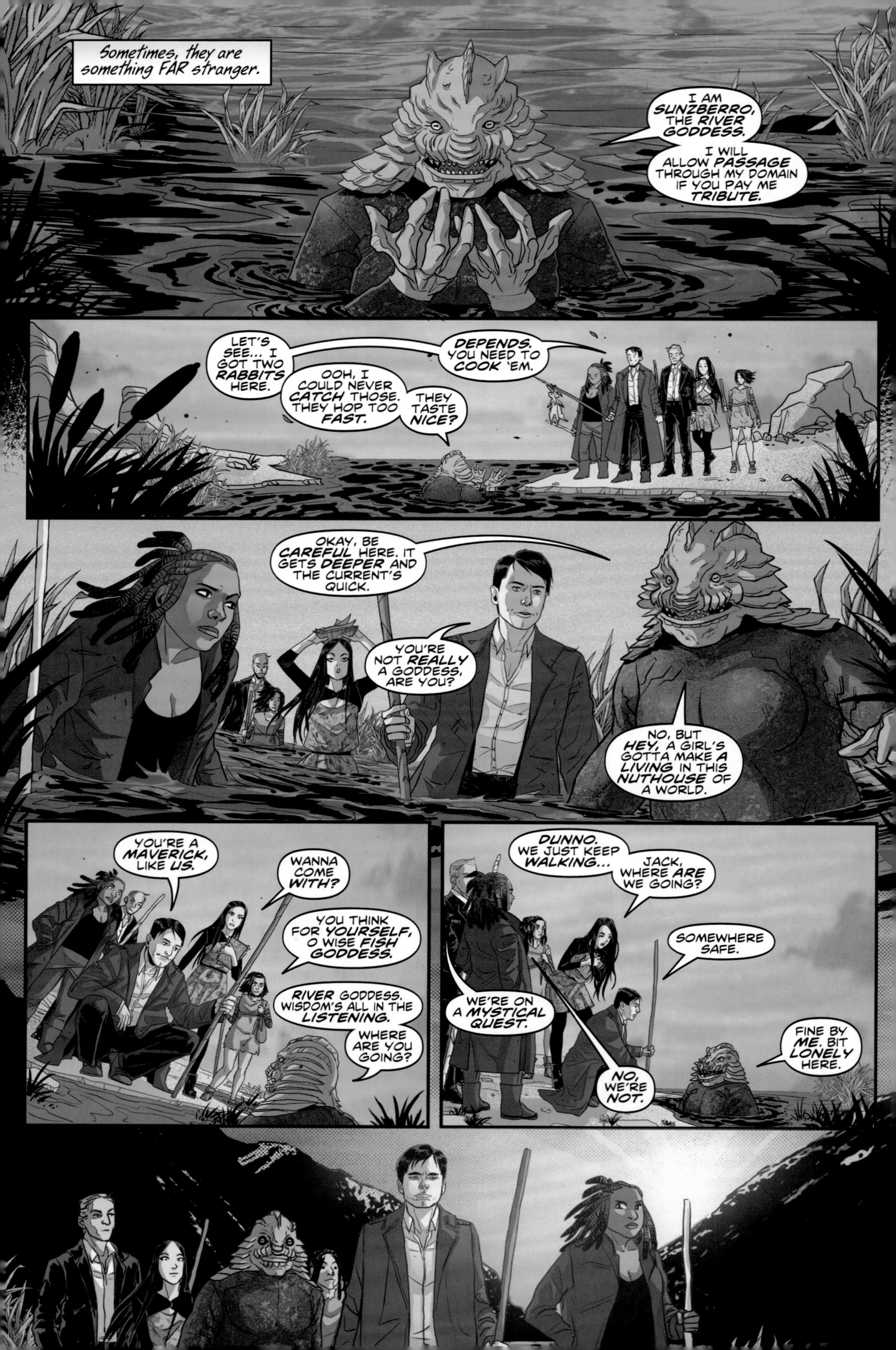
Sometimes, they are something FAR stranger.
I AM SUNZBERRO, THE RIVER GODDESS.
I WILL ALLOW PASSAGE THROUGH MY DOMAIN IF YOU PAY ME TRIBUTE.
LET'S SEE... I GOT TWO RABBITS HERE.
OOH, I COULD NEVER CATCH THOSE. THEY HOP TOO FAST.
THEY TASTE NICE?
DEPENDS. YOU NEED TO COOK 'EM.
OKAY, BE CAREFUL HERE. IT GETS DEEPER AND THE CURRENT'S QUICK.
YOU'RE NOT REALLY A GODDESS, ARE YOU?
NO, BUT HEY, A GIRL'S GOTTA MAKE A LIVING IN THIS NUTHOUSE OF A WORLD.
YOU'RE A MAVERICK, LIKE US.
WANNA COME WITH?
YOU THINK FOR YOURSELF, O WISE FISH GODDESS.
RIVER GODDESS. WISDOM'S ALL IN THE LISTENING.
WHERE ARE YOU GOING?
DUNNO. WE JUST KEEP WALKING...
JACK, WHERE ARE WE GOING?
SOMEWHERE SAFE.
WE'RE ON A MYSTICAL QUEST.
NO, WE'RE NOT.
FINE BY ME. BIT LONELY HERE.

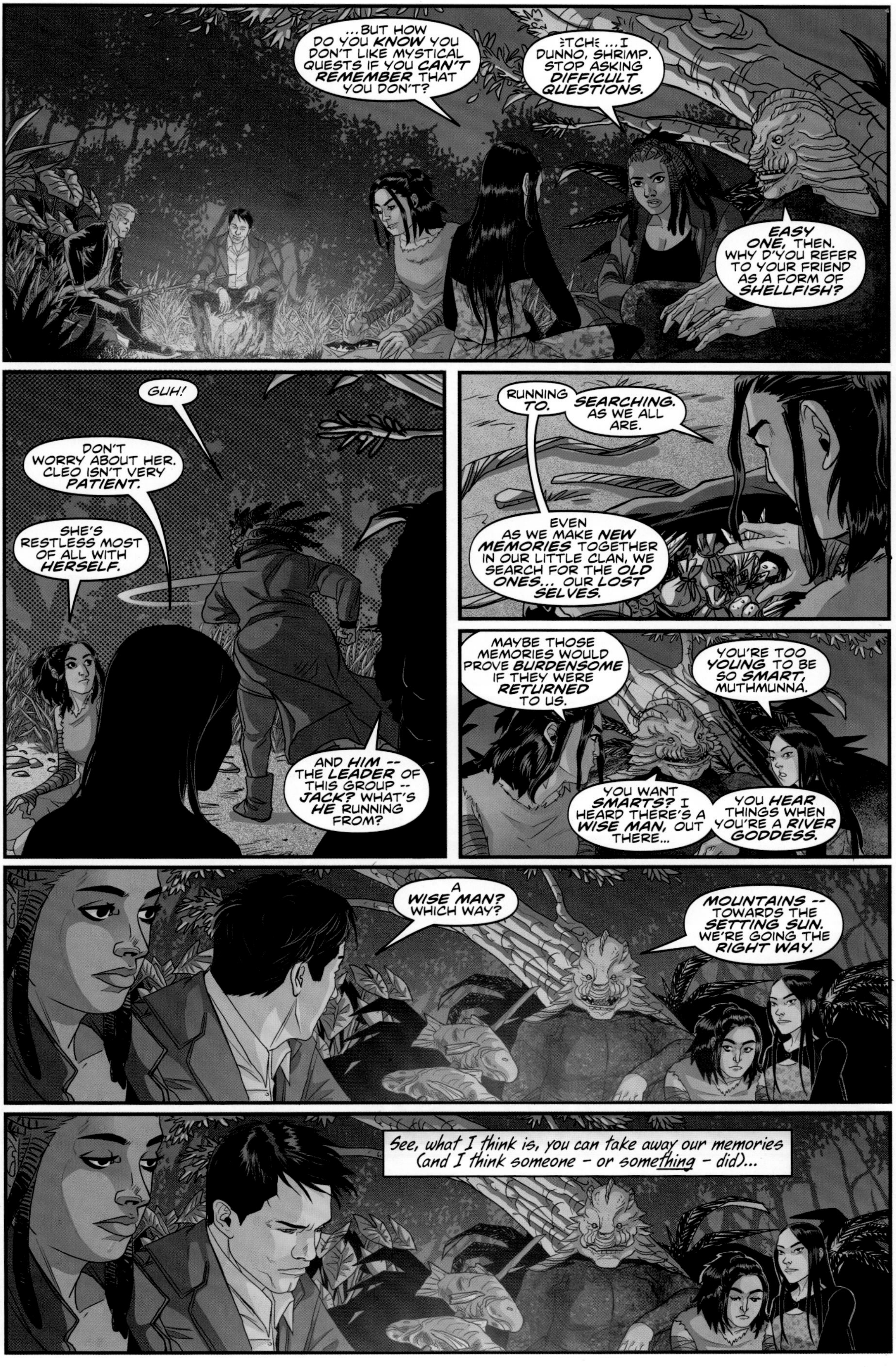
...BUT HOW DO YOU KNOW YOU DON'T LIKE MYSTICAL QUESTS IF YOU CAN'T REMEMBER THAT YOU DON'T?
TCH! ...I DUNNO, SHRIMP. STOP ASKING DIFFICULT QUESTIONS.
EASY ONE, THEN. WHY D'YOU REFER TO YOUR FRIEND AS A FORM OF SHELLFISH?
GUH!
DON'T WORRY ABOUT HER. CLEO ISN'T VERY PATIENT.
SHE'S RESTLESS MOST OF ALL WITH HERSELF.
AND HIM -- THE LEADER OF THIS GROUP -- JACK? WHAT'S HE RUNNING FROM?
RUNNING TO.
SEARCHING. AS WE ALL ARE.
EVEN AS WE MAKE NEW MEMORIES TOGETHER IN OUR LITTLE CLAN, WE SEARCH FOR THE OLD ONES... OUR LOST SELVES.
MAYBE THOSE MEMORIES WOULD PROVE BURDENSOME IF THEY WERE RETURNED TO US.
YOU'RE TOO YOUNG TO BE SO SMART, MUTHMUNNA.
YOU WANT SMARTS? I HEARD THERE'S A WISE MAN, OUT THERE...
YOU HEAR THINGS WHEN YOU'RE A RIVER GODDESS.
A WISE MAN? WHICH WAY?
MOUNTAINS -- TOWARDS THE SETTING SUN. WE'RE GOING THE RIGHT WAY.
See, what I think is, you can take away our memories (and I think someone - or something - did)...

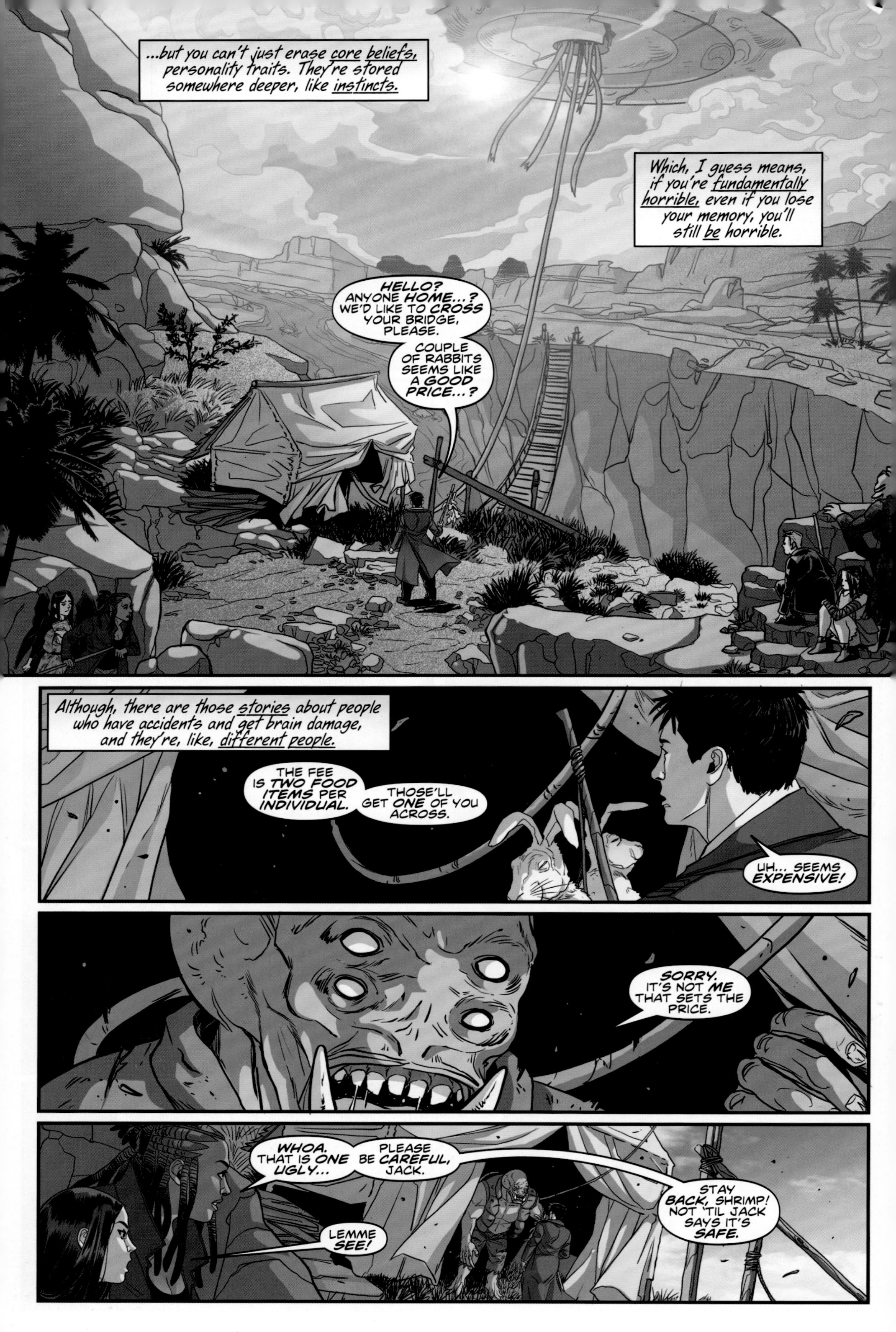
...but you can't just erase core beliefs, personality traits. They're stored somewhere deeper, like instincts.
Which, I guess means, if you're fundamentally horrible, even if you lose your memory, you'll still be horrible.
HELLO? ANYONE HOME...? WE'D LIKE TO CROSS YOUR BRIDGE, PLEASE.
COUPLE OF RABBITS SEEMS LIKE A GOOD PRICE...?
Although, there are those stories about people who have accidents and get brain damage, and they're, like, different people.
THE FEE IS TWO FOOD ITEMS PER INDIVIDUAL.
THOSE'LL GET ONE OF YOU ACROSS.
UH... SEEMS EXPENSIVE!
SORRY. IT'S NOT ME THAT SETS THE PRICE.
WHOA. THAT IS ONE UGLY...
PLEASE BE CAREFUL, JACK.
STAY BACK, SHRIMP! NOT 'TIL JACK SAYS IT'S SAFE.
LEMME SEE!

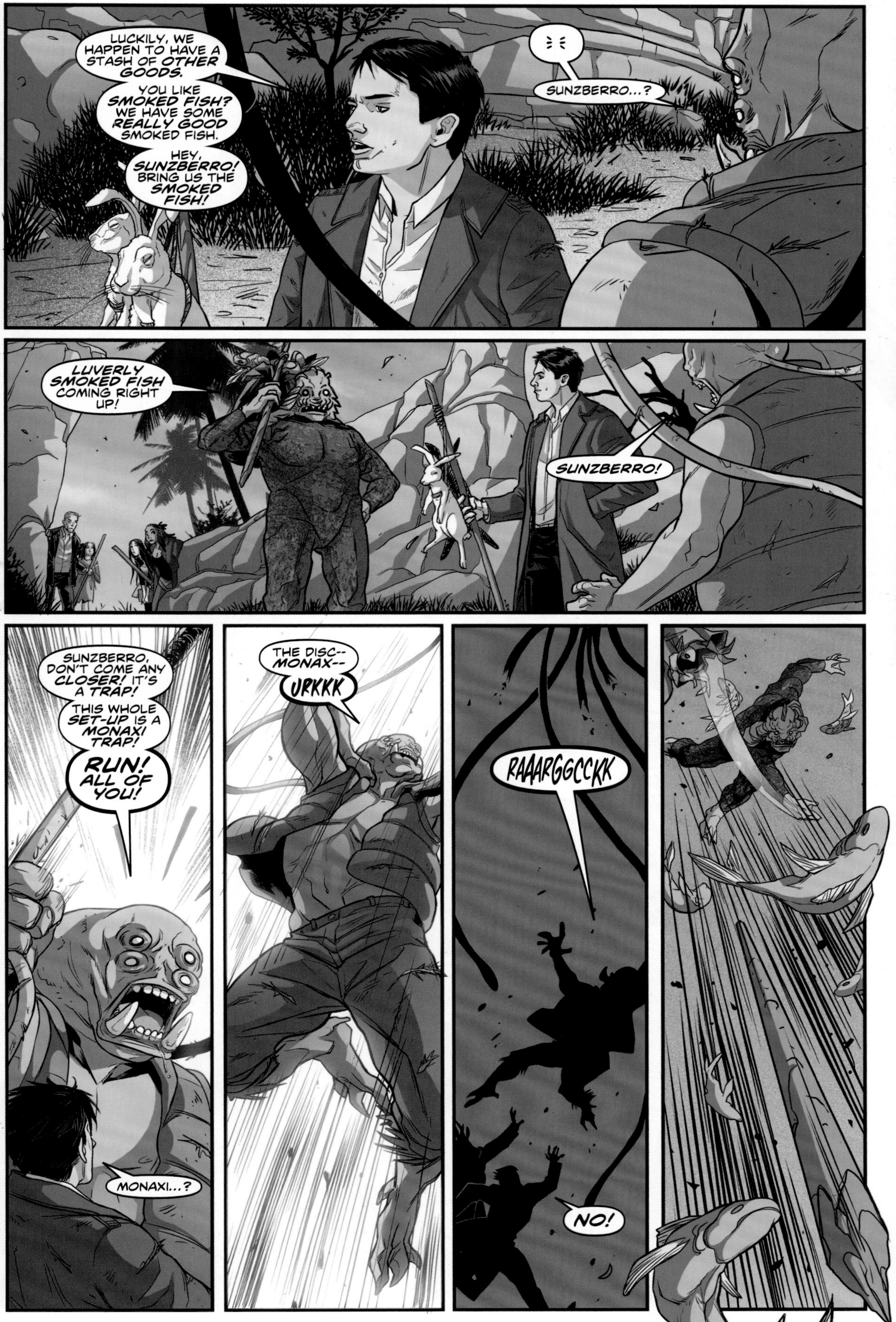
LUCKILY, WE HAPPEN TO HAVE A STASH OF OTHER GOODS.
YOU LIKE SMOKED FISH? WE HAVE SOME REALLY GOOD SMOKED FISH.
HEY, SUNZBERRO! BRING US THE SMOKED FISH!
...
SUNZBERRO...?
LUVERLY SMOKED FISH COMING RIGHT UP!
SUNZBERRO!
SUNZBERRO, DON'T COME ANY CLOSER! IT'S A TRAP!
THIS WHOLE SET-UP IS A MONAXI TRAP!
RUN! ALL OF YOU!
MONAXI...?
THE DISC-- MONAX--
URKKK
RAAARGGCCKK
NO!

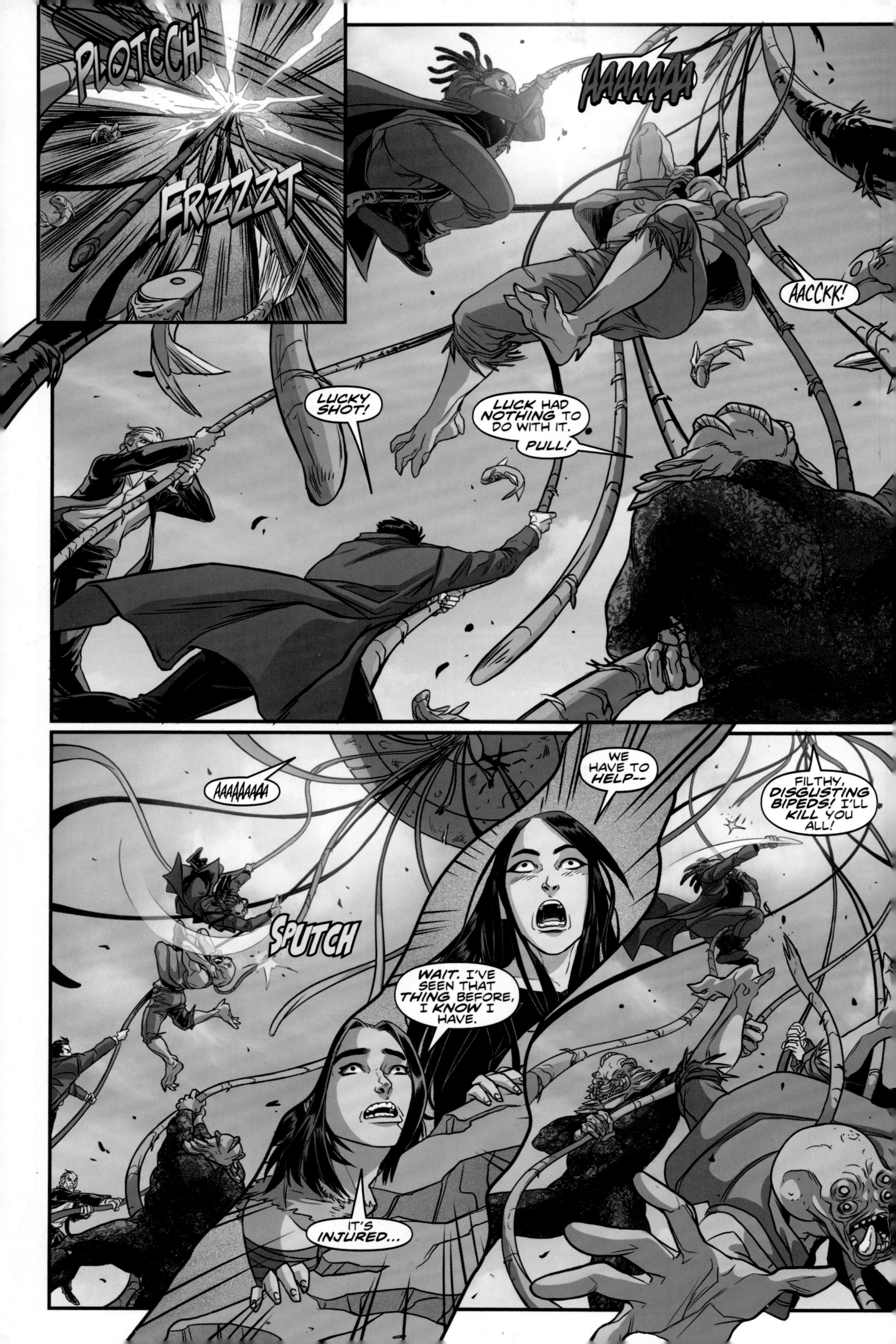
PLOTCCH
FRZZZT
AAAAAAA
AACCKK!
LUCKY SHOT!
LUCK HAD NOTHING TO DO WITH IT.
PULL!
AAAAAAAA
WE HAVE TO HELP--
FILTHY, DISGUSTING BIPEDS! I'LL KILL YOU ALL!
SPUTCH
WAIT. I'VE SEEN THAT THING BEFORE, I KNOW I HAVE.
IT'S INJURED...

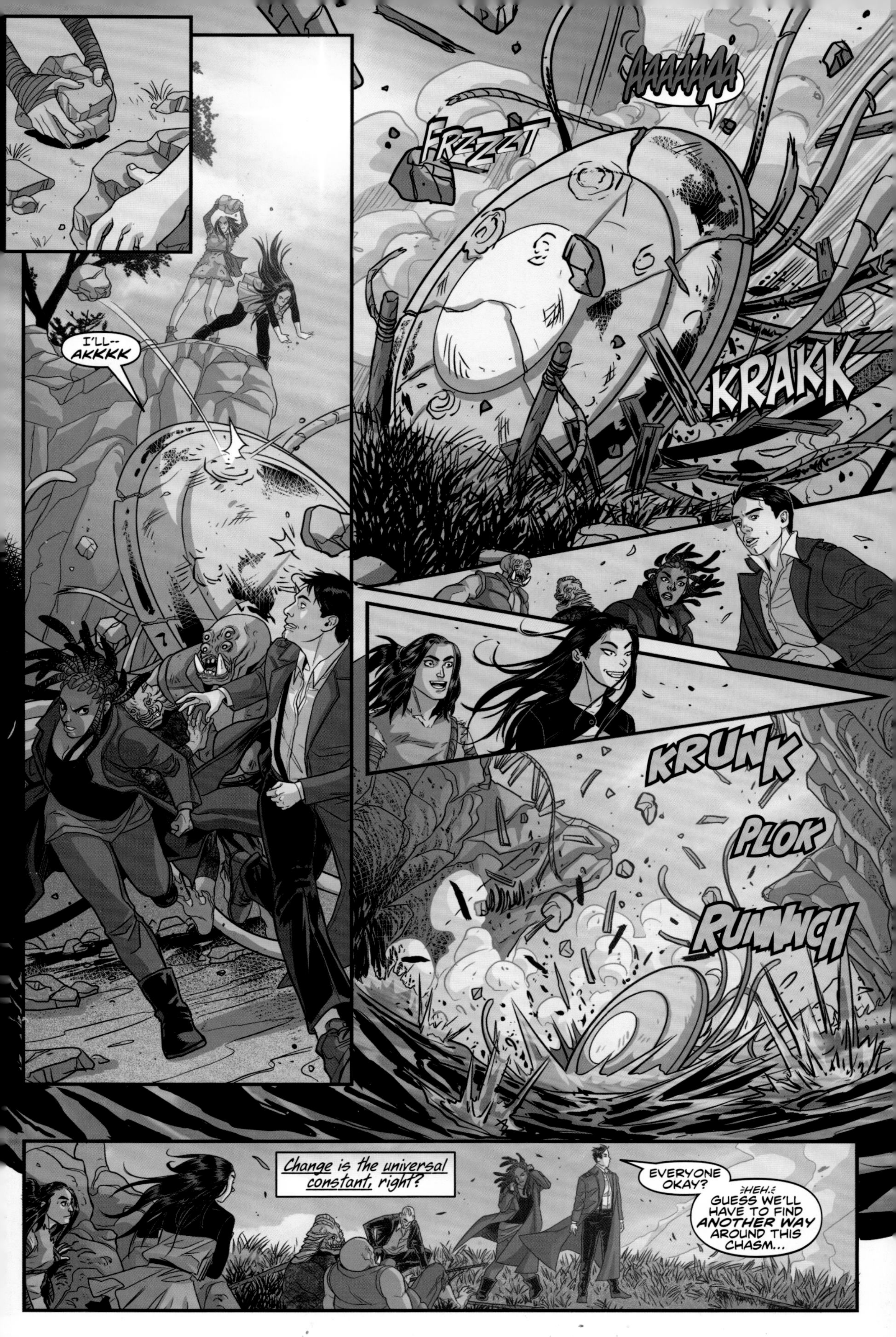
I'LL--
AKKKK
FRZZZT
AAAAAAA
KRAKK
KRUNK
PLOK
RUNNNCH
Change is the universal constant, right?
EVERYONE OKAY?
HEH. GUESS WE'LL HAVE TO FIND ANOTHER WAY AROUND THIS CHASM...

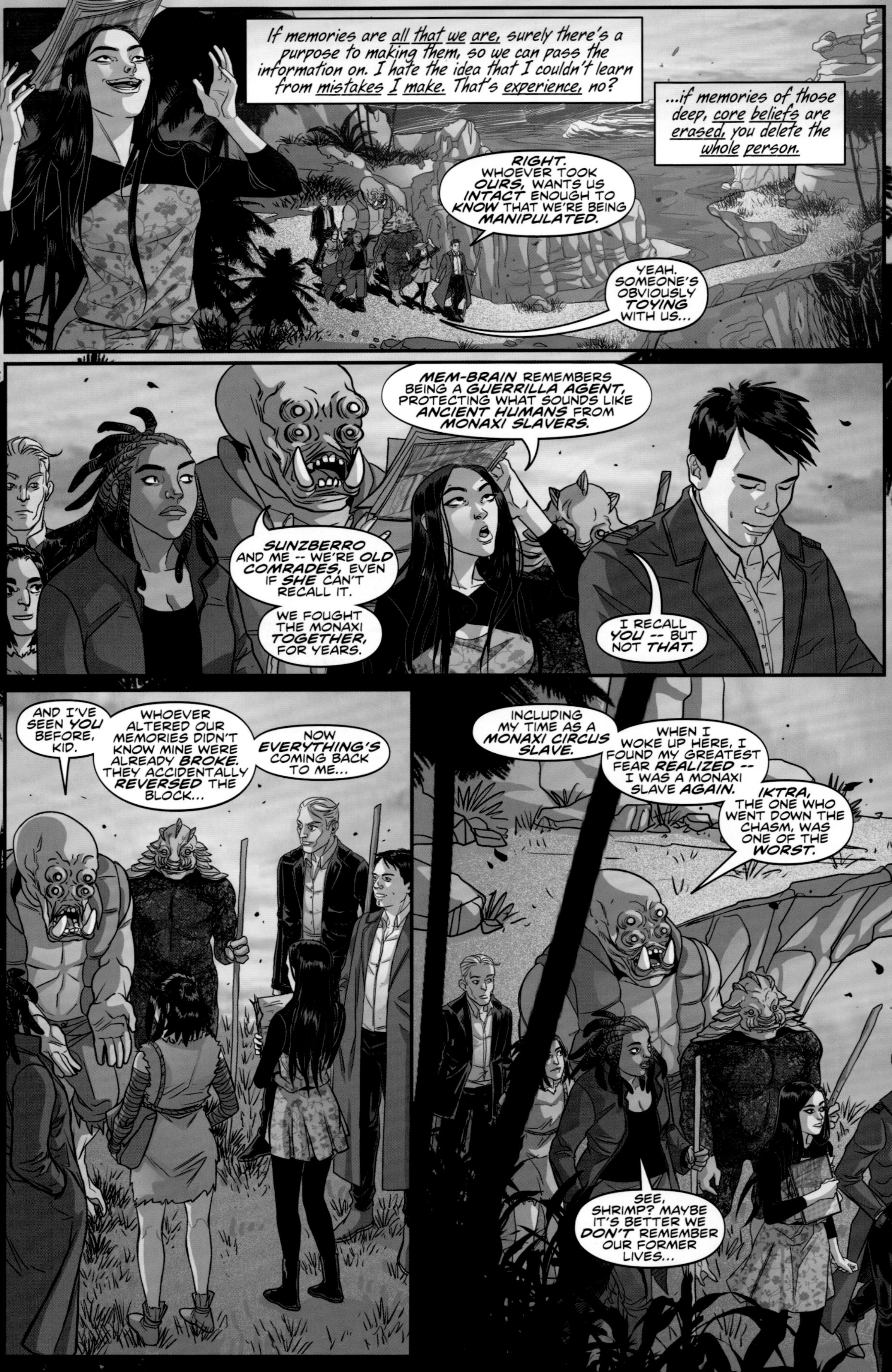
If memories are all that we are, surely there's a purpose to making them, so we can pass the information on. I hate the idea that I couldn't learn from mistakes I make. That's experience, no?
...if memories of those deep, core beliefs are erased, you delete the whole person.
RIGHT. WHOEVER TOOK OURS, WANTS US INTACT ENOUGH TO KNOW THAT WE'RE BEING MANIPULATED.
YEAH. SOMEONE'S OBVIOUSLY TOYING WITH US...
MEM-BRAIN REMEMBERS BEING A GUERRILLA AGENT, PROTECTING WHAT SOUNDS LIKE ANCIENT HUMANS FROM MONAXI SLAVERS.
SUNZBERRO AND ME -- WE'RE OLD COMRADES, EVEN IF SHE CAN'T RECALL IT.
WE FOUGHT THE MONAXI TOGETHER, FOR YEARS.
I RECALL YOU -- BUT NOT THAT.
AND I'VE SEEN YOU BEFORE, KID.
WHOEVER ALTERED OUR MEMORIES DIDN'T KNOW MINE WERE ALREADY BROKE. THEY ACCIDENTALLY REVERSED THE BLOCK...
NOW EVERYTHING'S COMING BACK TO ME...
INCLUDING MY TIME AS A MONAXI CIRCUS SLAVE.
WHEN I WOKE UP HERE, I FOUND MY GREATEST FEAR REALIZED -- I WAS A MONAXI SLAVE AGAIN.
IKTRA, THE ONE WHO WENT DOWN THE CHASM, WAS ONE OF THE WORST.
SEE, SHRIMP? MAYBE IT'S BETTER WE DON'T REMEMBER OUR FORMER LIVES...

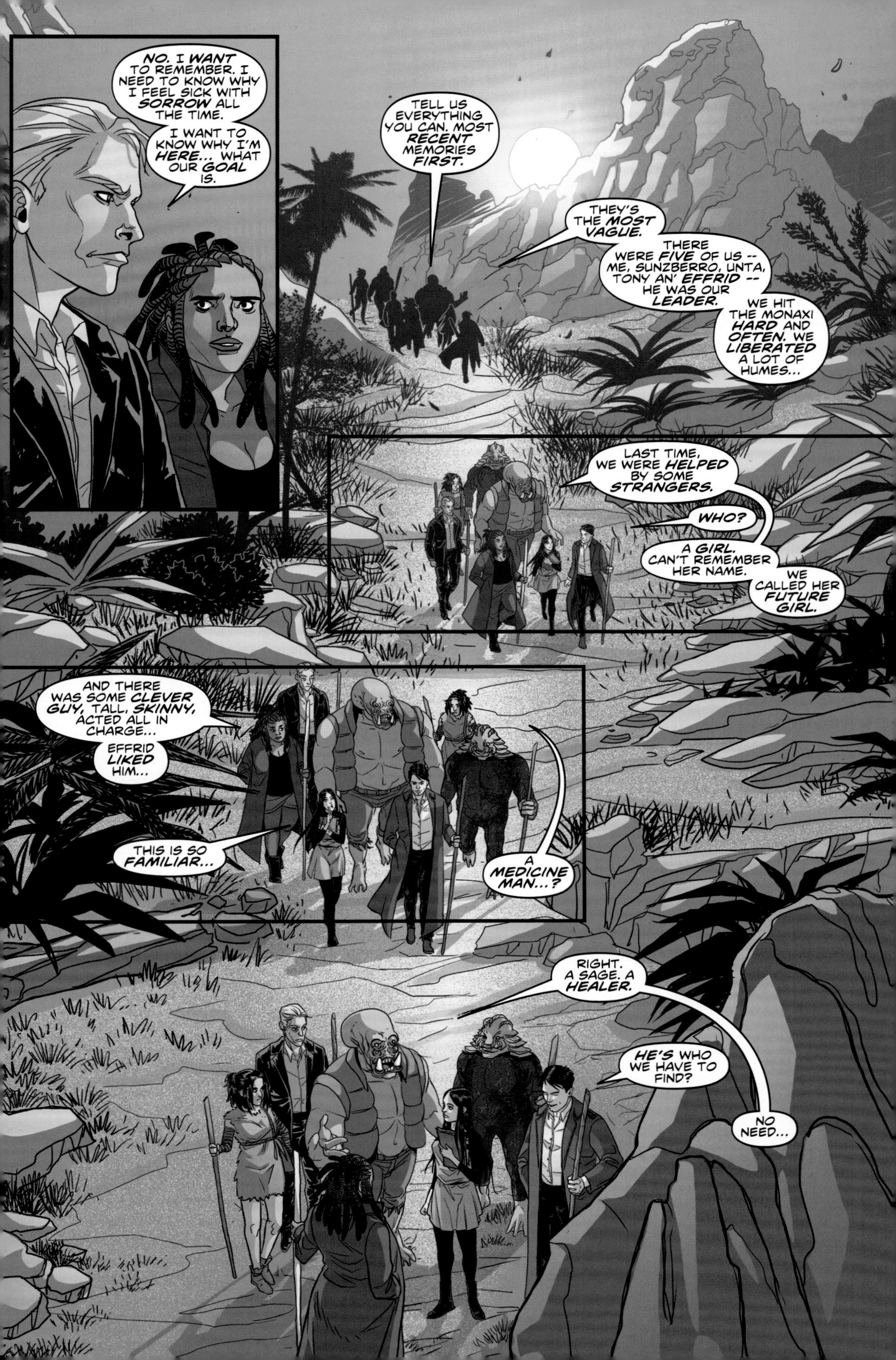
NO. I WANT TO REMEMBER. I NEED TO KNOW WHY I FEEL SICK WITH SORROW ALL THE TIME.
I WANT TO KNOW WHY I'M HERE... WHAT OUR GOAL IS.
TELL US EVERYTHING YOU CAN. MOST RECENT MEMORIES FIRST.
THEY'S THE MOST VAGUE.
THERE WERE FIVE OF US -- ME, SUNZBERRO, UNTA, TONY AN' EFFRID -- HE WAS OUR LEADER.
WE HIT THE MONAXI HARD AND OFTEN. WE LIBERATED A LOT OF HUMES...
LAST TIME, WE WERE HELPED BY SOME STRANGERS.
WHO?
A GIRL. CAN'T REMEMBER HER NAME.
WE CALLED HER FUTURE GIRL.
AND THERE WAS SOME CLEVER GUY, TALL, SKINNY, ACTED ALL IN CHARGE...
EFFRID LIKED HIM...
THIS IS SO FAMILIAR...
A MEDICINE MAN...?
RIGHT. A SAGE. A HEALER.
HE'S WHO WE HAVE TO FIND?
NO NEED...

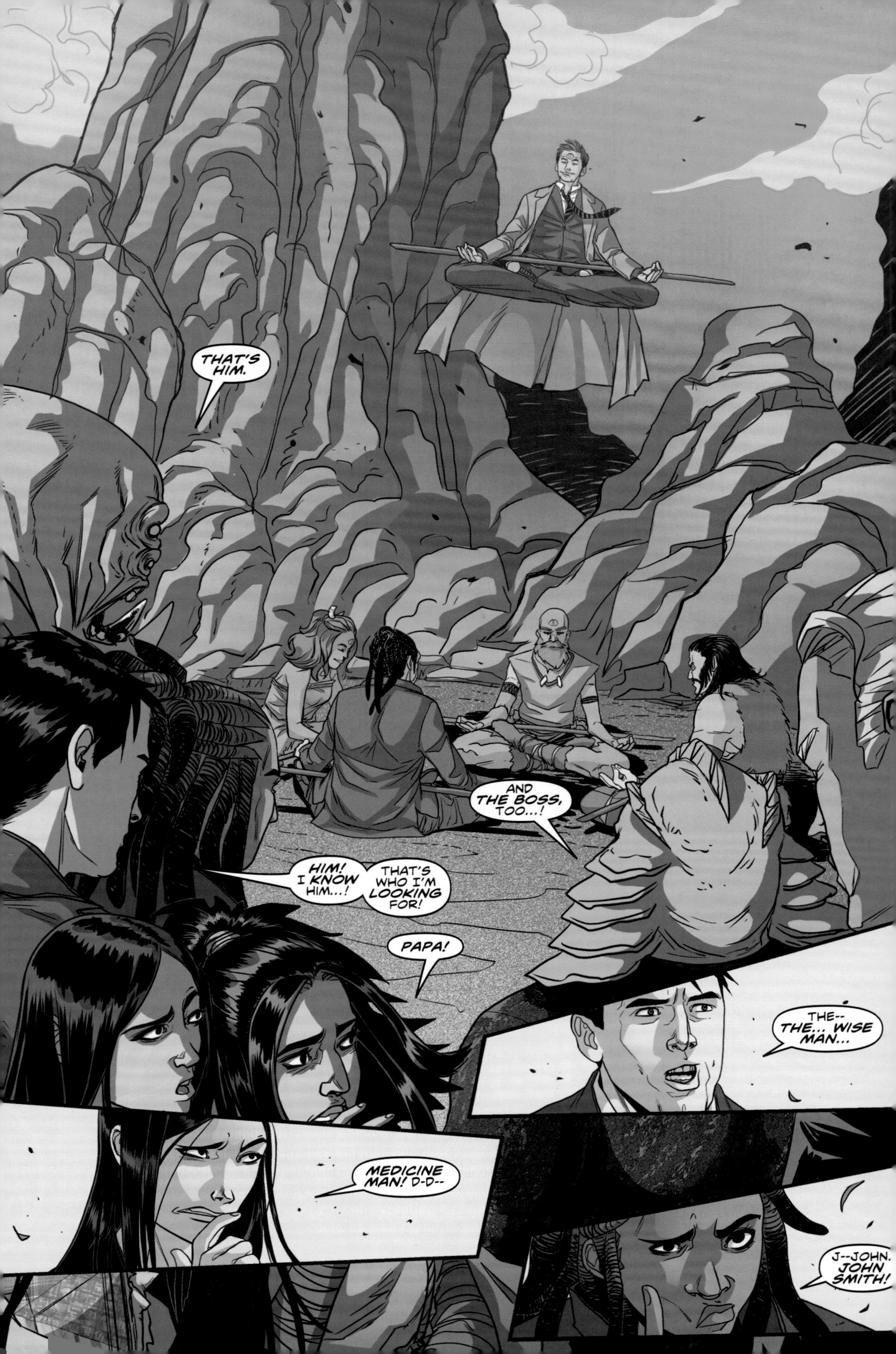
THAT'S HIM.
AND THE BOSS, TOO...!
HIM! I KNOW HIM...!
THAT'S WHO I'M LOOKING FOR!
PAPA!
THE-- THE... WISE MAN...
MEDICINE MAN! D-D--
J--JOHN. JOHN SMITH!

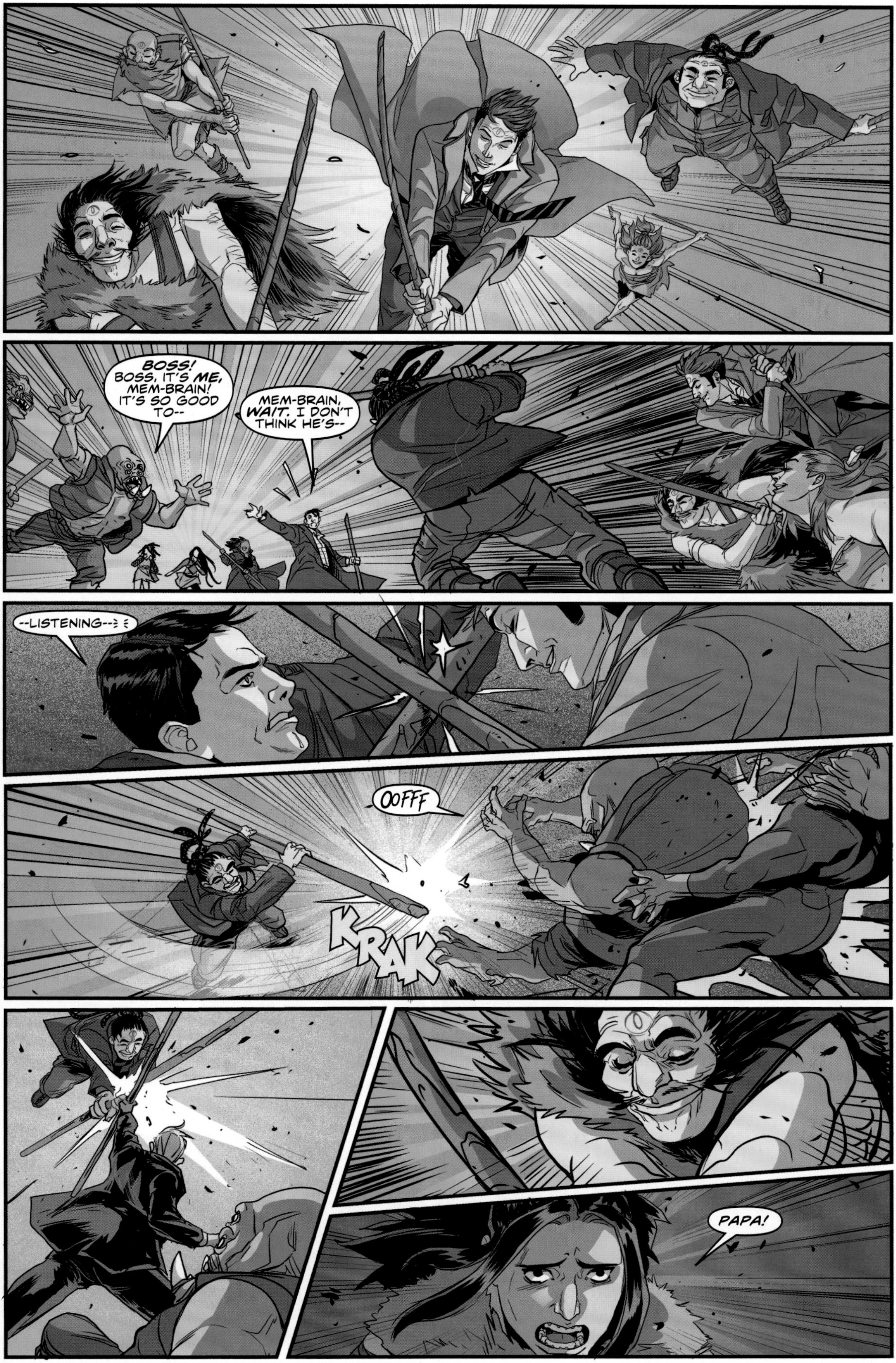

BOSS! BOSS, IT'S ME, MEM-BRAIN! IT'S SO GOOD TO--
MEM-BRAIN, WAIT. I DON'T THINK HE'S--
--LISTENING--
OOFFF
KRAK
PAPA!

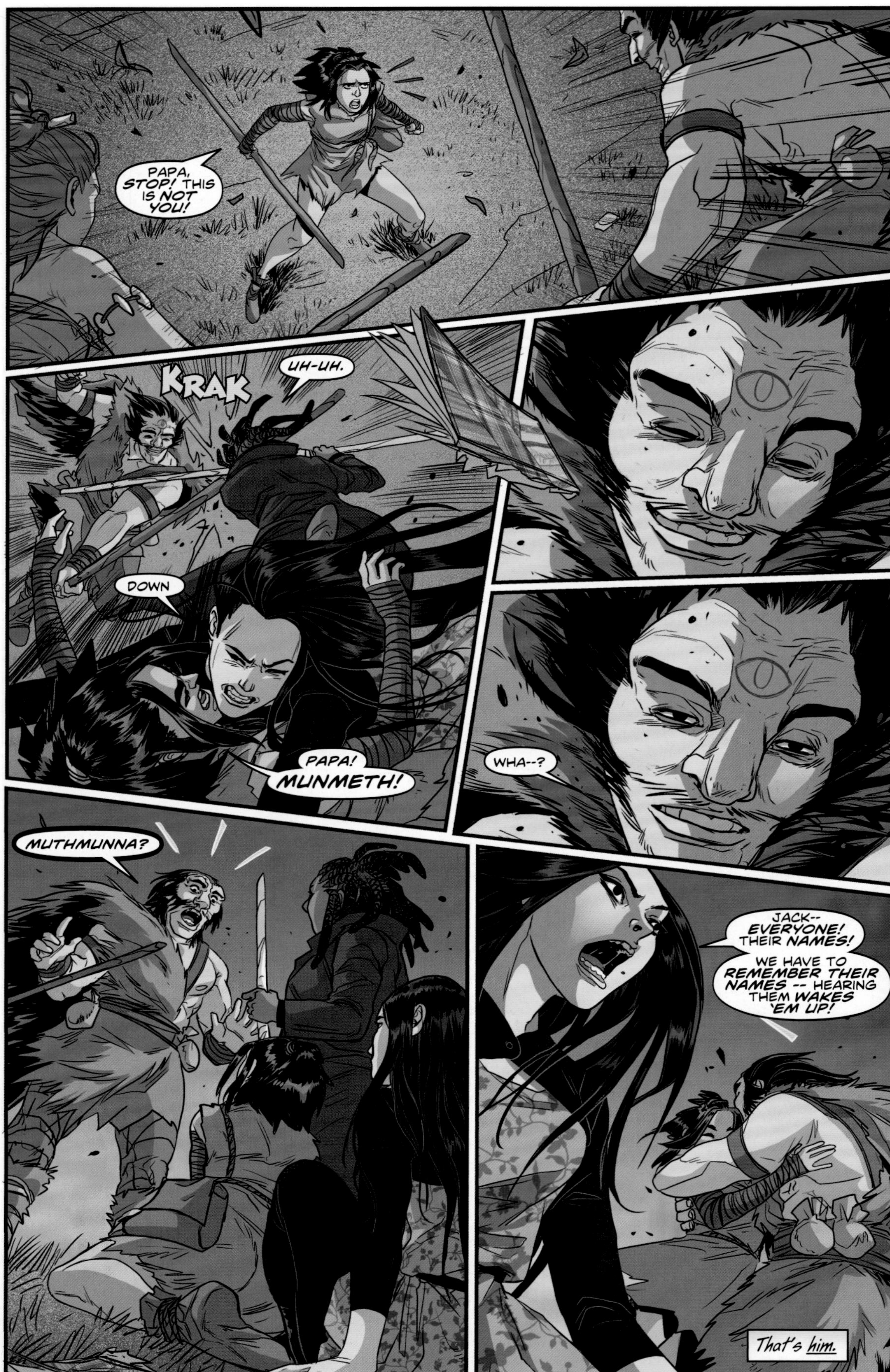
PAPA, STOP! THIS IS NOT YOU!
KRAK
UH-UH.
DOWN
PAPA! MUNMETH!
WHA--?
MUTHMUNNA?
JACK-- EVERYONE! THEIR NAMES!
WE HAVE TO REMEMBER THEIR NAMES -- HEARING THEM WAKES 'EM UP!
That's him.

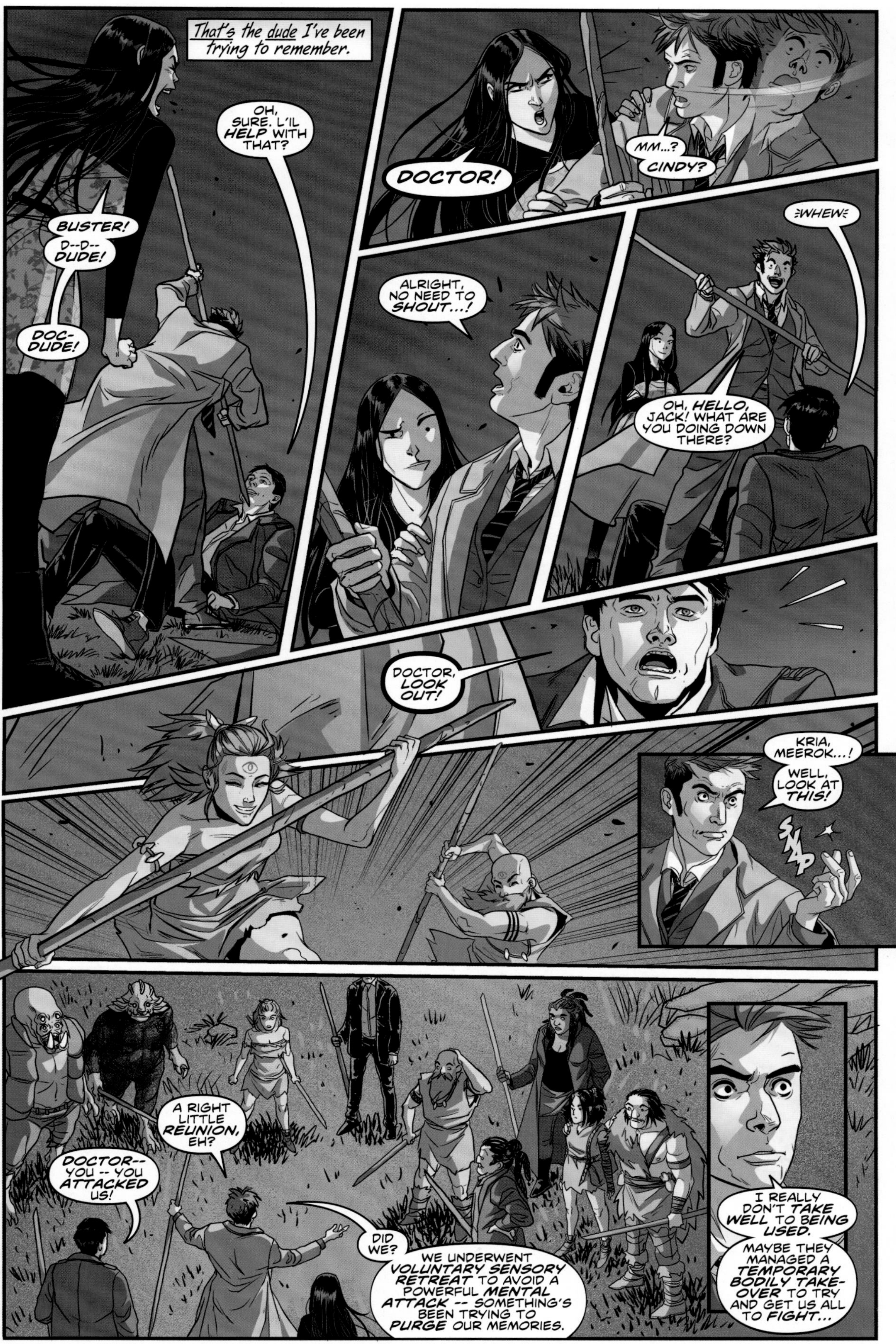
That's the dude I've been trying to remember.
OH, SURE. L'IL HELP WITH THAT?
BUSTER!
D--D-- DUDE!
DOC-DUDE!
DOCTOR!
MM...? CINDY?
ALRIGHT, NO NEED TO SHOUT...!
WHEW
OH, HELLO, JACK! WHAT ARE YOU DOING DOWN THERE?
DOCTOR, LOOK OUT!
KRIA, MEEROK...!
WELL, LOOK AT THIS!
SNAP
A RIGHT LITTLE REUNION, EH?
DOCTOR-- YOU -- YOU ATTACKED US!
DID WE?
WE UNDERWENT VOLUNTARY SENSORY RETREAT TO AVOID A POWERFUL MENTAL ATTACK -- SOMETHING'S BEEN TRYING TO PURGE OUR MEMORIES.
I REALLY DON'T TAKE WELL TO BEING USED.
MAYBE THEY MANAGED A TEMPORARY BODILY TAKE-OVER TO TRY AND GET US ALL TO FIGHT...

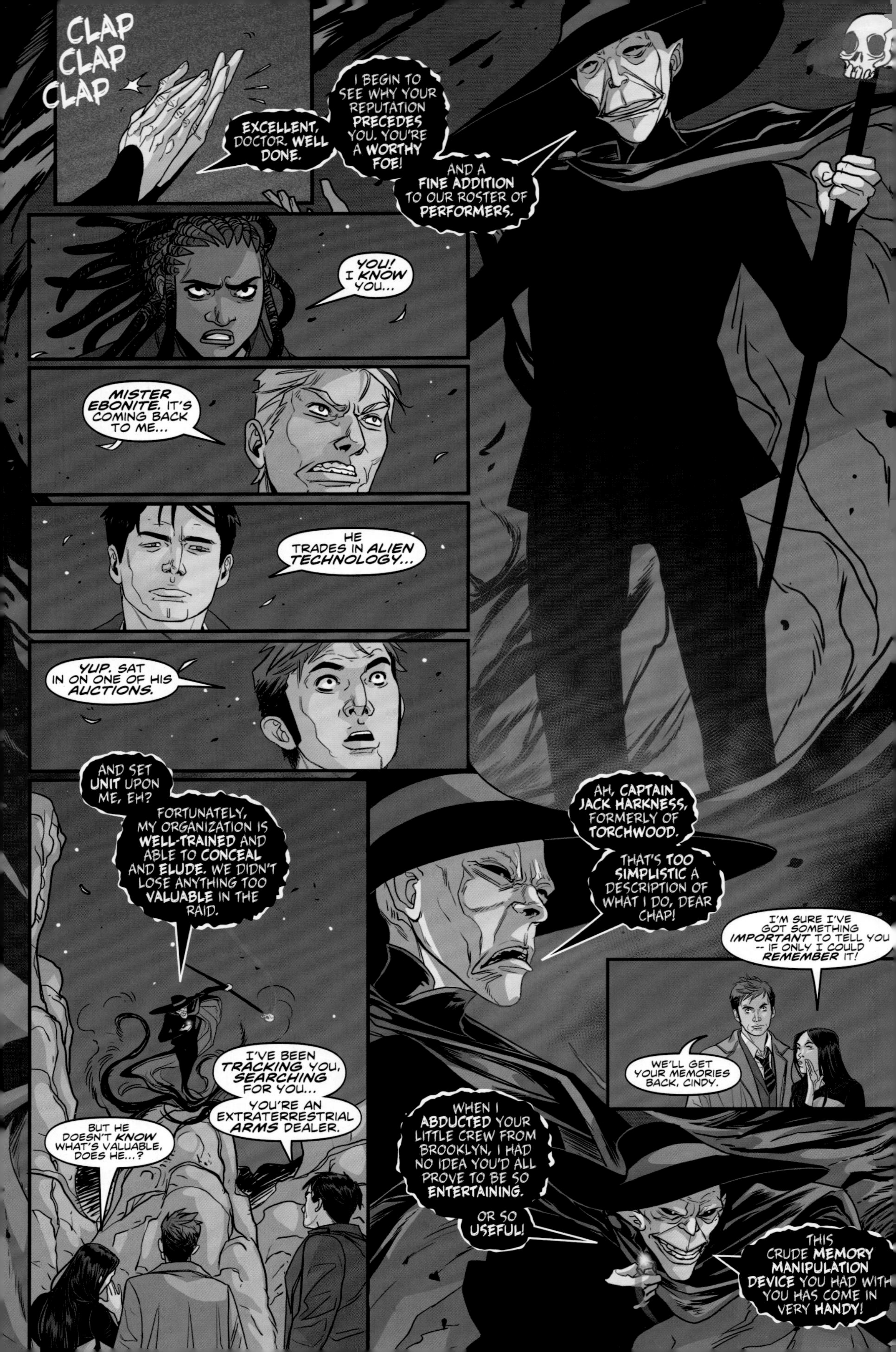
CLAP CLAP CLAP
EXCELLENT, DOCTOR. WELL DONE.
I BEGIN TO SEE WHY YOUR REPUTATION PRECEDES YOU. YOU'RE A WORTHY FOE!
AND A FINE ADDITION TO OUR ROSTER OF PERFORMERS.
YOU! I KNOW YOU...
MISTER EBONITE. IT'S COMING BACK TO ME...
HE TRADES IN ALIEN TECHNOLOGY...
YUP. SAT IN ON ONE OF HIS AUCTIONS.
AND SET UNIT UPON ME, EH?
FORTUNATELY, MY ORGANIZATION IS WELL-TRAINED AND ABLE TO CONCEAL AND ELUDE. WE DIDN'T LOSE ANYTHING TOO VALUABLE IN THE RAID.
I'VE BEEN TRACKING YOU, SEARCHING FOR YOU...
YOU'RE AN EXTRATERRESTRIAL ARMS DEALER.
BUT HE DOESN'T KNOW WHAT'S VALUABLE, DOES HE...?
AH, CAPTAIN JACK HARKNESS, FORMERLY OF TORCHWOOD.
THAT'S TOO SIMPLISTIC A DESCRIPTION OF WHAT I DO, DEAR CHAP!
I'M SURE I'VE GOT SOMETHING IMPORTANT TO TELL YOU -- IF ONLY I COULD REMEMBER IT!
WE'LL GET YOUR MEMORIES BACK, CINDY.
WHEN I ABDUCTED YOUR LITTLE CREW FROM BROOKLYN, I HAD NO IDEA YOU'D ALL PROVE TO BE SO ENTERTAINING.
OR SO USEFUL!
THIS CRUDE MEMORY MANIPULATION DEVICE YOU HAD WITH YOU HAS COME IN VERY HANDY!

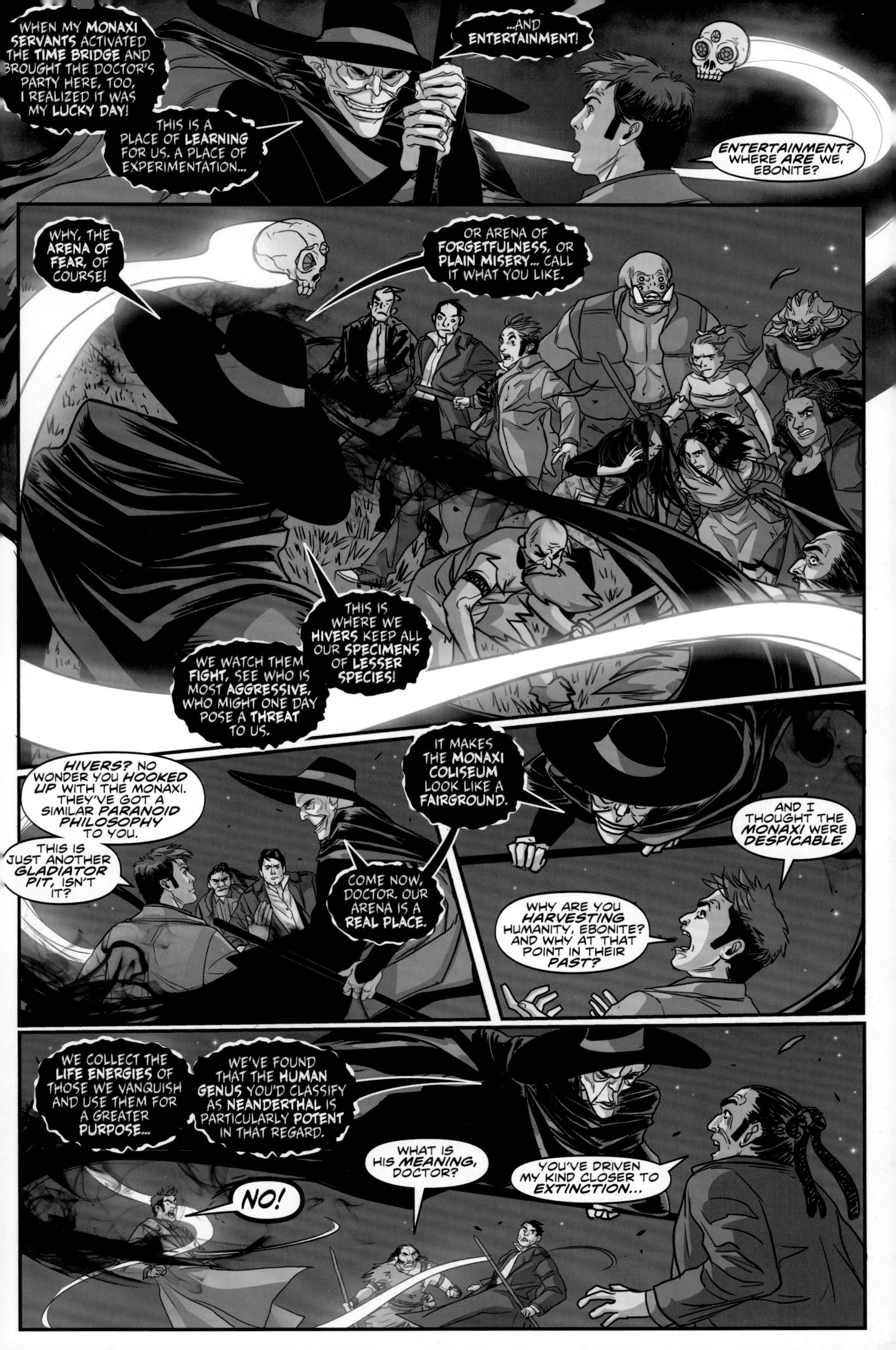

WHEN MY MONAXI SERVANTS ACTIVATED THE TIME BRIDGE AND BROUGHT THE DOCTOR'S PARTY HERE, TOO, I REALIZED IT WAS MY LUCKY DAY!
THIS IS A PLACE OF LEARNING FOR US. A PLACE OF EXPERIMENTATION...
...AND ENTERTAINMENT!
ENTERTAINMENT? WHERE ARE WE, EBONITE?
WHY, THE ARENA OF FEAR, OF COURSE!
OR ARENA OF FORGETFULNESS, OR PLAIN MISERY... CALL IT WHAT YOU LIKE.
THIS IS WHERE WE HIVERS KEEP ALL OUR SPECIMENS OF LESSER SPECIES!
WE WATCH THEM FIGHT, SEE WHO IS MOST AGGRESSIVE, WHO MIGHT ONE DAY POSE A THREAT TO US.
HIVERS? NO WONDER YOU HOOKED UP WITH THE MONAXI. THEY'VE GOT A SIMILAR PARANOID PHILOSOPHY TO YOU.
THIS IS JUST ANOTHER GLADIATOR PIT, ISN'T IT?
COME NOW, DOCTOR. OUR ARENA IS A REAL PLACE.
IT MAKES THE MONAXI COLISEUM LOOK LIKE A FAIRGROUND.
AND I THOUGHT THE MONAXI WERE DESPICABLE.
WHY ARE YOU HARVESTING HUMANITY, EBONITE? AND WHY AT THAT POINT IN THEIR PAST?
WE COLLECT THE LIFE ENERGIES OF THOSE WE VANQUISH AND USE THEM FOR A GREATER PURPOSE...
WE'VE FOUND THAT THE HUMAN GENUS YOU'D CLASSIFY AS NEANDERTHAL IS PARTICULARLY POTENT IN THAT REGARD.
NO!
WHAT IS HIS MEANING, DOCTOR?
YOU'VE DRIVEN MY KIND CLOSER TO EXTINCTION...

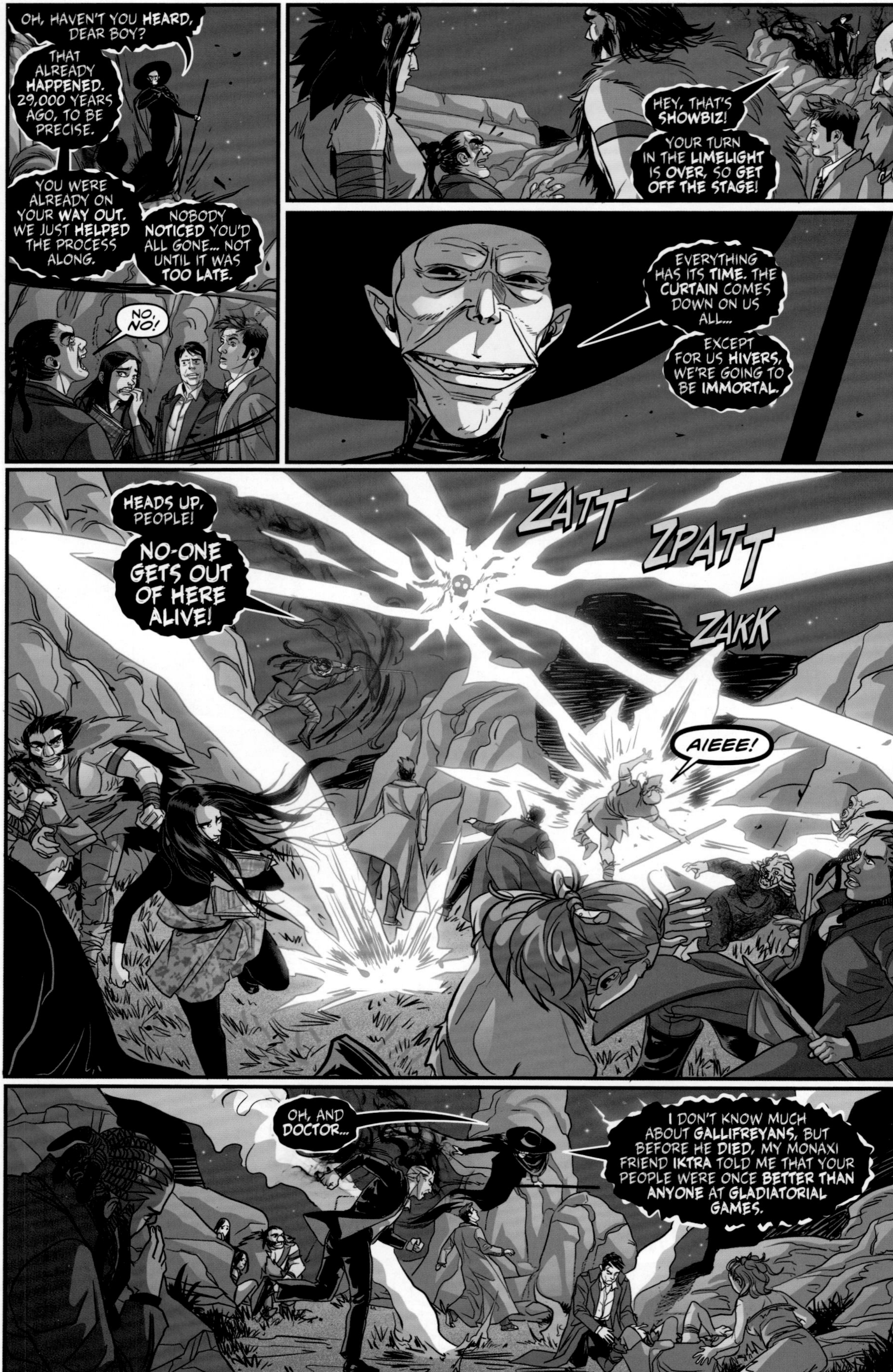
OH, HAVEN'T YOU HEARD, DEAR BOY?
THAT ALREADY HAPPENED. 29,000 YEARS AGO, TO BE PRECISE.
YOU WERE ALREADY ON YOUR WAY OUT. WE JUST HELPED THE PROCESS ALONG.
NOBODY NOTICED YOU'D ALL GONE... NOT UNTIL IT WAS TOO LATE.
HEY, THAT'S SHOWBIZ!
YOUR TURN IN THE LIMELIGHT IS OVER, SO GET OFF THE STAGE!
NO, NO!
EVERYTHING HAS ITS TIME. THE CURTAIN COMES DOWN ON US ALL...
EXCEPT FOR US HIVERS, WE'RE GOING TO BE IMMORTAL.
HEADS UP, PEOPLE!
NO-ONE GETS OUT OF HERE ALIVE!
ZATT
ZPATT
ZAKK
AIEEE!
OH, AND DOCTOR...
I DON'T KNOW MUCH ABOUT GALLIFREYANS, BUT BEFORE HE DIED, MY MONAXI FRIEND IKTRA TOLD ME THAT YOUR PEOPLE WERE ONCE BETTER THAN ANYONE AT GLADIATORIAL GAMES.

LITTLE BIT OF **HYPOCRISY** IN YOUR **MORAL OUTRAGE**...?

WE'LL BE **WATCHING**. DO BE CAREFUL, EVERYONE!

YOUR **ENEMIES** COULD BE... OOH, ABSOLUTELY ANYBODY!

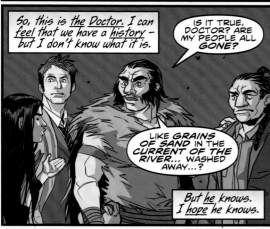

So, this is the Doctor. I can feel that we have a history – but I don't know what it is.

IS IT TRUE, DOCTOR? ARE MY PEOPLE ALL **GONE**?

LIKE **GRAINS OF SAND** IN THE **CURRENT OF THE RIVER**... WASHED AWAY...?

But he knows. I hope he knows.

Because that would give me a little hope. Which we all really need right now.

DOCTOR...?

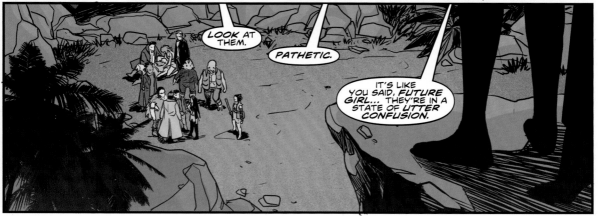

LOOK AT THEM.

PATHETIC.

IT'S LIKE YOU SAID, **FUTURE GIRL**... THEY'RE IN A STATE OF **UTTER CONFUSION.**

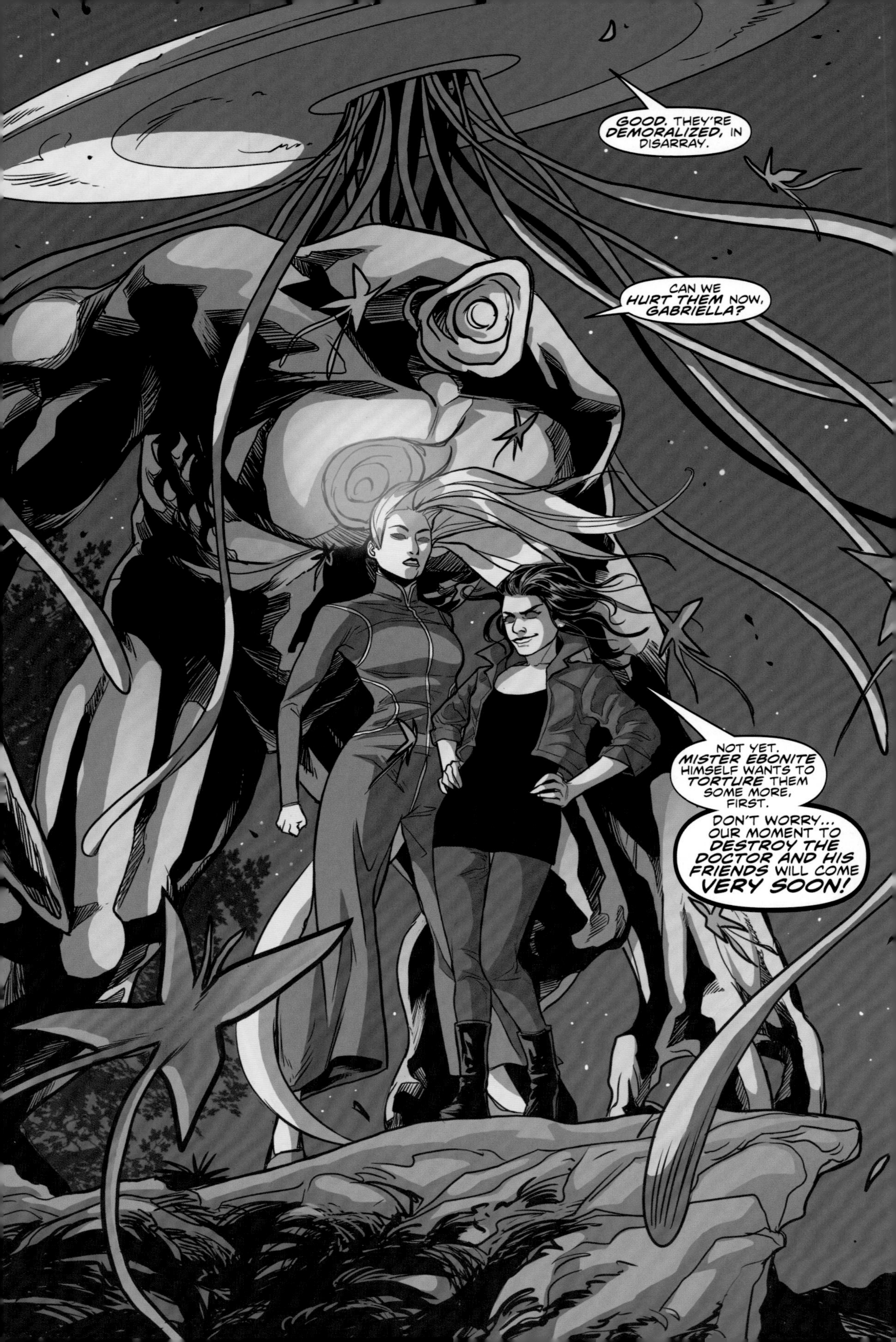

GOOD. THEY'RE DEMORALIZED, IN DISARRAY.
CAN WE HURT THEM NOW, GABRIELLA?
NOT YET. MISTER EBONITE HIMSELF WANTS TO TORTURE THEM SOME MORE, FIRST.
DON'T WORRY... OUR MOMENT TO DESTROY THE DOCTOR AND HIS FRIENDS WILL COME VERY SOON!

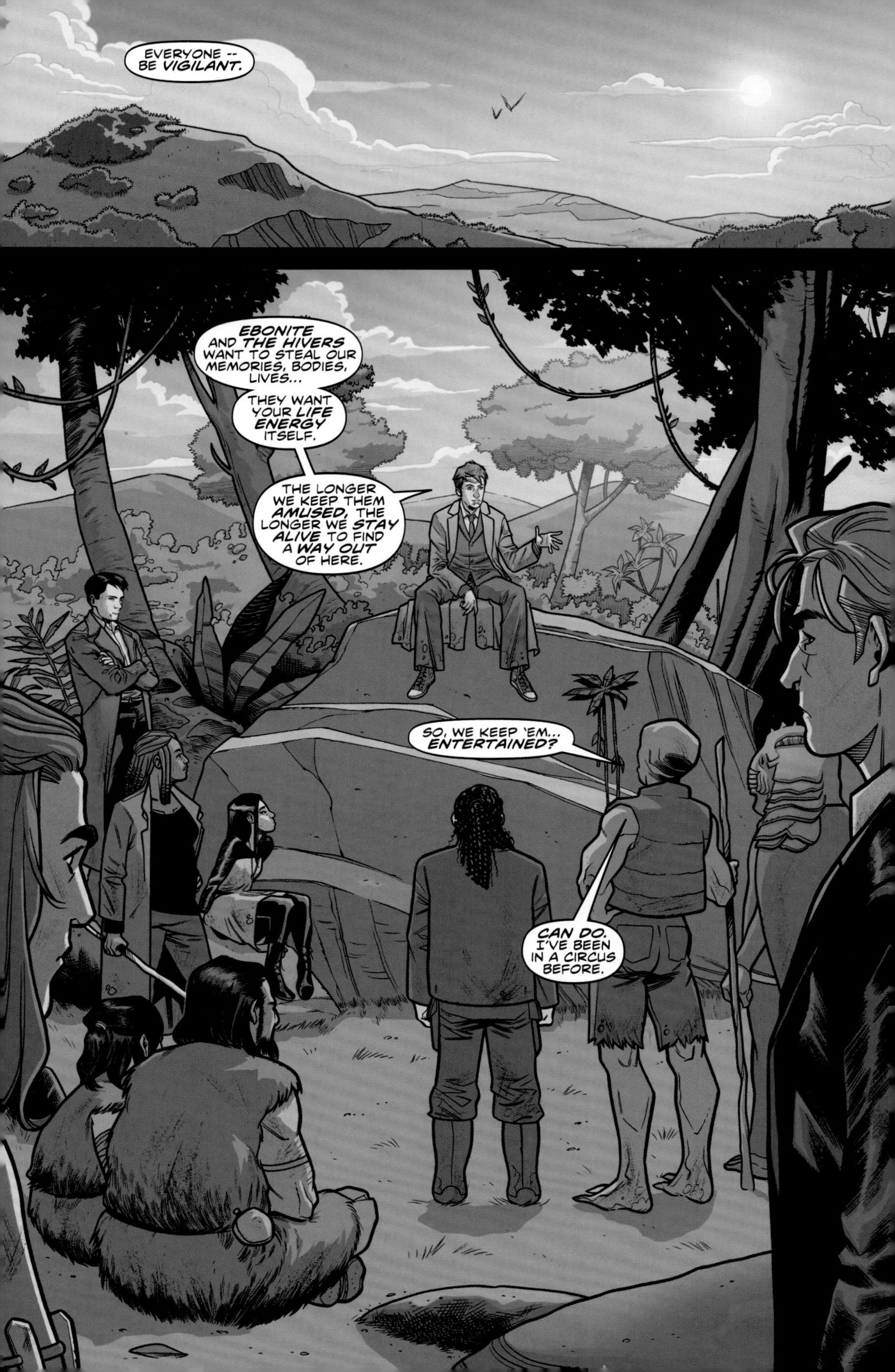
EVERYONE -- BE VIGILANT.
EBONITE AND THE HIVERS WANT TO STEAL OUR MEMORIES, BODIES, LIVES...
THEY WANT YOUR LIFE ENERGY ITSELF.
THE LONGER WE KEEP THEM AMUSED, THE LONGER WE STAY ALIVE TO FIND A WAY OUT OF HERE.
SO, WE KEEP 'EM... ENTERTAINED?
CAN DO. I'VE BEEN IN A CIRCUS BEFORE.

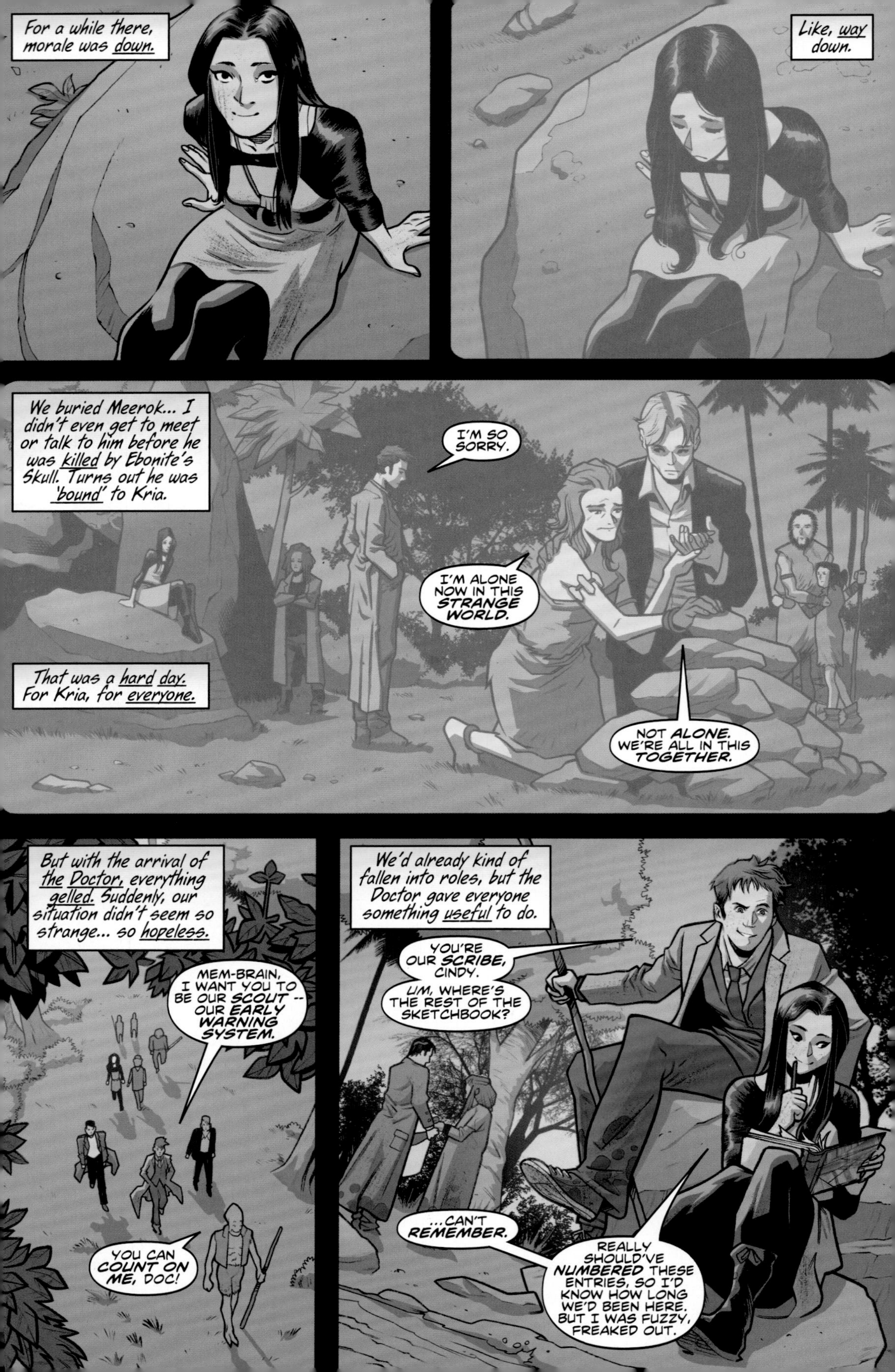
For a while there, morale was down.
Like, way down.
We buried Meerok... I didn't even get to meet or talk to him before he was killed by Ebonite's Skull. Turns out he was 'bound' to Kria.
I'M SO SORRY.
I'M ALONE NOW IN THIS STRANGE WORLD.
That was a hard day. For Kria, for everyone.
NOT ALONE. WE'RE ALL IN THIS TOGETHER.
But with the arrival of the Doctor, everything gelled. Suddenly, our situation didn't seem so strange... so hopeless.
MEM-BRAIN, I WANT YOU TO BE OUR SCOUT -- OUR EARLY WARNING SYSTEM.
YOU CAN COUNT ON ME, DOC!
We'd already kind of fallen into roles, but the Doctor gave everyone something useful to do.
YOU'RE OUR SCRIBE, CINDY.
UM, WHERE'S THE REST OF THE SKETCHBOOK?
...CAN'T REMEMBER.
REALLY SHOULD'VE NUMBERED THESE ENTRIES, SO I'D KNOW HOW LONG WE'D BEEN HERE. BUT I WAS FUZZY, FREAKED OUT.

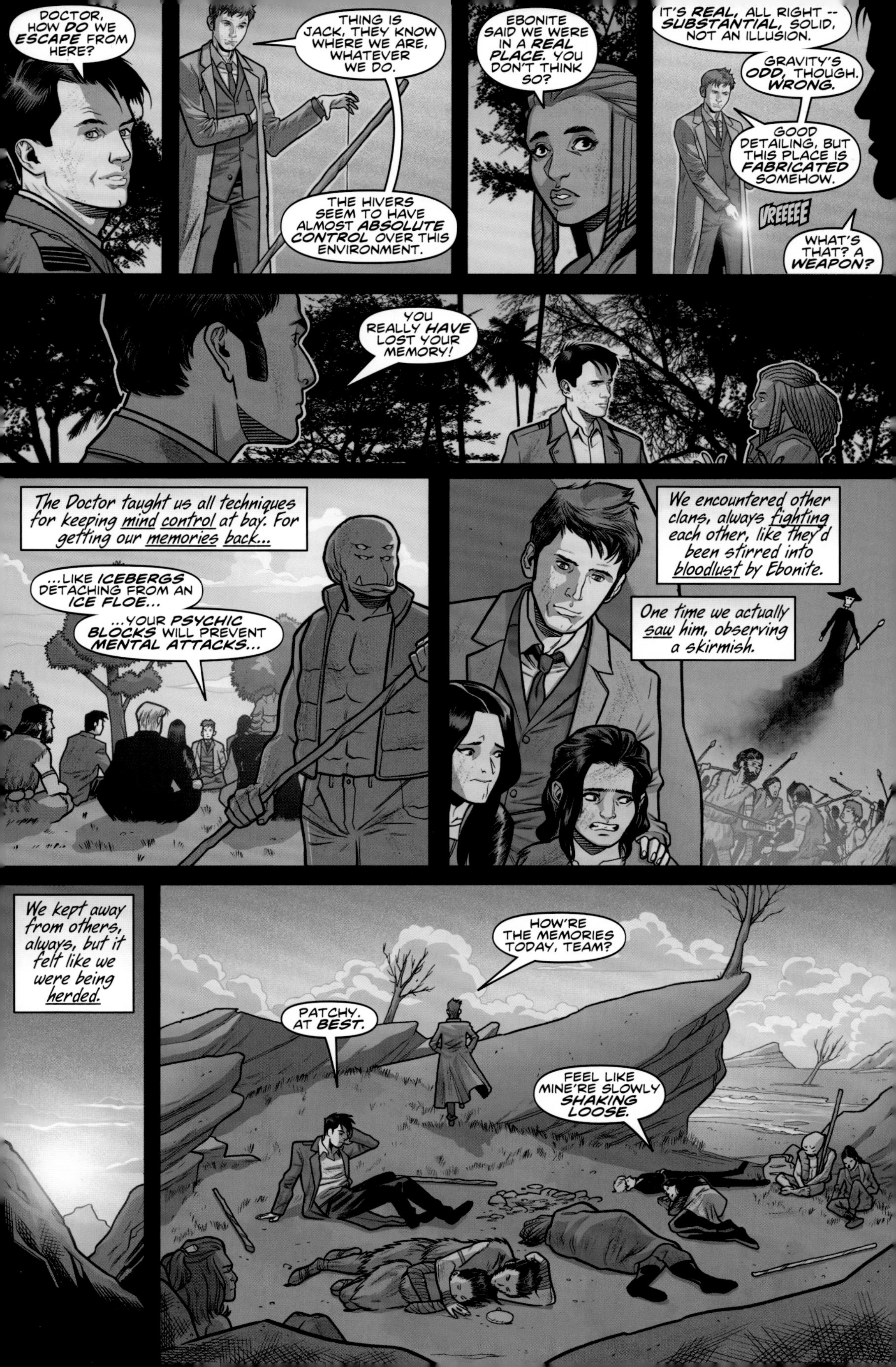
DOCTOR, HOW DO WE ESCAPE FROM HERE?
THING IS JACK, THEY KNOW WHERE WE ARE, WHATEVER WE DO.
THE HIVERS SEEM TO HAVE ALMOST ABSOLUTE CONTROL OVER THIS ENVIRONMENT.
EBONITE SAID WE WERE IN A REAL PLACE. YOU DON'T THINK SO?
IT'S REAL, ALL RIGHT -- SUBSTANTIAL, SOLID, NOT AN ILLUSION.
GRAVITY'S ODD, THOUGH. WRONG.
GOOD DETAILING, BUT THIS PLACE IS FABRICATED SOMEHOW.
VREEEEE
WHAT'S THAT? A WEAPON?
YOU REALLY HAVE LOST YOUR MEMORY!
The Doctor taught us all techniques for keeping mind control at bay. For getting our memories back...
...LIKE ICEBERGS DETACHING FROM AN ICE FLOE...
...YOUR PSYCHIC BLOCKS WILL PREVENT MENTAL ATTACKS...
We encountered other clans, always fighting each other, like they'd been stirred into bloodlust by Ebonite.
One time we actually saw him, observing a skirmish.
We kept away from others, always, but it felt like we were being herded.
HOW'RE THE MEMORIES TODAY, TEAM?
PATCHY. AT BEST.
FEEL LIKE MINE'RE SLOWLY SHAKING LOOSE.

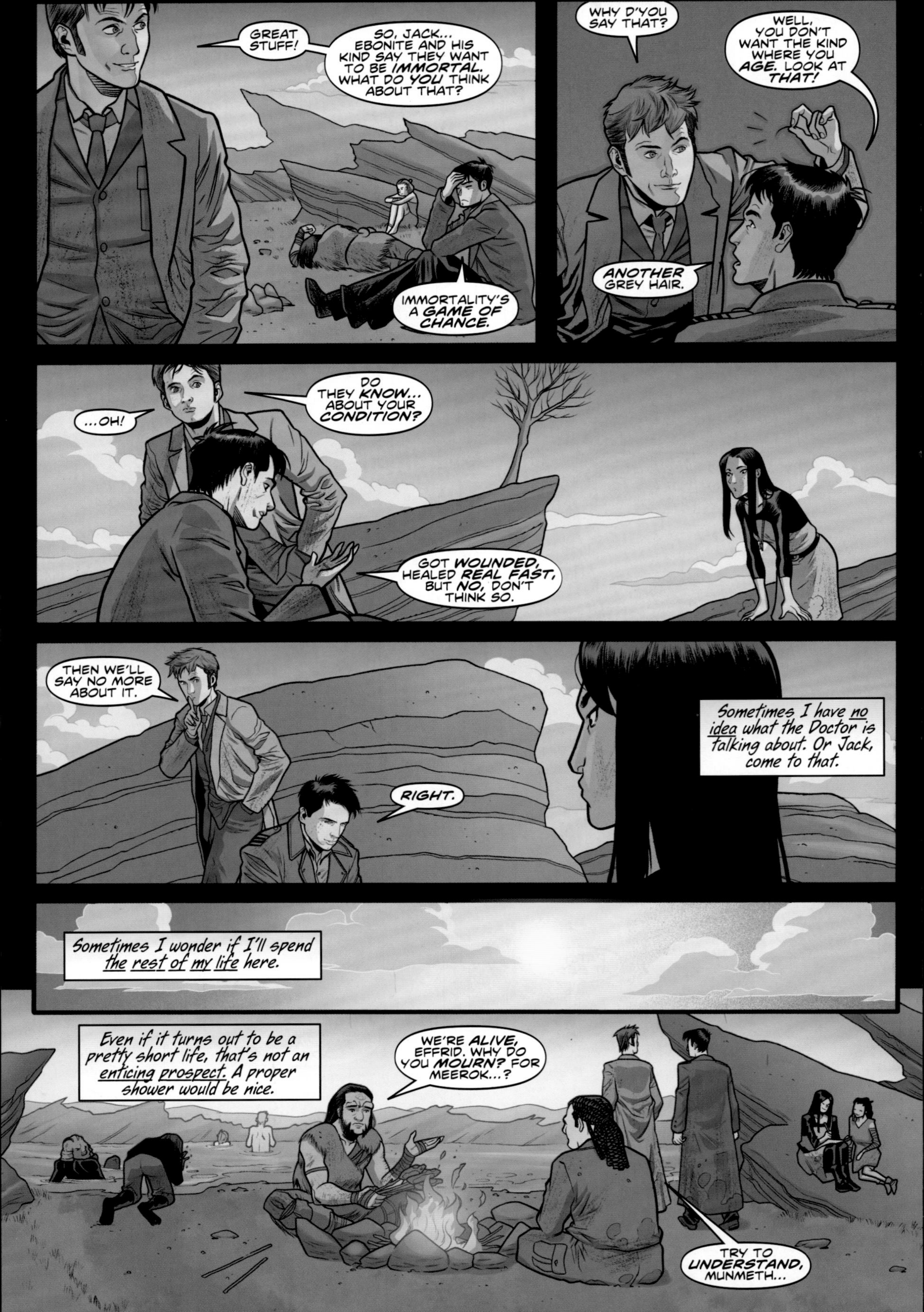
GREAT STUFF!
SO, JACK... EBONITE AND HIS KIND SAY THEY WANT TO BE IMMORTAL. WHAT DO YOU THINK ABOUT THAT?
IMMORTALITY'S A GAME OF CHANCE.
WHY D'YOU SAY THAT?
WELL, YOU DON'T WANT THE KIND WHERE YOU AGE. LOOK AT THAT!
ANOTHER GREY HAIR.
DO THEY KNOW... ABOUT YOUR CONDITION?
...OH!
GOT WOUNDED, HEALED REAL FAST, BUT NO, DON'T THINK SO.
THEN WE'LL SAY NO MORE ABOUT IT.
RIGHT.
Sometimes I have no idea what the Doctor is talking about. Or Jack, come to that.
Sometimes I wonder if I'll spend the rest of my life here.
Even if it turns out to be a pretty short life, that's not an enticing prospect. A proper shower would be nice.
WE'RE ALIVE, EFFRID. WHY DO YOU MOURN? FOR MEEROK...?
TRY TO UNDERSTAND, MUNMETH...

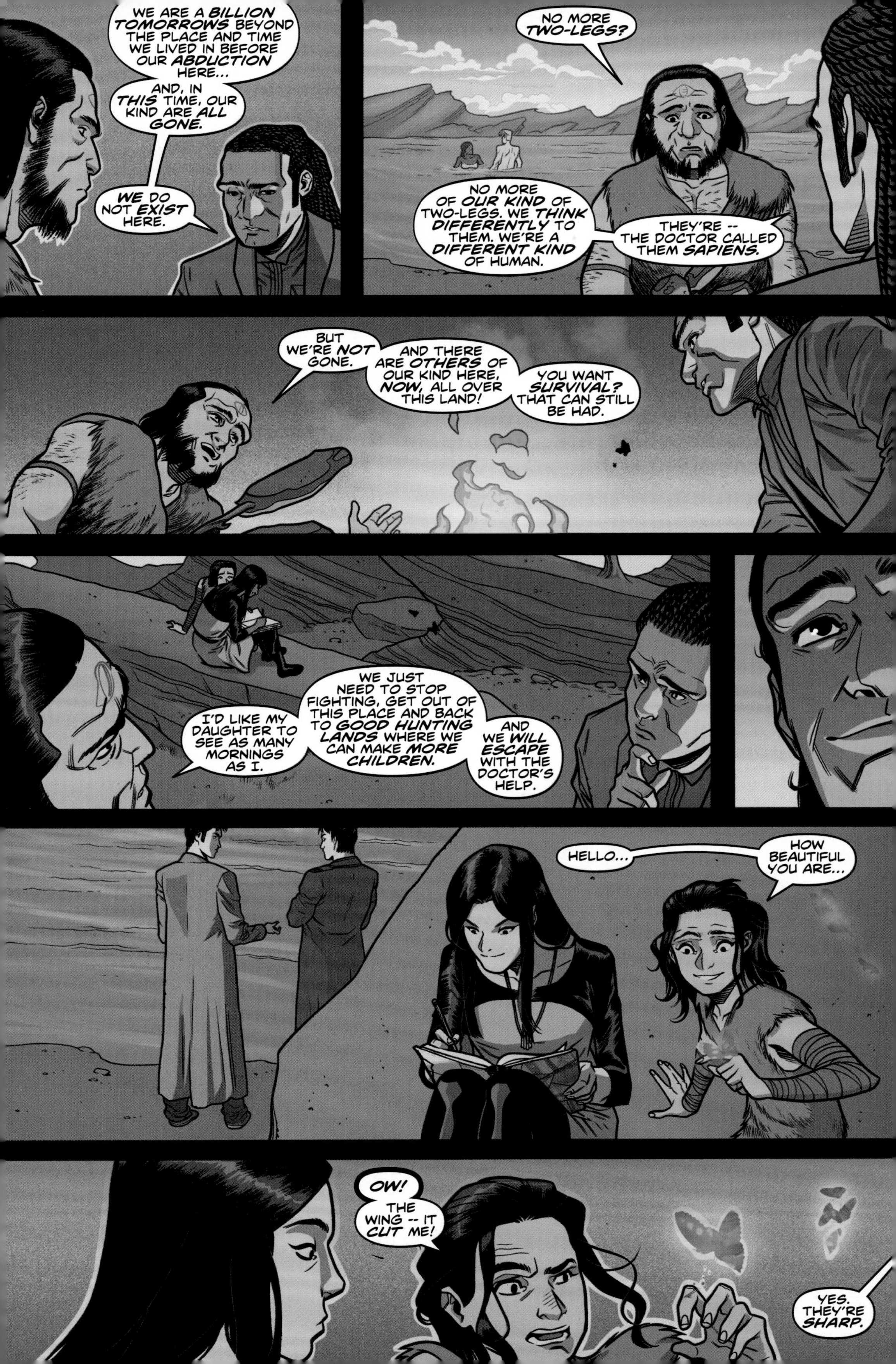
WE ARE A BILLION TOMORROWS BEYOND THE PLACE AND TIME WE LIVED IN BEFORE OUR ABDUCTION HERE...
AND, IN THIS TIME, OUR KIND ARE ALL GONE.
WE DO NOT EXIST HERE.
NO MORE TWO-LEGS?
NO MORE OF OUR KIND OF TWO-LEGS. WE THINK DIFFERENTLY TO THEM. WE'RE A DIFFERENT KIND OF HUMAN.
THEY'RE -- THE DOCTOR CALLED THEM SAPIENS.
BUT WE'RE NOT GONE.
AND THERE ARE OTHERS OF OUR KIND HERE, NOW, ALL OVER THIS LAND!
YOU WANT SURVIVAL? THAT CAN STILL BE HAD.
I'D LIKE MY DAUGHTER TO SEE AS MANY MORNINGS AS I.
WE JUST NEED TO STOP FIGHTING, GET OUT OF THIS PLACE AND BACK TO GOOD HUNTING LANDS WHERE WE CAN MAKE MORE CHILDREN.
AND WE WILL ESCAPE WITH THE DOCTOR'S HELP.
HELLO...
HOW BEAUTIFUL YOU ARE...
OW!
THE WING -- IT CUT ME!
YES. THEY'RE SHARP.

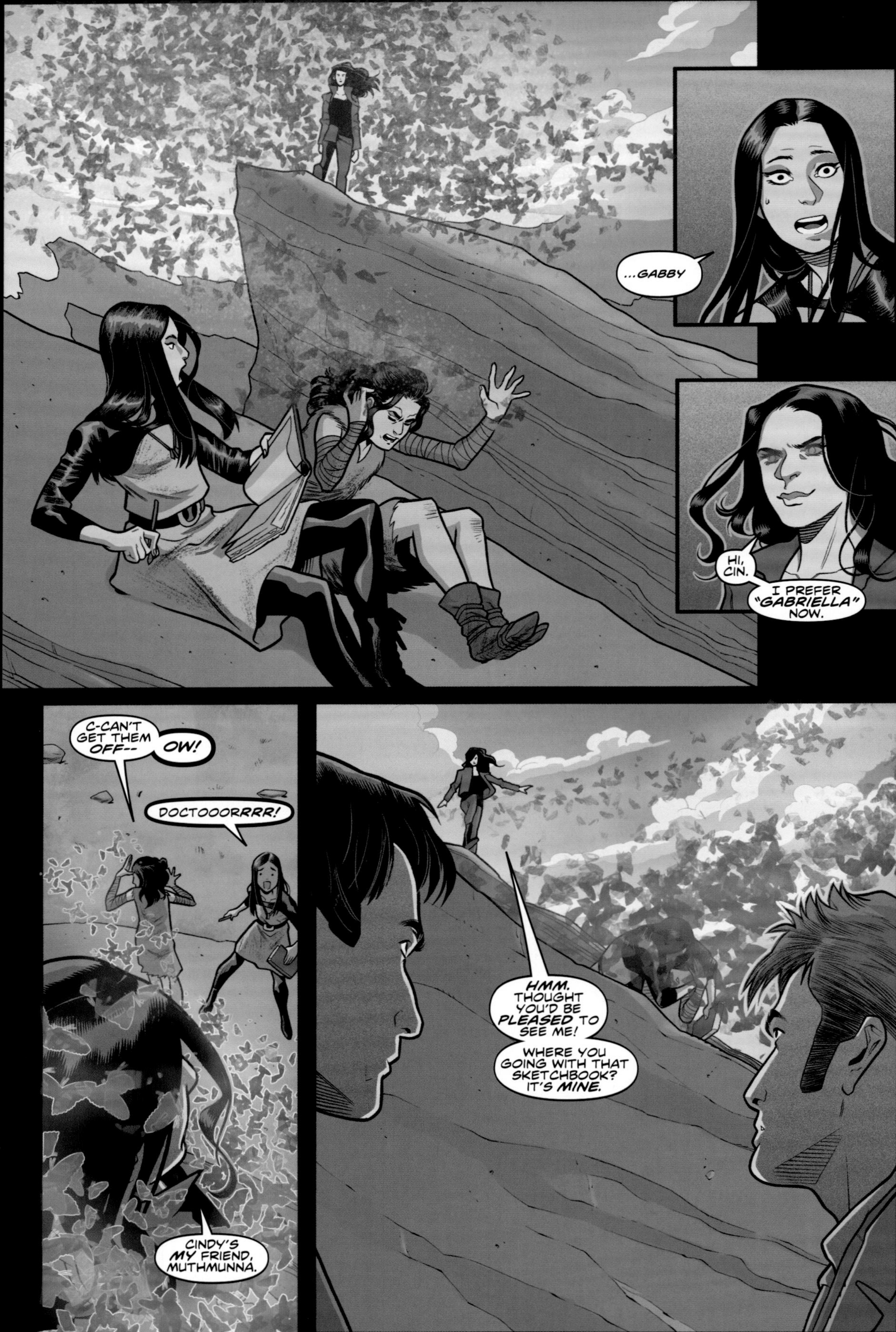
...GABBY
HI, CIN.
I PREFER "GABRIELLA" NOW.
C-CAN'T GET THEM OFF--
OW!
DOCTOOORRRR!
CINDY'S MY FRIEND, MUTHMUNNA.
HMM. THOUGHT YOU'D BE PLEASED TO SEE ME!
WHERE YOU GOING WITH THAT SKETCHBOOK? IT'S MINE.

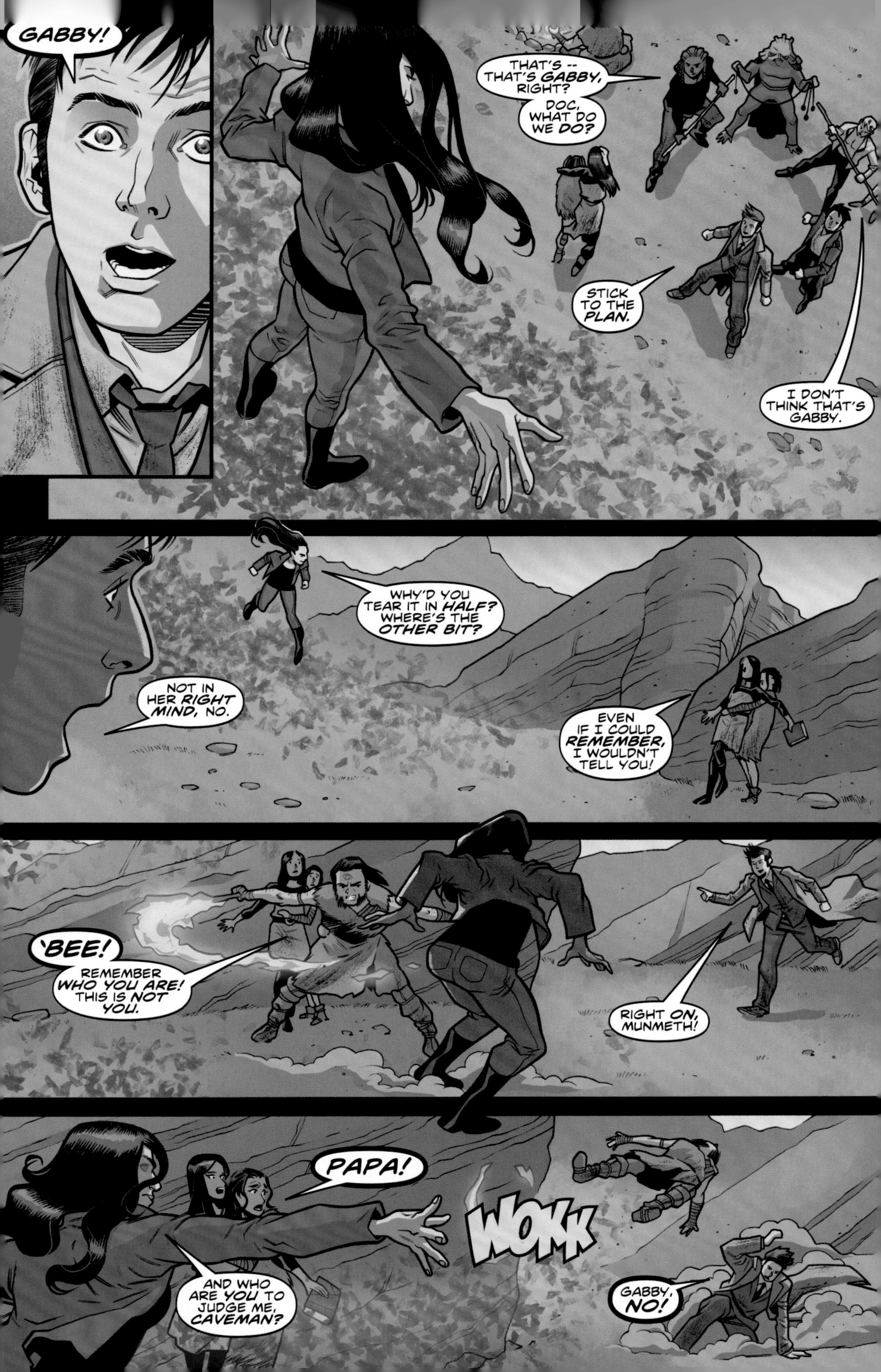
GABBY!
THAT'S -- THAT'S GABBY, RIGHT?
DOC, WHAT DO WE DO?
STICK TO THE PLAN.
I DON'T THINK THAT'S GABBY.
WHY'D YOU TEAR IT IN HALF? WHERE'S THE OTHER BIT?
NOT IN HER RIGHT MIND, NO.
EVEN IF I COULD REMEMBER, I WOULDN'T TELL YOU!
'BEE! REMEMBER WHO YOU ARE! THIS IS NOT YOU.
RIGHT ON, MUNMETH!
PAPA!
WOKK
AND WHO ARE YOU TO JUDGE ME, CAVEMAN?
GABBY, NO!

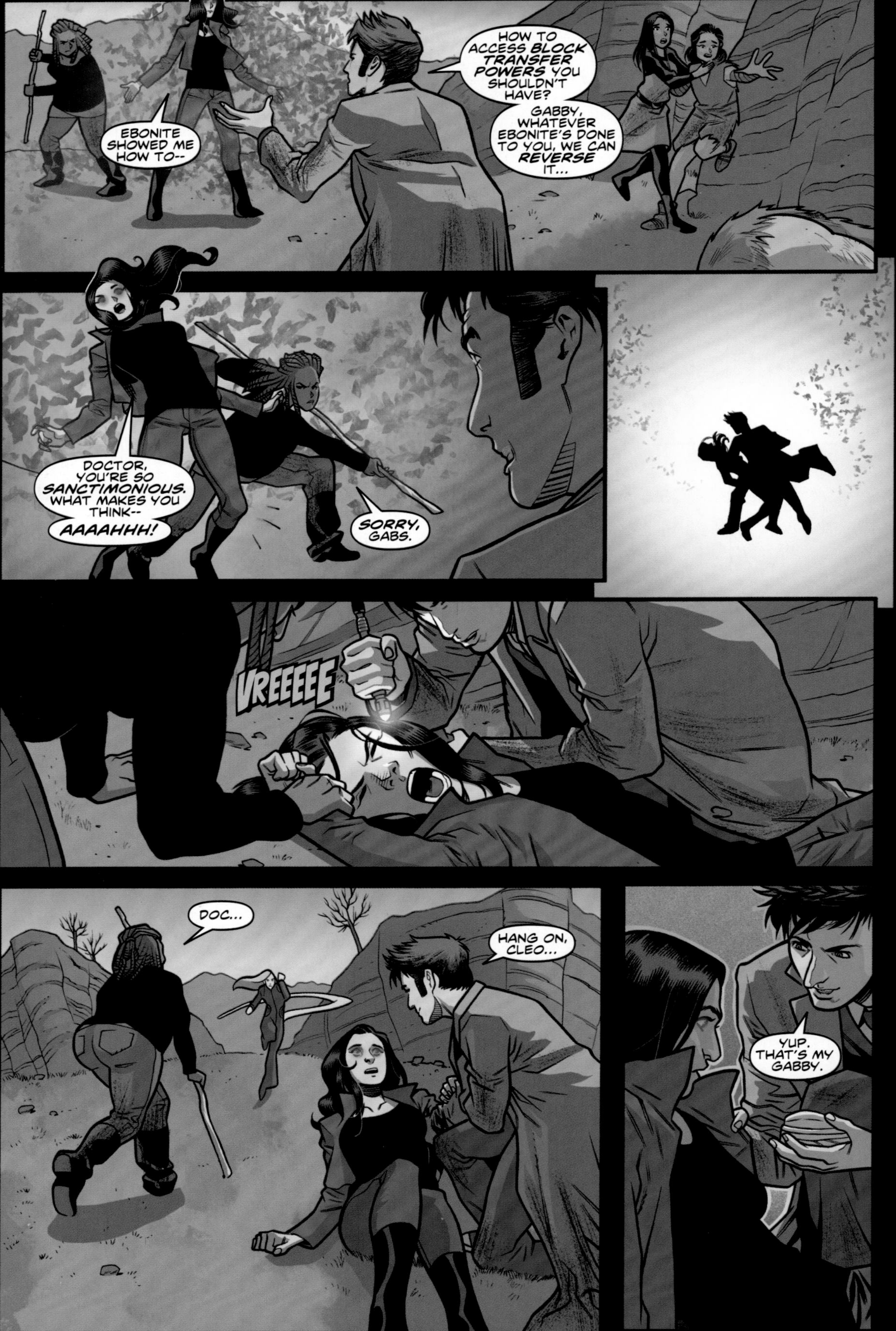
EBONITE SHOWED ME HOW TO--
HOW TO ACCESS BLOCK TRANSFER POWERS YOU SHOULDN'T HAVE?
GABBY, WHATEVER EBONITE'S DONE TO YOU, WE CAN REVERSE IT...
DOCTOR, YOU'RE SO SANCTIMONIOUS. WHAT MAKES YOU THINK-- AAAAHHH!
SORRY, GABS.
VREEEEE
DOC...
HANG ON, CLEO...
YUP. THAT'S MY GABBY.

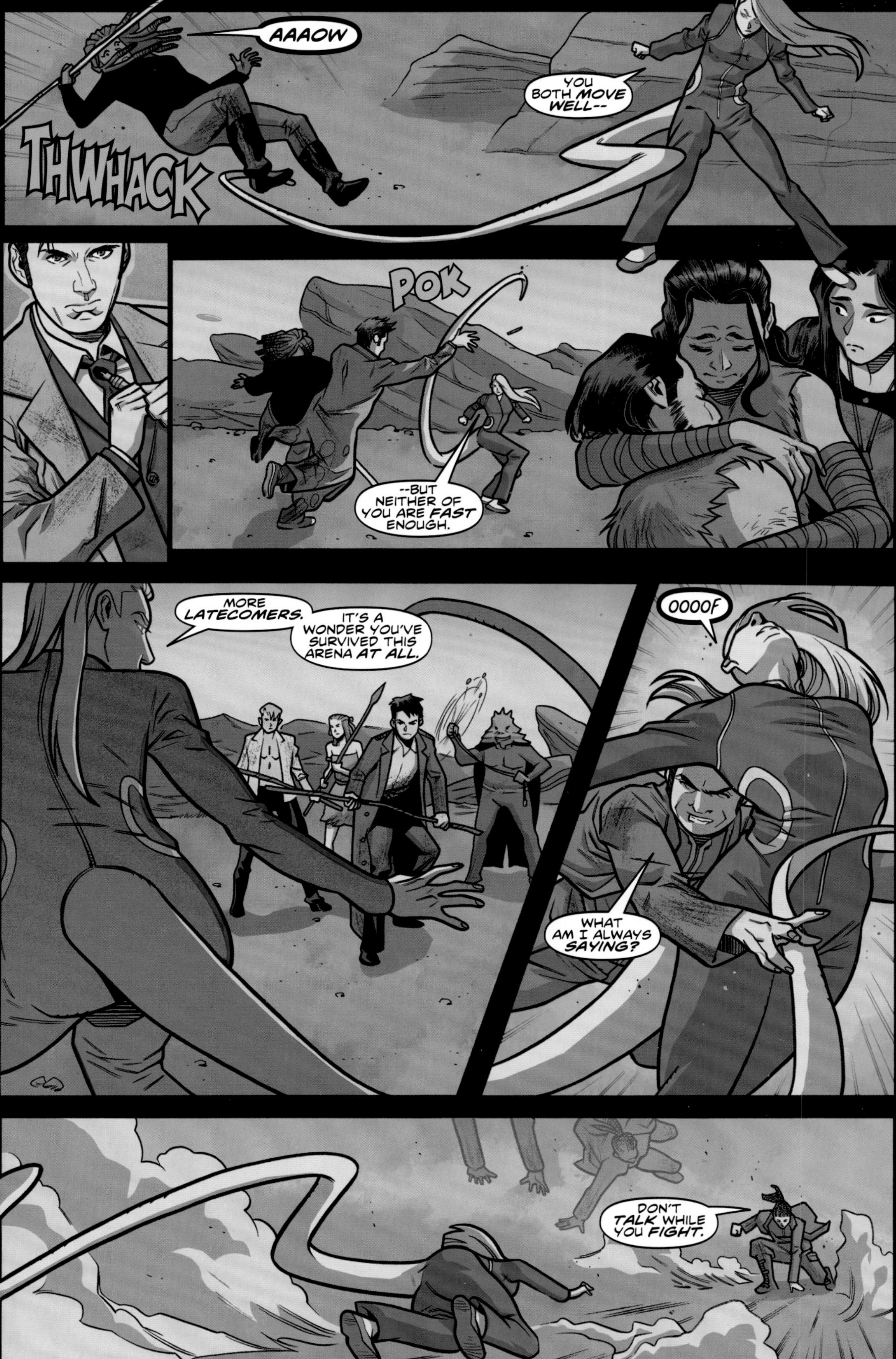
AAAOW
THWHACK
YOU BOTH MOVE WELL--
POK
--BUT NEITHER OF YOU ARE FAST ENOUGH.
MORE LATECOMERS.
IT'S A WONDER YOU'VE SURVIVED THIS ARENA AT ALL.
OOOOF
WHAT AM I ALWAYS SAYING?
DON'T TALK WHILE YOU FIGHT.

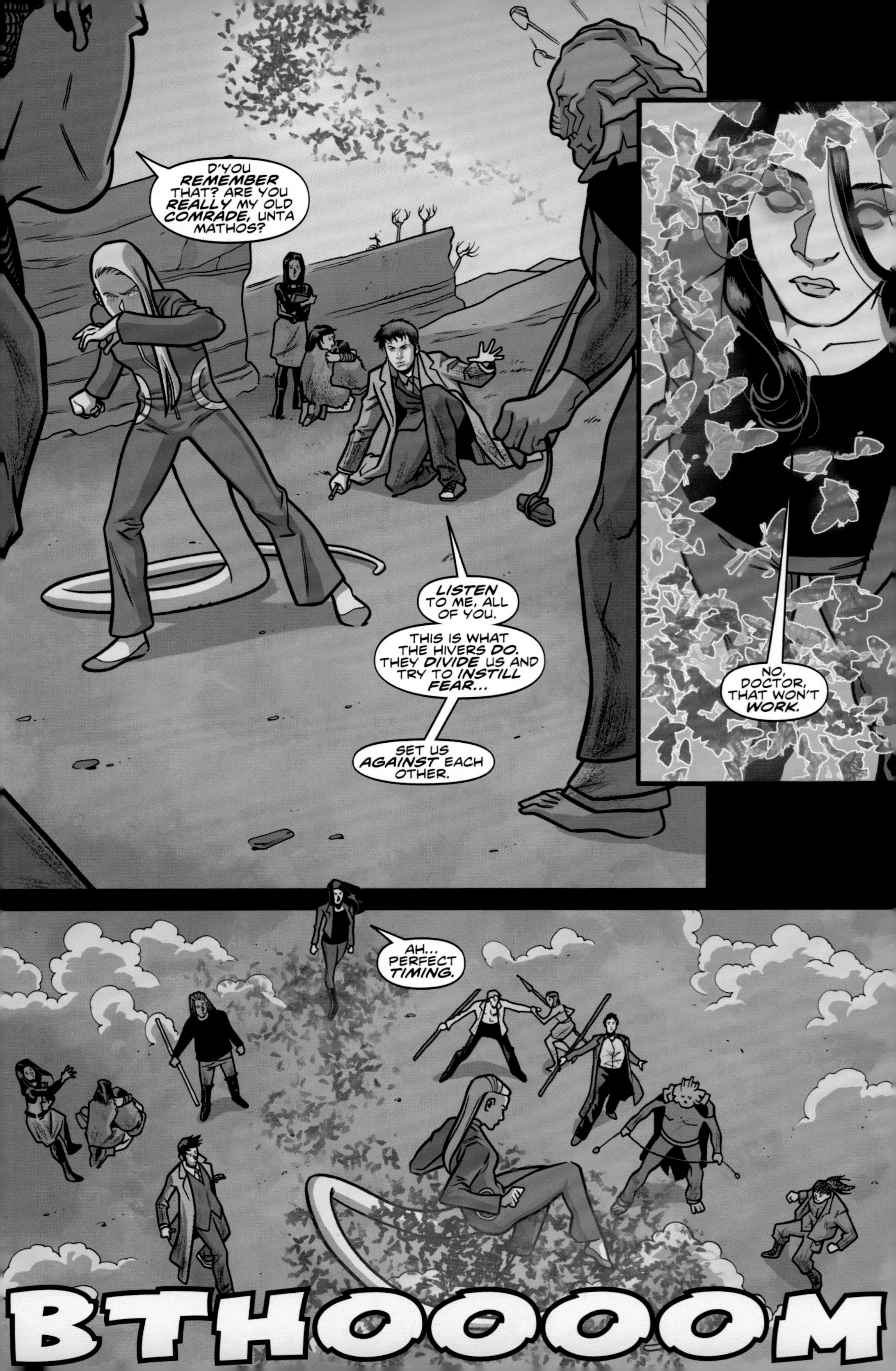
D'YOU REMEMBER THAT? ARE YOU REALLY MY OLD COMRADE, UNTA MATHOS?
LISTEN TO ME, ALL OF YOU.
THIS IS WHAT THE HIVERS DO. THEY DIVIDE US AND TRY TO INSTILL FEAR...
SET US AGAINST EACH OTHER.
NO, DOCTOR, THAT WON'T WORK.
AH... PERFECT TIMING.
BTHOOOOOM

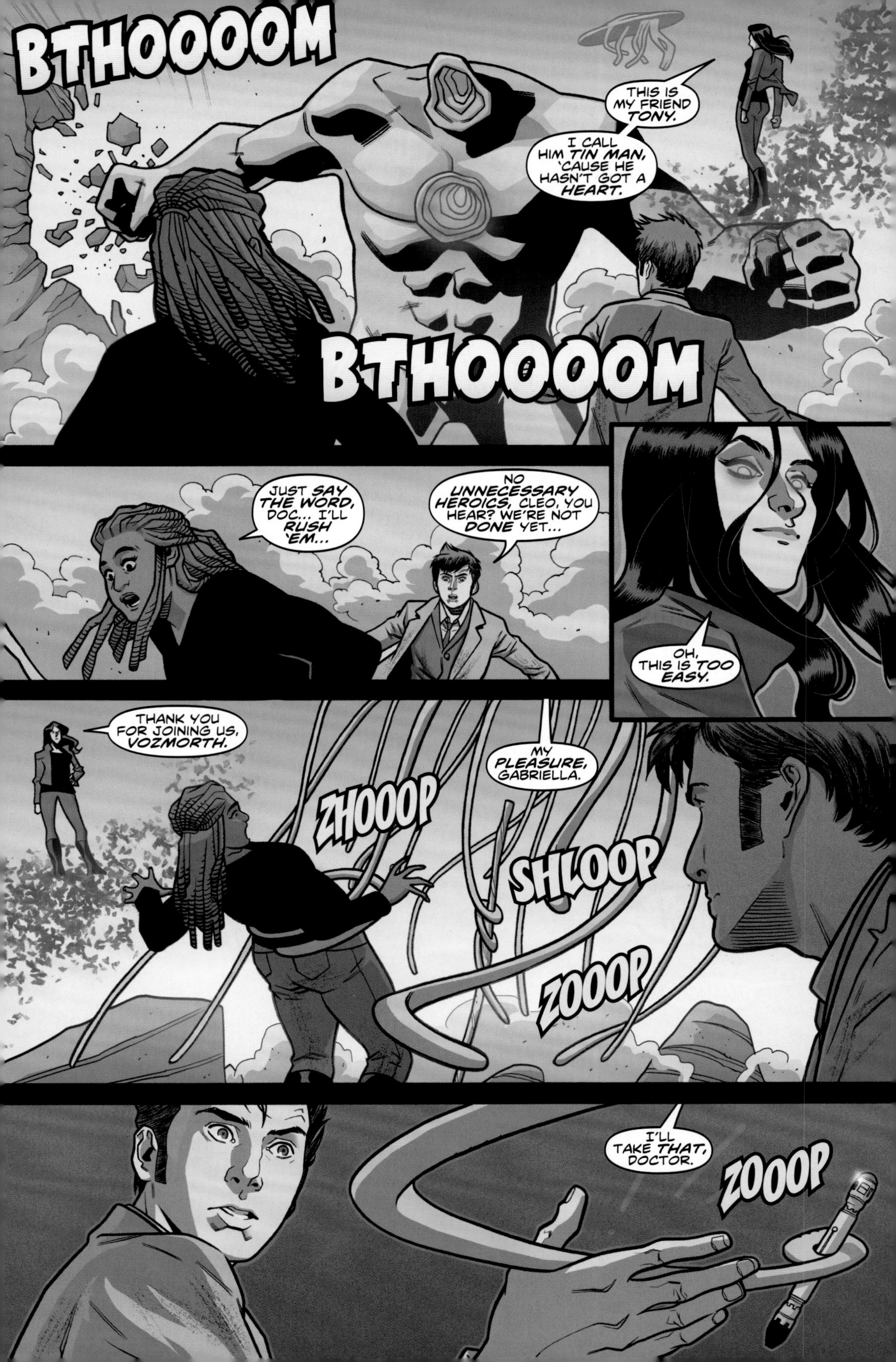
BTHOOOOM
THIS IS MY FRIEND TONY.
I CALL HIM TIN MAN, 'CAUSE HE HASN'T GOT A HEART.
BTHOOOOM
JUST SAY THE WORD, DOC... I'LL RUSH 'EM...
NO UNNECESSARY HEROICS, CLEO, YOU HEAR? WE'RE NOT DONE YET...
OH, THIS IS TOO EASY.
THANK YOU FOR JOINING US, VOZMORTH.
MY PLEASURE, GABRIELLA.
ZHOOOP
SHLOOP
ZOOOP
I'LL TAKE THAT, DOCTOR.
ZOOOP

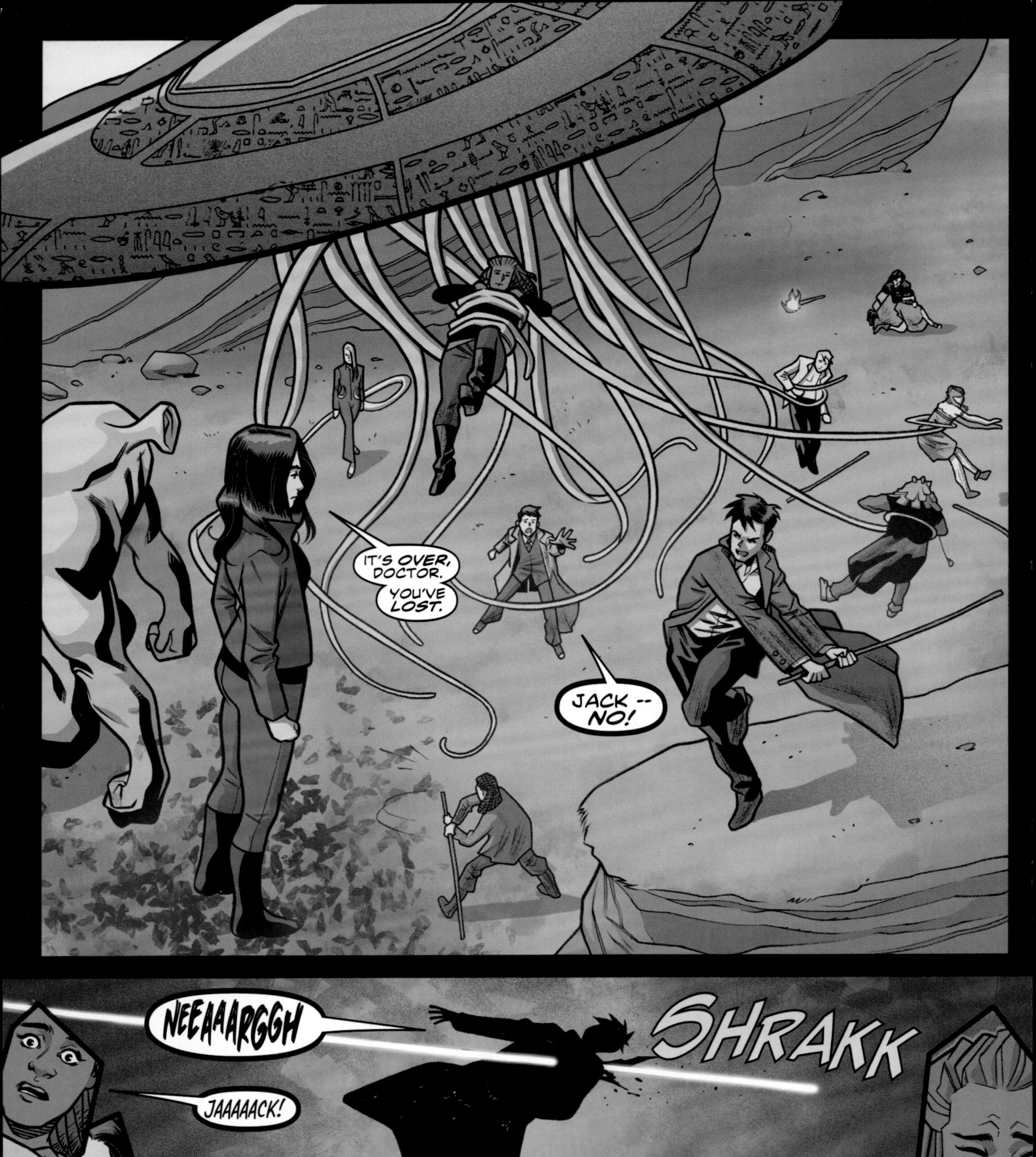
IT'S OVER, DOCTOR. YOU'VE LOST.
JACK -- NO!
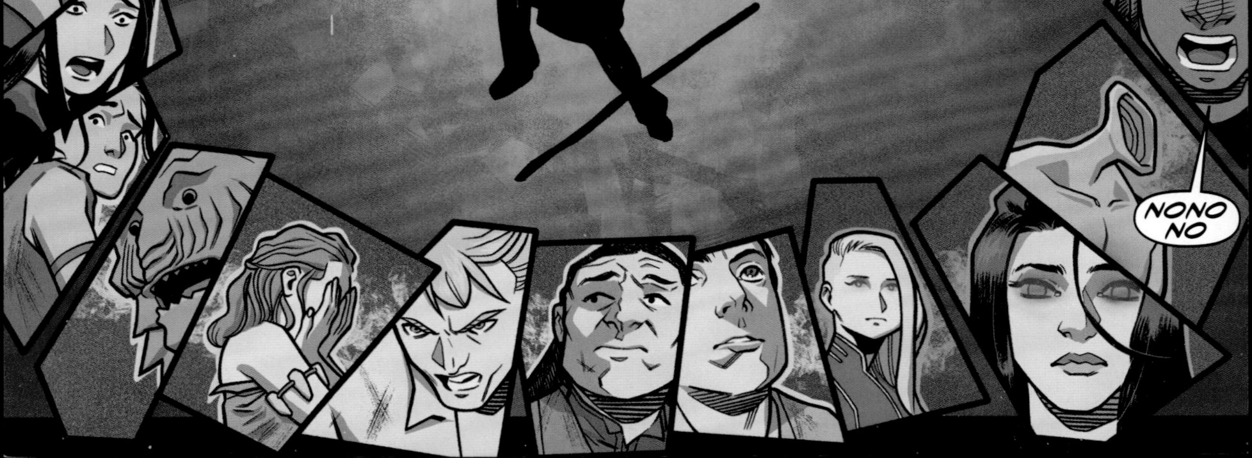
NEEAAARGGH
SHRAKK
JAAAAACK!
NONO NO

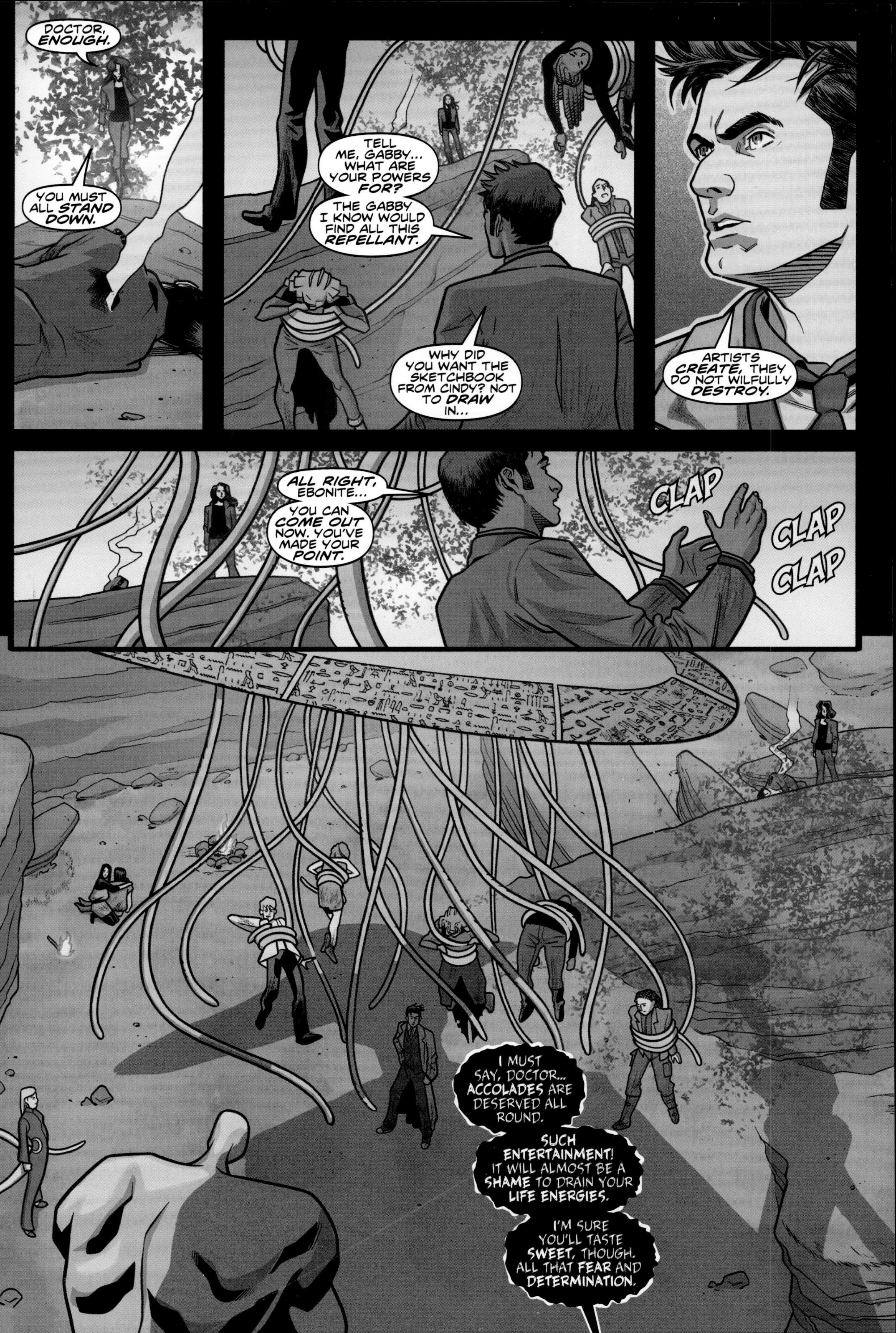
DOCTOR, ENOUGH.
YOU MUST ALL STAND DOWN.
TELL ME, GABBY... WHAT ARE YOUR POWERS FOR?
THE GABBY I KNOW WOULD FIND ALL THIS REPELLANT.
WHY DID YOU WANT THE SKETCHBOOK FROM CINDY? NOT TO DRAW IN...
ARTISTS CREATE, THEY DO NOT WILFULLY DESTROY.
ALL RIGHT, EBONITE...
YOU CAN COME OUT NOW. YOU'VE MADE YOUR POINT.
CLAP
CLAP
CLAP
I MUST SAY, DOCTOR... ACCOLADES ARE DESERVED ALL ROUND.
SUCH ENTERTAINMENT! IT WILL ALMOST BE A SHAME TO DRAIN YOUR LIFE ENERGIES.
I'M SURE YOU'LL TASTE SWEET, THOUGH. ALL THAT FEAR AND DETERMINATION.

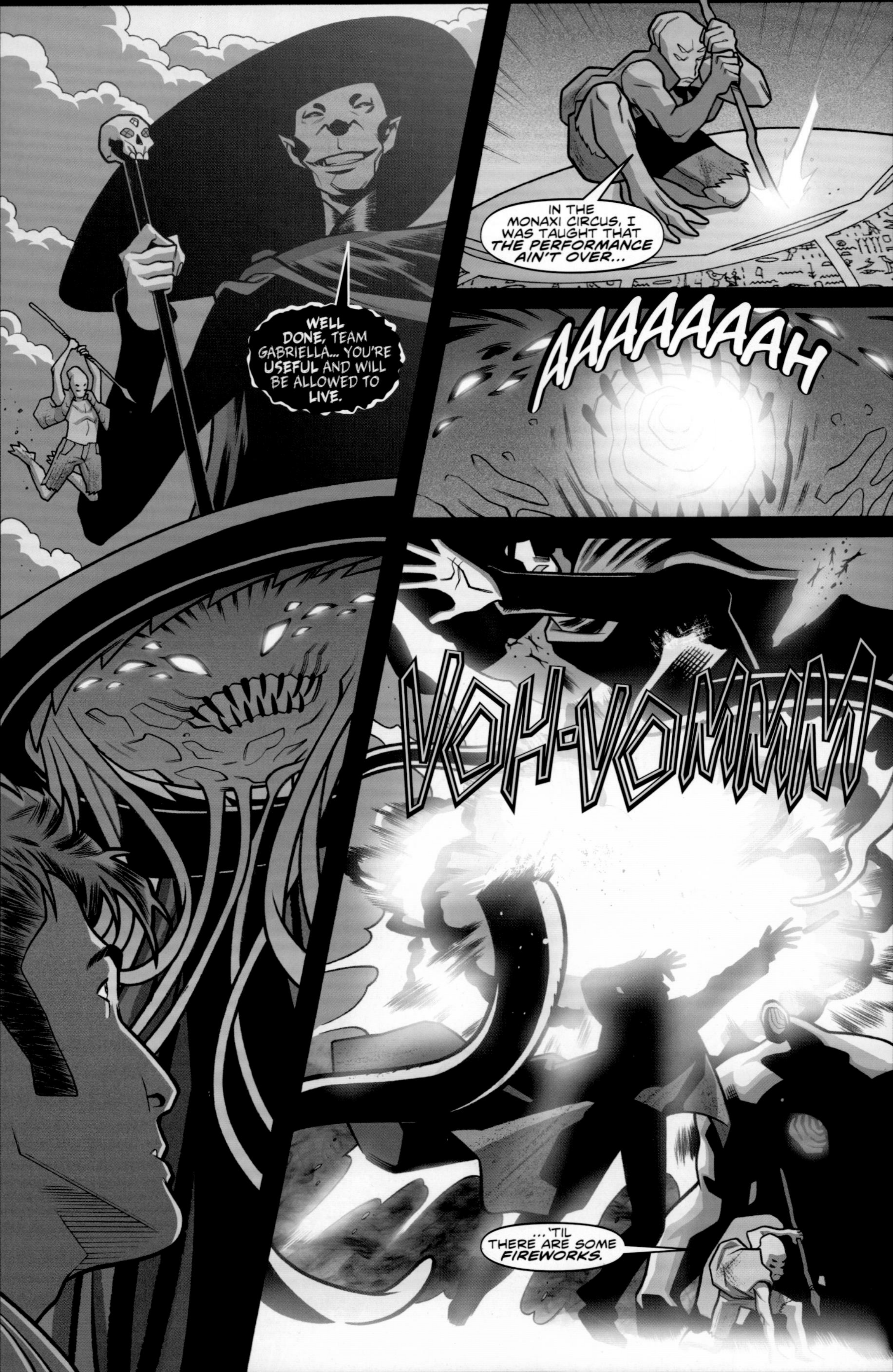
WELL DONE, TEAM GABRIELLA... YOU'RE USEFUL AND WILL BE ALLOWED TO LIVE.
IN THE MONAXI CIRCUS, I WAS TAUGHT THAT THE PERFORMANCE AIN'T OVER...
AAAAAAAAH
VOH-VOMMMM
...'TIL THERE ARE SOME FIREWORKS.

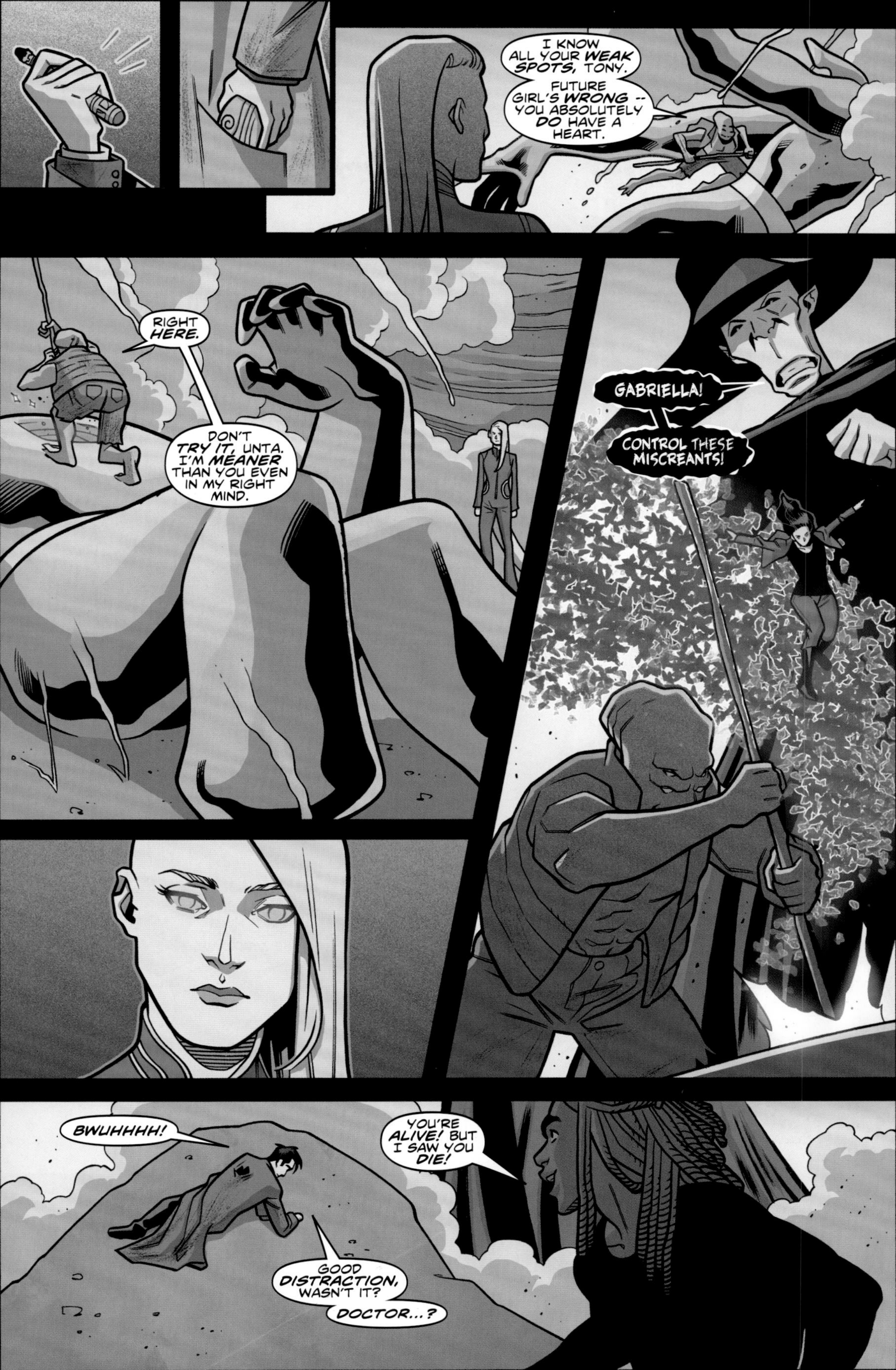
I KNOW ALL YOUR WEAK SPOTS, TONY.
FUTURE GIRL'S WRONG -- YOU ABSOLUTELY DO HAVE A HEART.
RIGHT HERE.
DON'T TRY IT, UNTA. I'M MEANER THAN YOU EVEN IN MY RIGHT MIND.
GABRIELLA!
CONTROL THESE MISCREANTS!
BWUHHHH!
YOU'RE ALIVE! BUT I SAW YOU DIE!
GOOD DISTRACTION, WASN'T IT?
DOCTOR...?

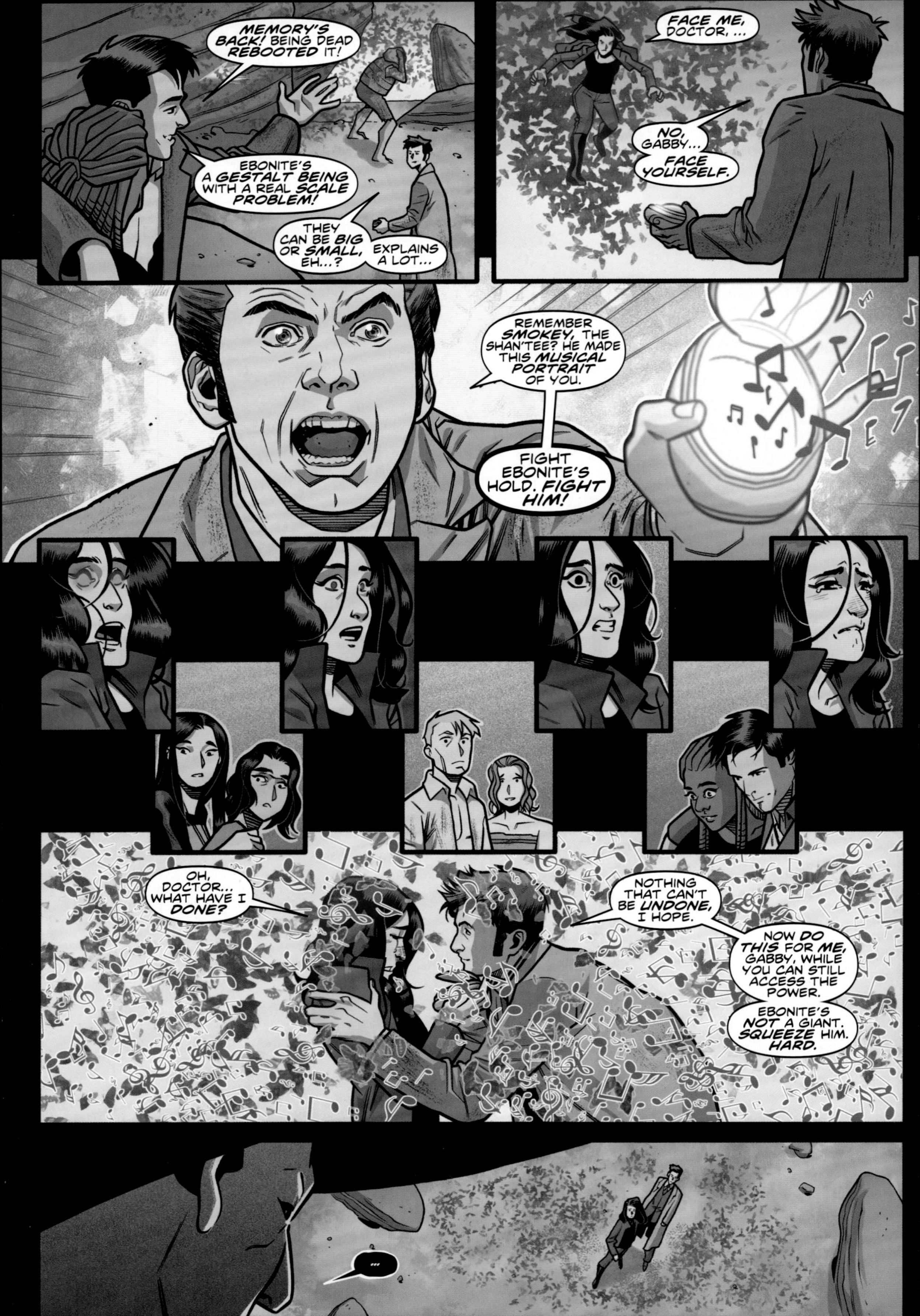
MEMORY'S BACK! BEING DEAD REBOOTED IT!
EBONITE'S A GESTALT BEING WITH A REAL SCALE PROBLEM!
THEY CAN BE BIG OR SMALL, EH...?
EXPLAINS A LOT...
FACE ME, DOCTOR, ...
NO, GABBY... FACE YOURSELF.
REMEMBER SMOKEY, THE SHAN'TEE? HE MADE THIS MUSICAL PORTRAIT OF YOU.
FIGHT EBONITE'S HOLD. FIGHT HIM!
OH, DOCTOR... WHAT HAVE I DONE?
NOTHING THAT CAN'T BE UNDONE, I HOPE.
NOW DO THIS FOR ME, GABBY, WHILE YOU CAN STILL ACCESS THE POWER.
EBONITE'S NOT A GIANT. SQUEEZE HIM. HARD.
...

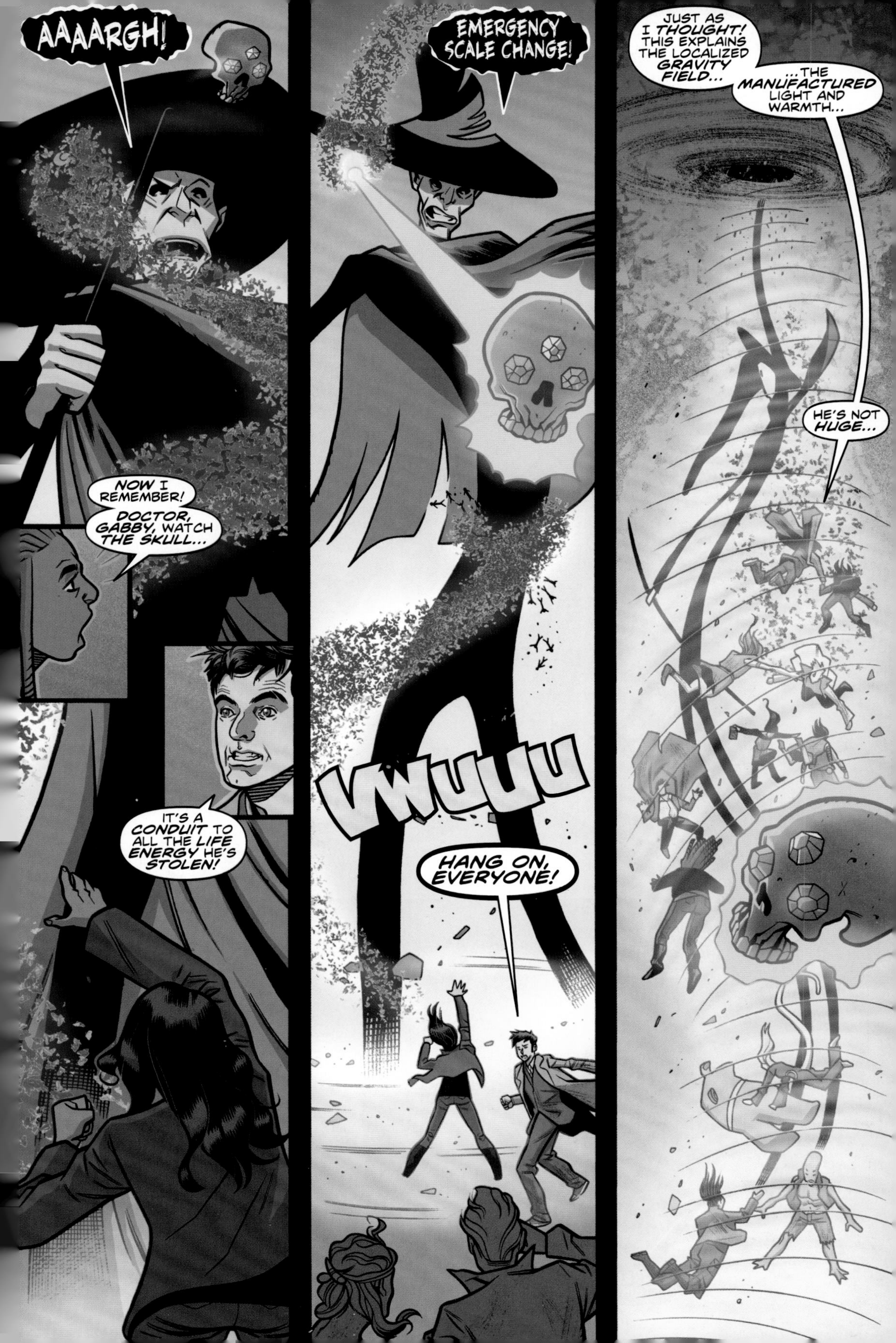
AAAARGH!
NOW I REMEMBER! DOCTOR, GABBY, WATCH THE SKULL...
IT'S A CONDUIT TO ALL THE LIFE ENERGY HE'S STOLEN!
EMERGENCY SCALE CHANGE!
VWUUU
HANG ON, EVERYONE!
JUST AS I THOUGHT! THIS EXPLAINS THE LOCALIZED GRAVITY FIELD...
...THE MANUFACTURED LIGHT AND WARMTH...
HE'S NOT HUGE...

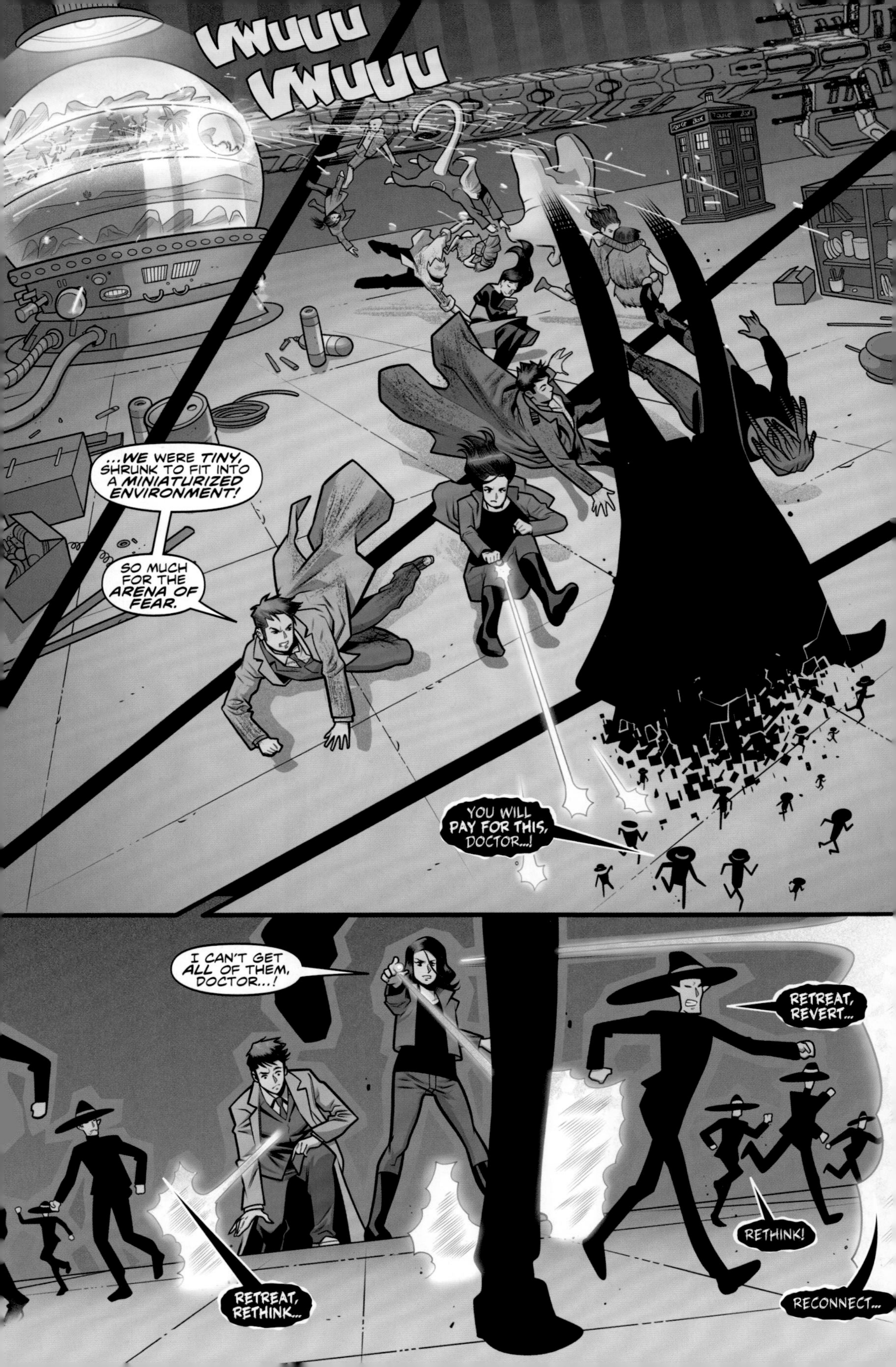
VWUUU VWUUU
...WE WERE TINY, SHRUNK TO FIT INTO A MINIATURIZED ENVIRONMENT!
SO MUCH FOR THE ARENA OF FEAR.
YOU WILL PAY FOR THIS, DOCTOR...!
I CAN'T GET ALL OF THEM, DOCTOR...!
RETREAT, REVERT...
RETHINK!
RETREAT, RETHINK...
RECONNECT...

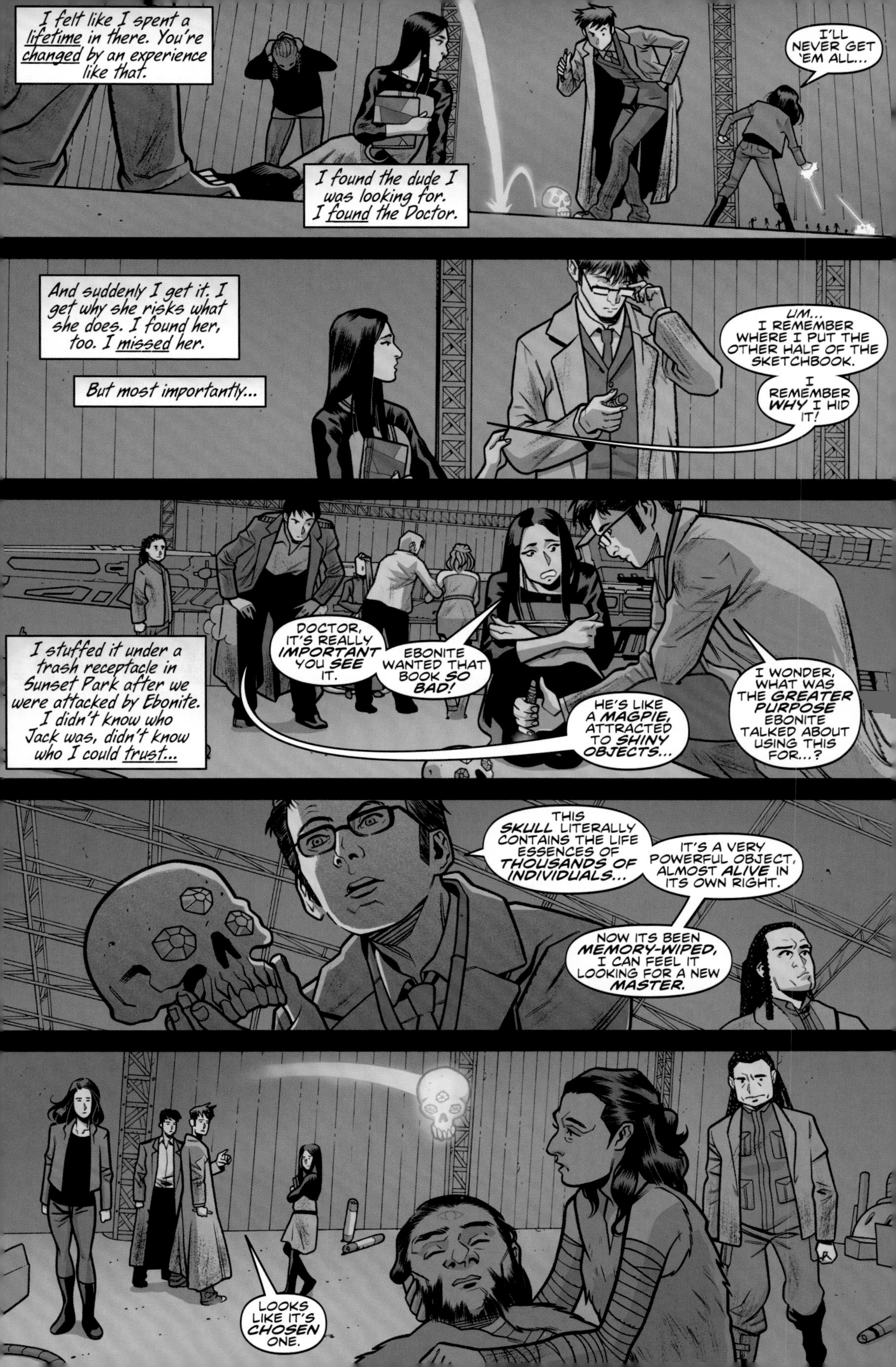

I felt like I spent a lifetime in there. You're changed by an experience like that.
I'LL NEVER GET 'EM ALL...
I found the dude I was looking for. I found the Doctor.
And suddenly I get it. I get why she risks what she does. I found her, too. I missed her.
But most importantly...
UM... I REMEMBER WHERE I PUT THE OTHER HALF OF THE SKETCHBOOK.
I REMEMBER WHY I HID IT!
I stuffed it under a trash receptacle in Sunset Park after we were attacked by Ebonite. I didn't know who Jack was, didn't know who I could trust...
DOCTOR, IT'S REALLY IMPORTANT YOU SEE IT.
EBONITE WANTED THAT BOOK SO BAD!
HE'S LIKE A MAGPIE, ATTRACTED TO SHINY OBJECTS...
I WONDER, WHAT WAS THE GREATER PURPOSE EBONITE TALKED ABOUT USING THIS FOR...?
THIS SKULL LITERALLY CONTAINS THE LIFE ESSENCES OF THOUSANDS OF INDIVIDUALS...
IT'S A VERY POWERFUL OBJECT, ALMOST ALIVE IN ITS OWN RIGHT.
NOW ITS BEEN MEMORY-WIPED, I CAN FEEL IT LOOKING FOR A NEW MASTER.
LOOKS LIKE IT'S CHOSEN ONE.

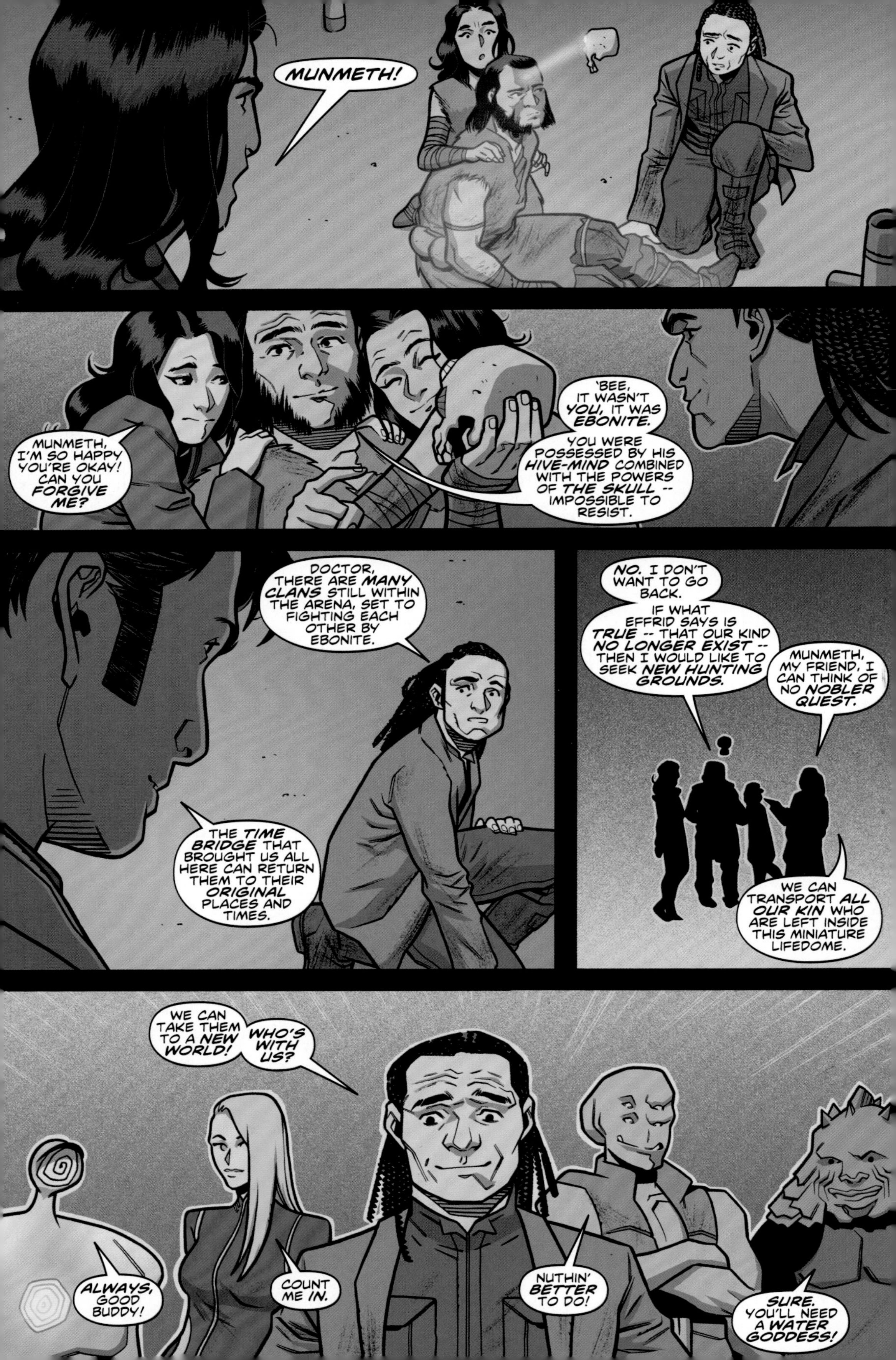
MUNMETH!
MUNMETH, I'M SO HAPPY YOU'RE OKAY! CAN YOU FORGIVE ME?
'BEE, IT WASN'T YOU, IT WAS EBONITE.
YOU WERE POSSESSED BY HIS HIVE-MIND COMBINED WITH THE POWERS OF THE SKULL -- IMPOSSIBLE TO RESIST.
DOCTOR, THERE ARE MANY CLANS STILL WITHIN THE ARENA, SET TO FIGHTING EACH OTHER BY EBONITE.
THE TIME BRIDGE THAT BROUGHT US ALL HERE CAN RETURN THEM TO THEIR ORIGINAL PLACES AND TIMES.
NO. I DON'T WANT TO GO BACK.
IF WHAT EFFRID SAYS IS TRUE -- THAT OUR KIND NO LONGER EXIST -- THEN I WOULD LIKE TO SEEK NEW HUNTING GROUNDS.
MUNMETH, MY FRIEND, I CAN THINK OF NO NOBLER QUEST.
WE CAN TRANSPORT ALL OUR KIN WHO ARE LEFT INSIDE THIS MINIATURE LIFEDOME.
WE CAN TAKE THEM TO A NEW WORLD!
WHO'S WITH US?
ALWAYS, GOOD BUDDY!
COUNT ME IN.
NUTHIN' BETTER TO DO!
SURE. YOU'LL NEED A WATER GODDESS!

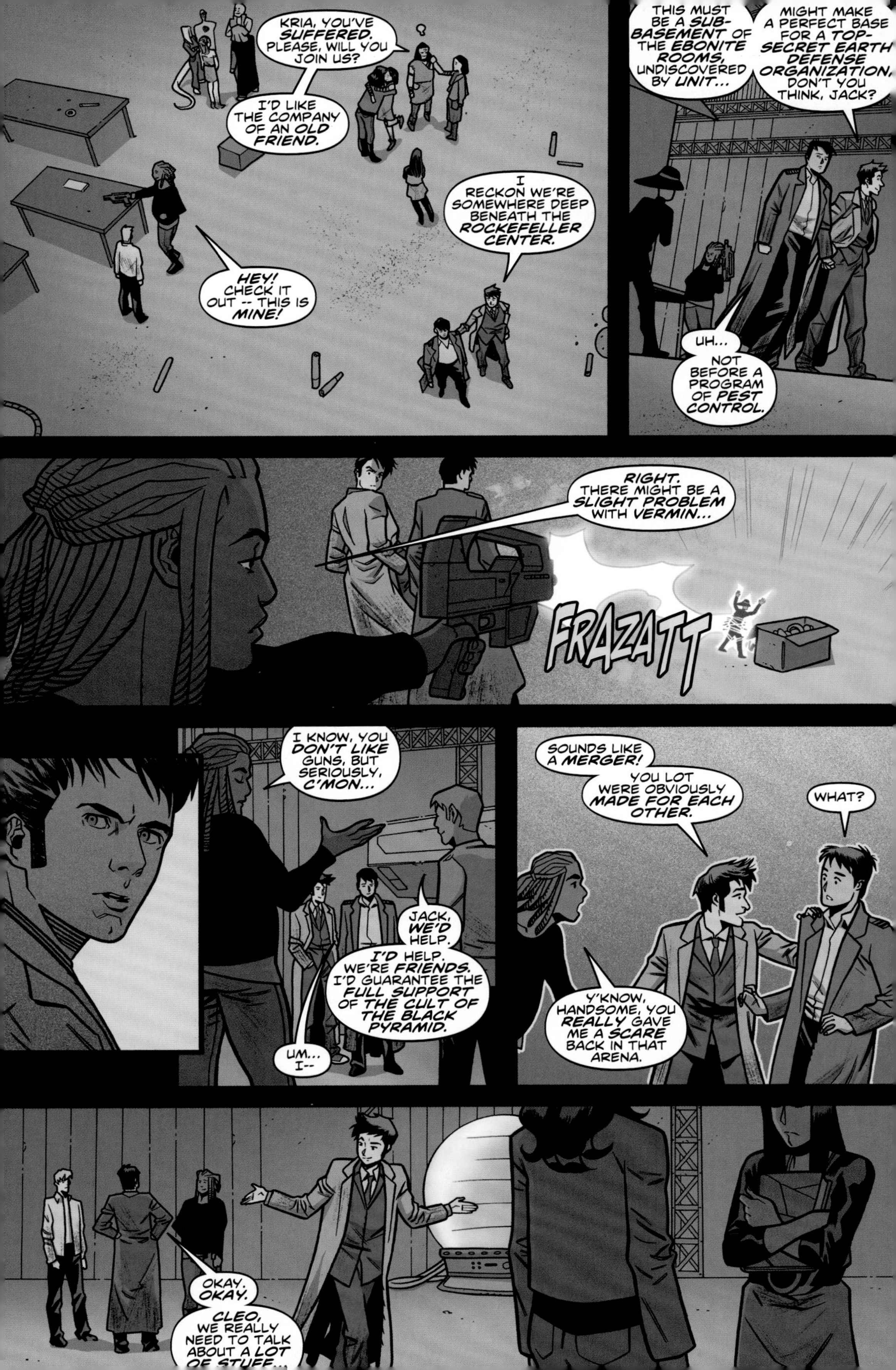

KRIA, YOU'VE SUFFERED. PLEASE, WILL YOU JOIN US?
I'D LIKE THE COMPANY OF AN OLD FRIEND.
I RECKON WE'RE SOMEWHERE DEEP BENEATH THE ROCKEFELLER CENTER.
HEY! CHECK IT OUT -- THIS IS MINE!
THIS MUST BE A SUB-BASEMENT OF THE EBONITE ROOMS, UNDISCOVERED BY UNIT...
MIGHT MAKE A PERFECT BASE FOR A TOP-SECRET EARTH DEFENSE ORGANIZATION, DON'T YOU THINK, JACK?
UH...
NOT BEFORE A PROGRAM OF PEST CONTROL.
RIGHT. THERE MIGHT BE A SLIGHT PROBLEM WITH VERMIN...
FRAZATT
I KNOW, YOU DON'T LIKE GUNS, BUT SERIOUSLY, C'MON...
JACK, WE'D HELP.
I'D HELP. WE'RE FRIENDS. I'D GUARANTEE THE FULL SUPPORT OF THE CULT OF THE BLACK PYRAMID.
UM... I--
SOUNDS LIKE A MERGER!
YOU LOT WERE OBVIOUSLY MADE FOR EACH OTHER.
WHAT?
Y'KNOW, HANDSOME, YOU REALLY GAVE ME A SCARE BACK IN THAT ARENA.
OKAY. OKAY.
CLEO, WE REALLY NEED TO TALK ABOUT A LOT OF STUFF...

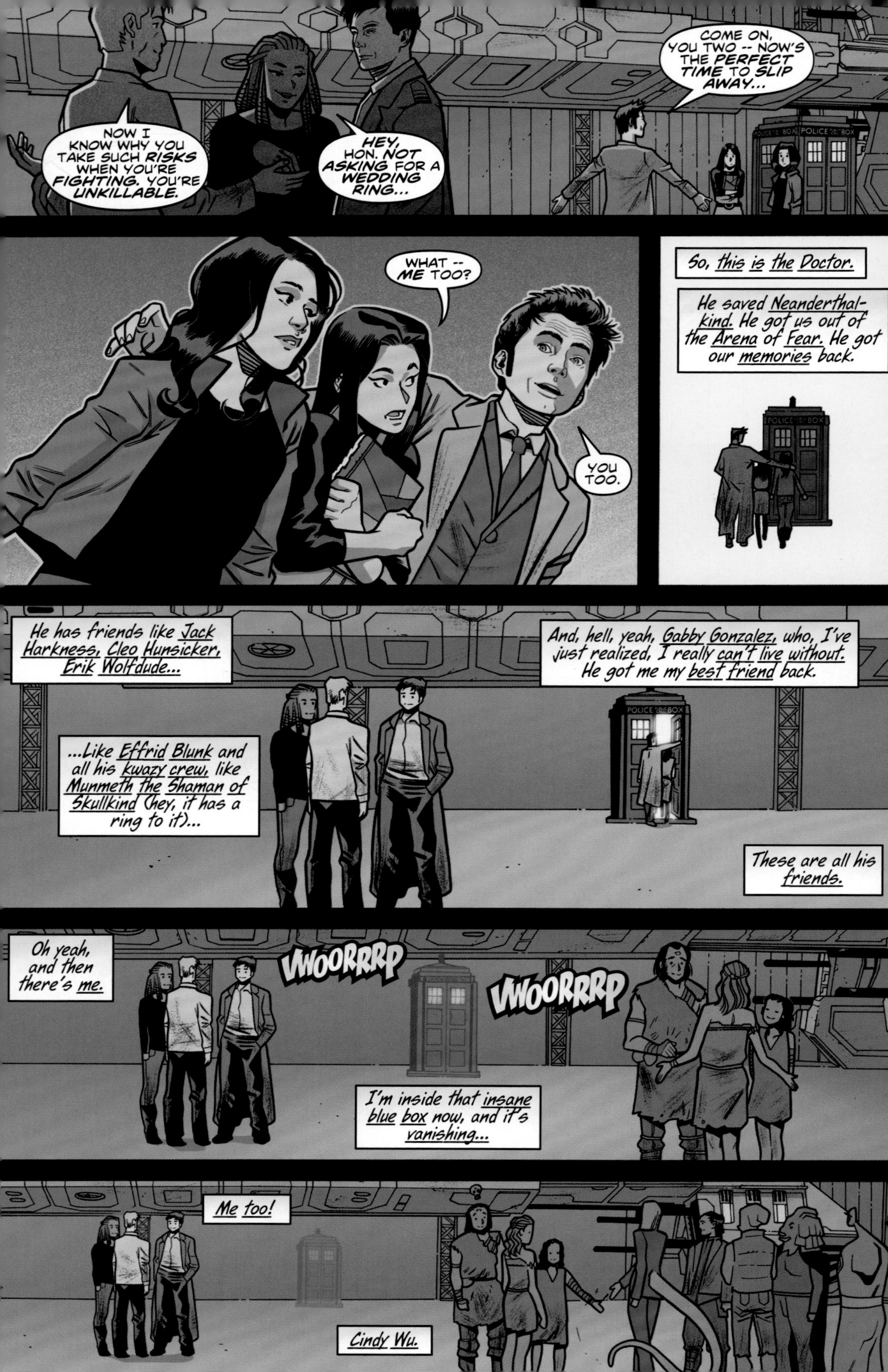

NOW I KNOW WHY YOU TAKE SUCH RISKS WHEN YOU'RE FIGHTING. YOU'RE UNKILLABLE.
HEY, HON. NOT ASKING FOR A WEDDING RING...
COME ON, YOU TWO -- NOW'S THE PERFECT TIME TO SLIP AWAY...
POLICE BOX
WHAT -- ME TOO?
YOU TOO.
So, this is the Doctor.
He saved Neanderthal-kind. He got us out of the Arena of Fear. He got our memories back.
He has friends like Jack Harkness, Cleo Hunsicker, Erik Wolfdude...
...Like Effrid Blunk and all his kwazy crew, like Munmeth the Shaman of Skullkind (hey, it has a ring to it)...
And, hell, yeah, Gabby Gonzalez, who, I've just realized, I really can't live without. He got me my best friend back.
These are all his friends.
Oh yeah, and then there's me.
VWOORRRP
VWOORRRP
I'm inside that insane blue box now, and it's vanishing...
Me too!
Cindy Wu.

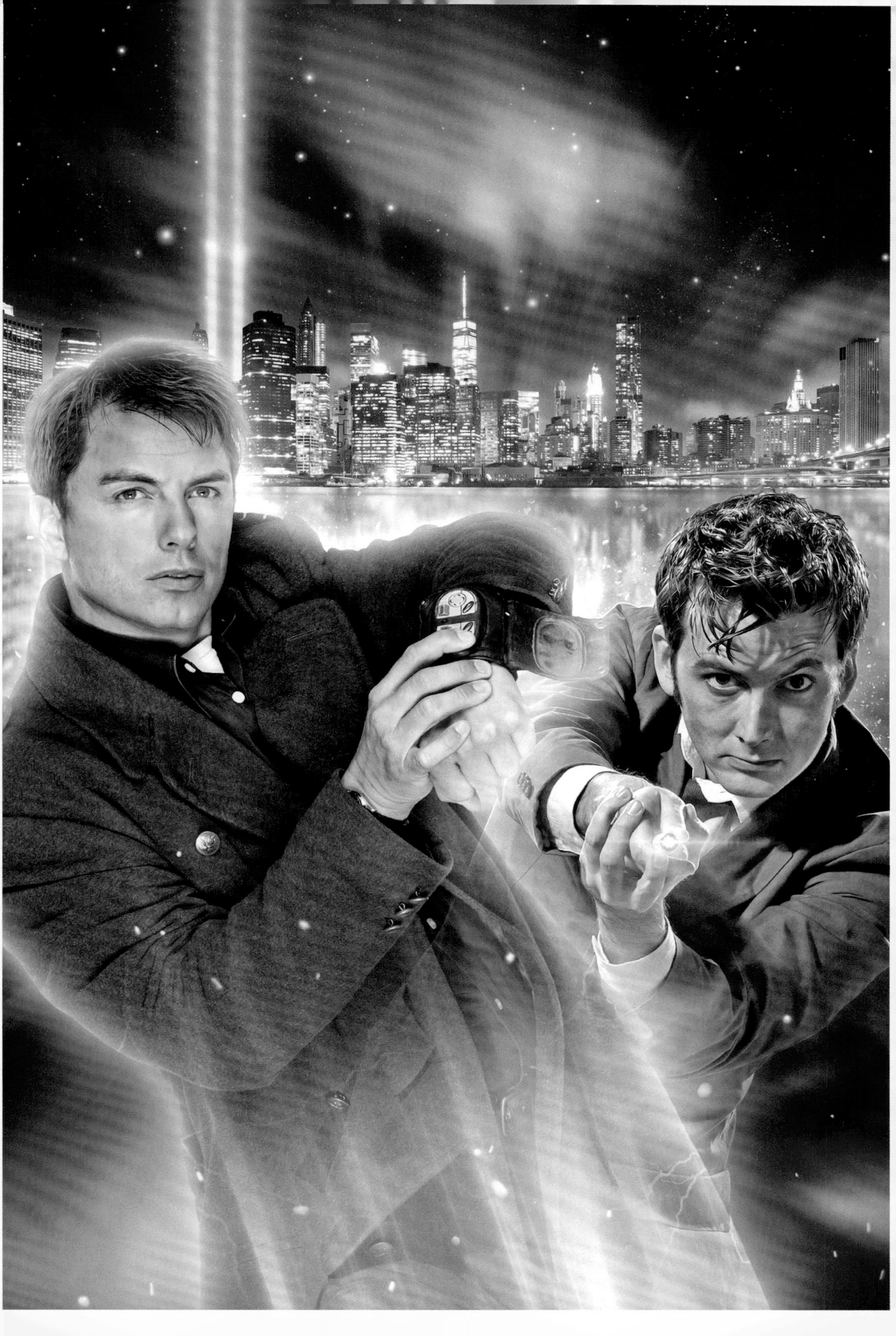

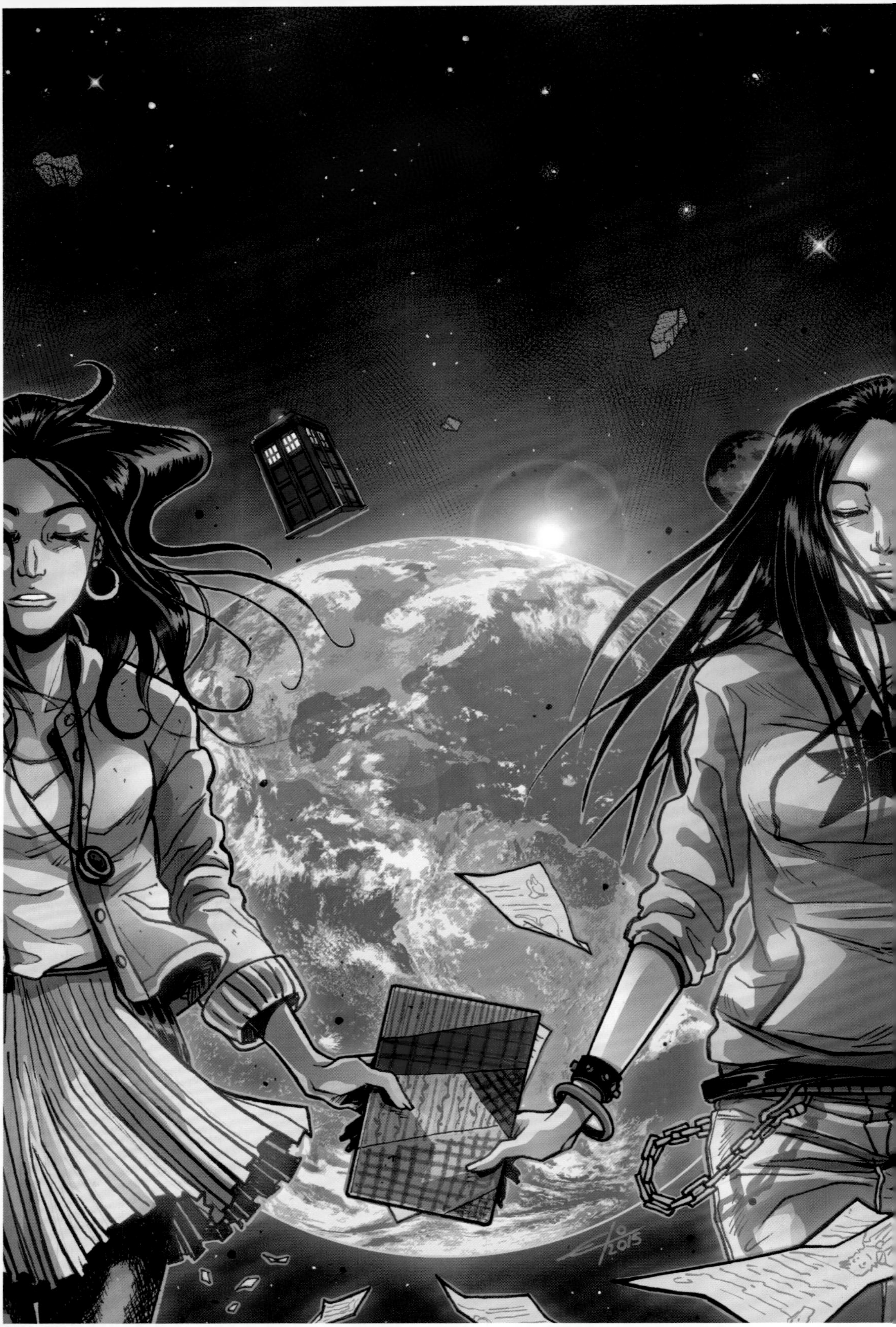

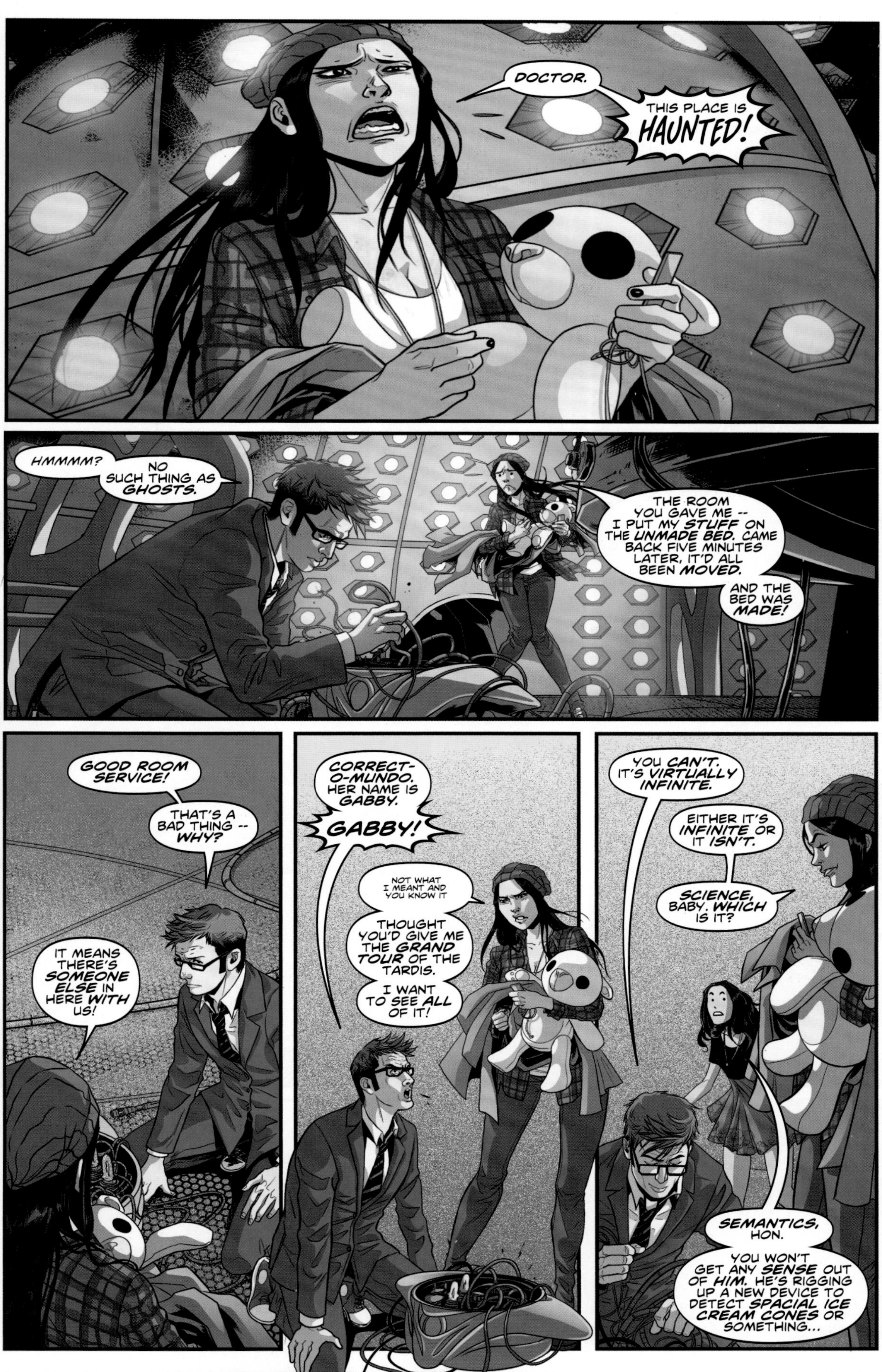

DOCTOR.
THIS PLACE IS HAUNTED!
HMMMM?
NO SUCH THING AS GHOSTS.
THE ROOM YOU GAVE ME -- I PUT MY STUFF ON THE UNMADE BED. CAME BACK FIVE MINUTES LATER, IT'D ALL BEEN MOVED.
AND THE BED WAS MADE!
GOOD ROOM SERVICE!
THAT'S A BAD THING -- WHY?
IT MEANS THERE'S SOMEONE ELSE IN HERE WITH US!
CORRECT-O-MUNDO. HER NAME IS GABBY.
GABBY!
NOT WHAT I MEANT AND YOU KNOW IT
THOUGHT YOU'D GIVE ME THE GRAND TOUR OF THE TARDIS.
I WANT TO SEE ALL OF IT!
YOU CAN'T. IT'S VIRTUALLY INFINITE.
EITHER IT'S INFINITE OR IT ISN'T.
SCIENCE, BABY. WHICH IS IT?
SEMANTICS, HON.
YOU WON'T GET ANY SENSE OUT OF HIM. HE'S RIGGING UP A NEW DEVICE TO DETECT SPACIAL ICE CREAM CONES OR SOMETHING...

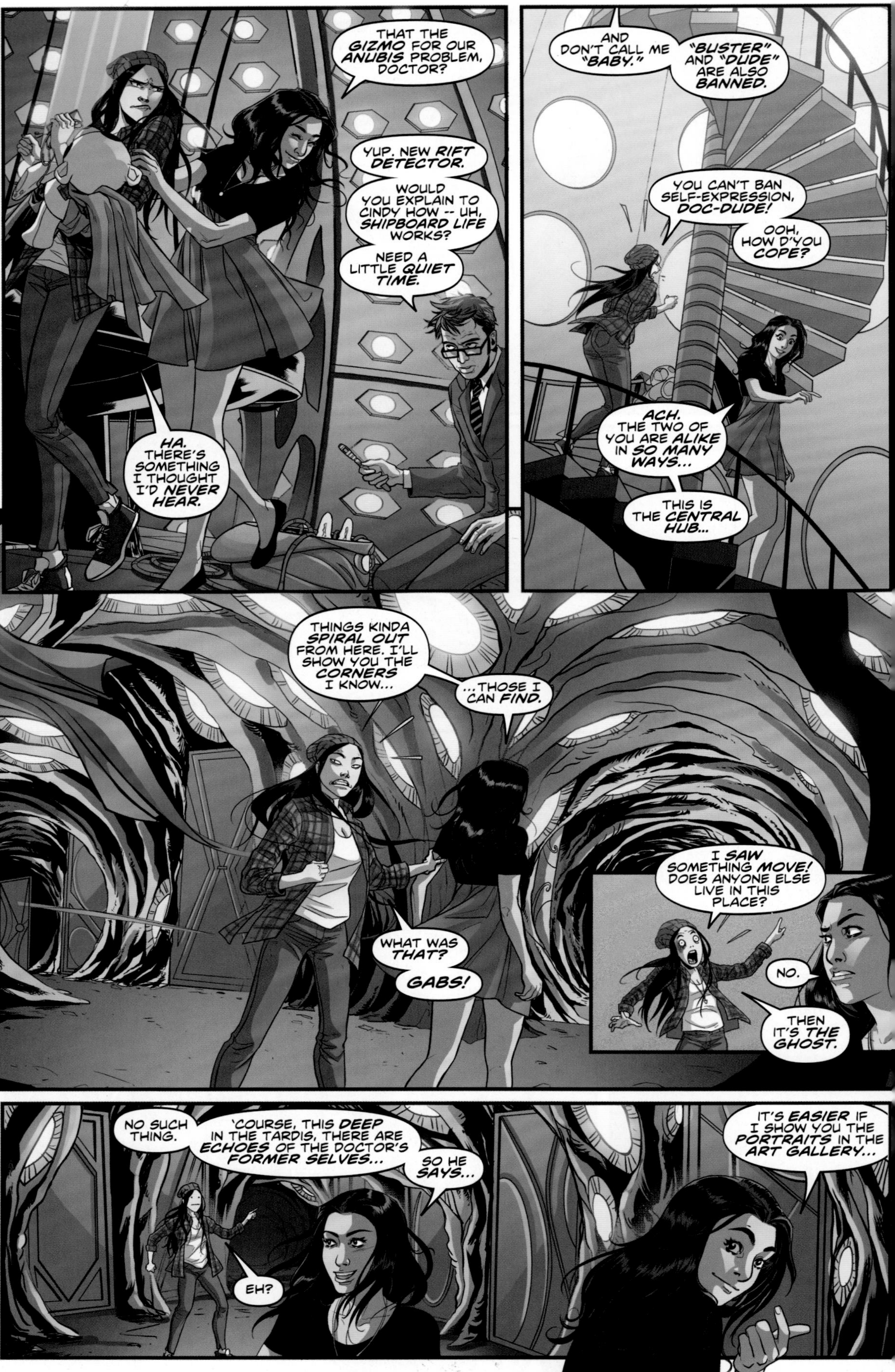

THAT THE GIZMO FOR OUR ANUBIS PROBLEM, DOCTOR?
YUP. NEW RIFT DETECTOR.
WOULD YOU EXPLAIN TO CINDY HOW -- UH, SHIPBOARD LIFE WORKS?
NEED A LITTLE QUIET TIME.
HA. THERE'S SOMETHING I THOUGHT I'D NEVER HEAR.
AND DON'T CALL ME "BABY."
"BUSTER" AND "DUDE" ARE ALSO BANNED.
YOU CAN'T BAN SELF-EXPRESSION, DOC-DUDE!
OOH, HOW D'YOU COPE?
ACH. THE TWO OF YOU ARE ALIKE IN SO MANY WAYS...
THIS IS THE CENTRAL HUB...
THINGS KINDA SPIRAL OUT FROM HERE. I'LL SHOW YOU THE CORNERS I KNOW...
...THOSE I CAN FIND.
WHAT WAS THAT?
GABS!
I SAW SOMETHING MOVE! DOES ANYONE ELSE LIVE IN THIS PLACE?
NO.
THEN IT'S THE GHOST.
NO SUCH THING.
'COURSE, THIS DEEP IN THE TARDIS, THERE ARE ECHOES OF THE DOCTOR'S FORMER SELVES...
SO HE SAYS...
EH?
IT'S EASIER IF I SHOW YOU THE PORTRAITS IN THE ART GALLERY...

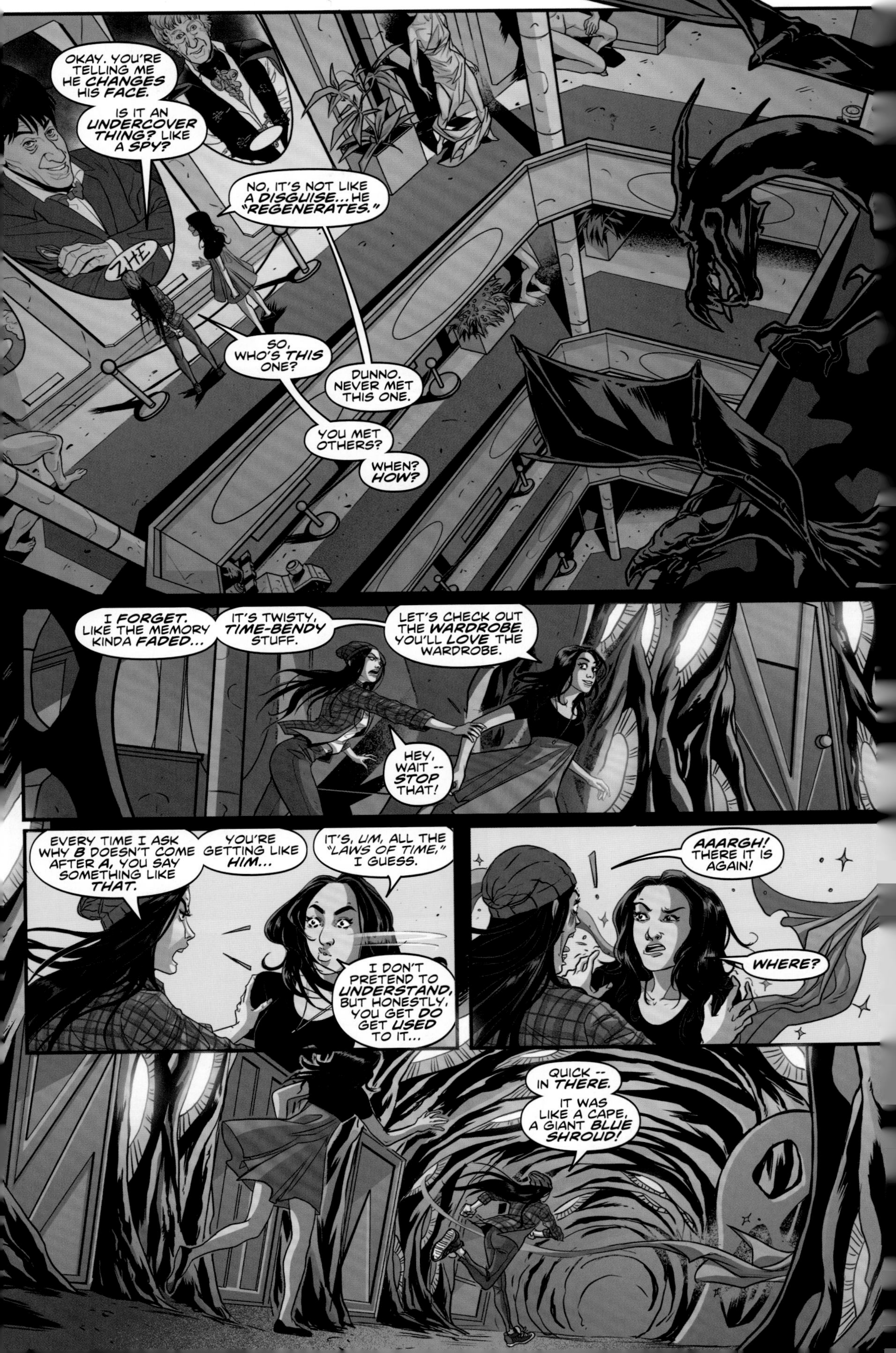

OKAY. YOU'RE TELLING ME HE CHANGES HIS FACE.
IS IT AN UNDERCOVER THING? LIKE A SPY?
NO, IT'S NOT LIKE A DISGUISE... HE "REGENERATES."
ZHE
SO, WHO'S THIS ONE?
DUNNO. NEVER MET THIS ONE.
YOU MET OTHERS?
WHEN? HOW?
I FORGET. LIKE THE MEMORY KINDA FADED...
IT'S TWISTY, TIME-BENDY STUFF.
LET'S CHECK OUT THE WARDROBE. YOU'LL LOVE THE WARDROBE.
HEY, WAIT -- STOP THAT!
EVERY TIME I ASK WHY B DOESN'T COME AFTER A, YOU SAY SOMETHING LIKE THAT.
YOU'RE GETTING LIKE HIM...
IT'S, UM, ALL THE "LAWS OF TIME," I GUESS.
I DON'T PRETEND TO UNDERSTAND, BUT HONESTLY, YOU GET DO GET USED TO IT...
AAARGH! THERE IT IS AGAIN!
!
WHERE?
QUICK -- IN THERE.
IT WAS LIKE A CAPE, A GIANT BLUE SHROUD!

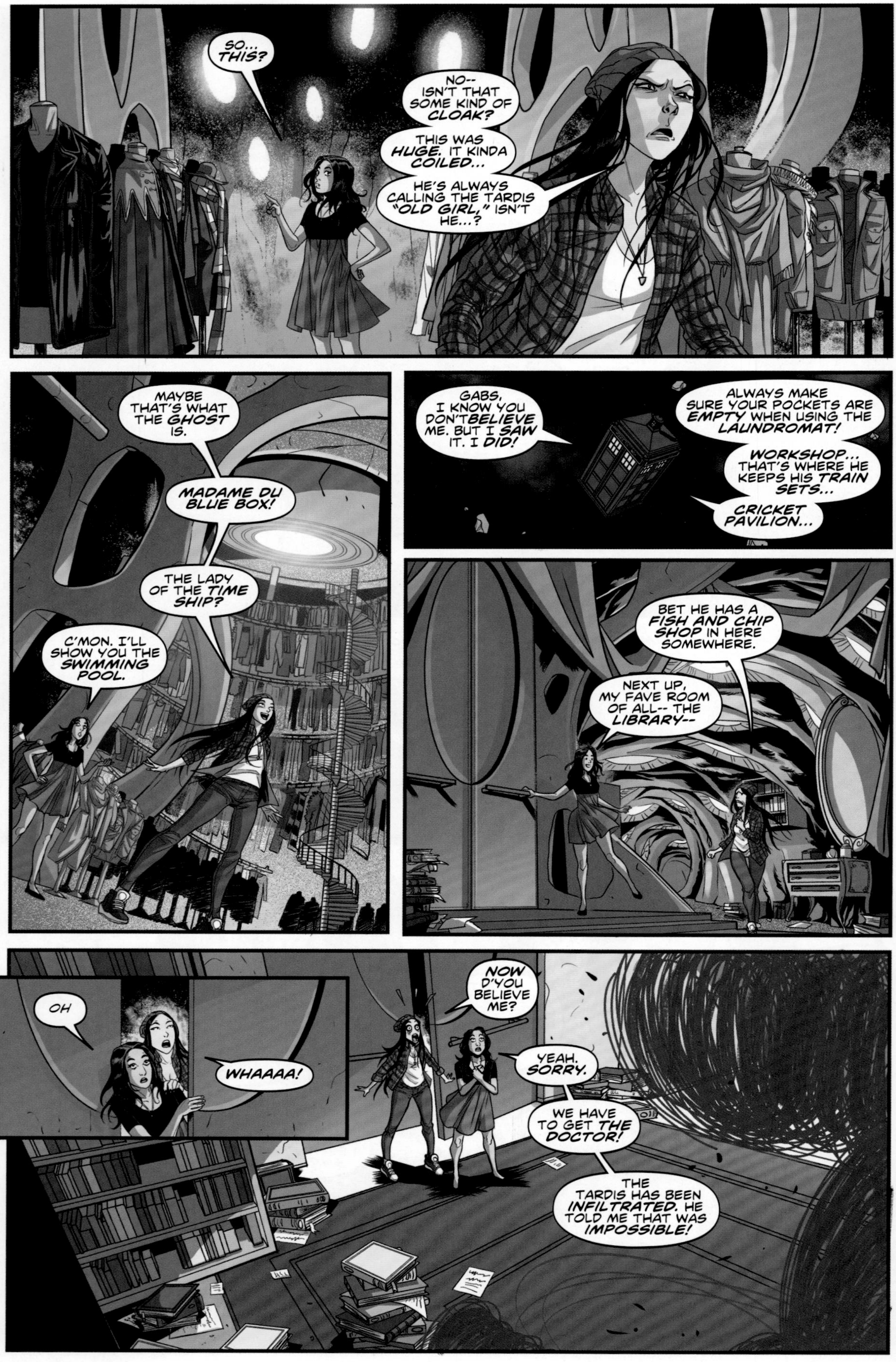
SO... THIS?
NO-- ISN'T THAT SOME KIND OF CLOAK?
THIS WAS HUGE. IT KINDA COILED...
HE'S ALWAYS CALLING THE TARDIS "OLD GIRL," ISN'T HE...?
MAYBE THAT'S WHAT THE GHOST IS.
MADAME DU BLUE BOX!
THE LADY OF THE TIME SHIP?
C'MON. I'LL SHOW YOU THE SWIMMING POOL.
GABS, I KNOW YOU DON'T BELIEVE ME. BUT I SAW IT. I DID!
ALWAYS MAKE SURE YOUR POCKETS ARE EMPTY WHEN USING THE LAUNDROMAT!
WORKSHOP... THAT'S WHERE HE KEEPS HIS TRAIN SETS...
CRICKET PAVILION...
BET HE HAS A FISH AND CHIP SHOP IN HERE SOMEWHERE.
NEXT UP, MY FAVE ROOM OF ALL-- THE LIBRARY--
OH
WHAAAA!
NOW D'YOU BELIEVE ME?
YEAH. SORRY.
WE HAVE TO GET THE DOCTOR!
THE TARDIS HAS BEEN INFILTRATED. HE TOLD ME THAT WAS IMPOSSIBLE!

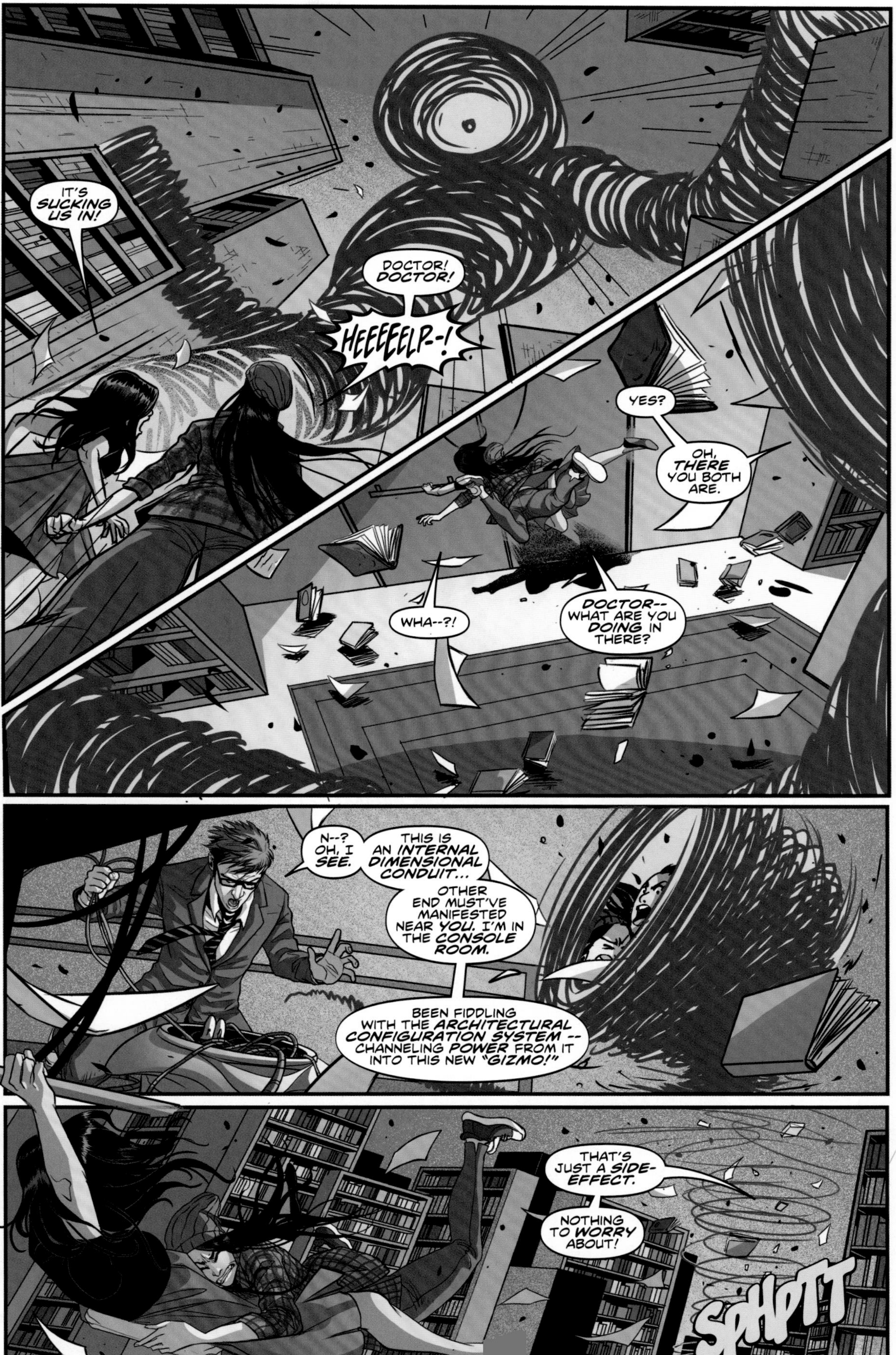
IT'S SUCKING US IN!
DOCTOR! DOCTOR!
HEEEEELP--!
YES?
OH, THERE YOU BOTH ARE.
WHA--?!
DOCTOR-- WHAT ARE YOU DOING IN THERE?
N--? OH, I SEE.
THIS IS AN INTERNAL DIMENSIONAL CONDUIT...
OTHER END MUST'VE MANIFESTED NEAR YOU. I'M IN THE CONSOLE ROOM.
BEEN FIDDLING WITH THE ARCHITECTURAL CONFIGURATION SYSTEM -- CHANNELING POWER FROM IT INTO THIS NEW "GIZMO!"
THAT'S JUST A SIDE-EFFECT.
NOTHING TO WORRY ABOUT!
SPHPTT

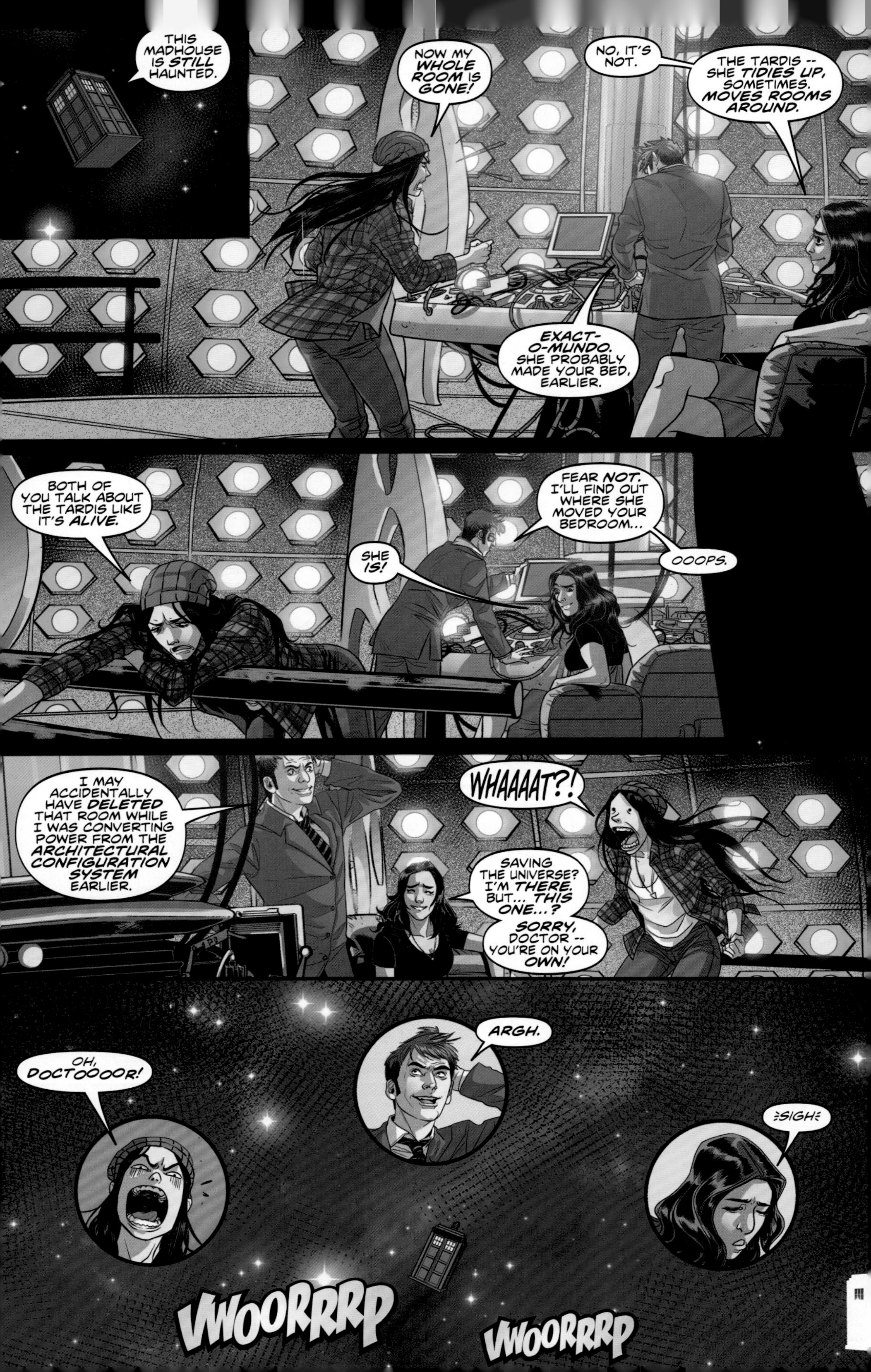
THIS MADHOUSE IS STILL HAUNTED.
NOW MY WHOLE ROOM IS GONE!
NO, IT'S NOT.
THE TARDIS -- SHE TIDIES UP, SOMETIMES. MOVES ROOMS AROUND.
EXACT-O-MUNDO. SHE PROBABLY MADE YOUR BED, EARLIER.
BOTH OF YOU TALK ABOUT THE TARDIS LIKE IT'S ALIVE.
SHE IS!
FEAR NOT. I'LL FIND OUT WHERE SHE MOVED YOUR BEDROOM...
OOOPS.
I MAY ACCIDENTALLY HAVE DELETED THAT ROOM WHILE I WAS CONVERTING POWER FROM THE ARCHITECTURAL CONFIGURATION SYSTEM EARLIER.
WHAAAAT?!
SAVING THE UNIVERSE? I'M THERE. BUT... THIS ONE...?
SORRY, DOCTOR -- YOU'RE ON YOUR OWN!
OH, DOCTOOOOR!
ARGH.
SIGH
VWOORRRP
VWOORRRP

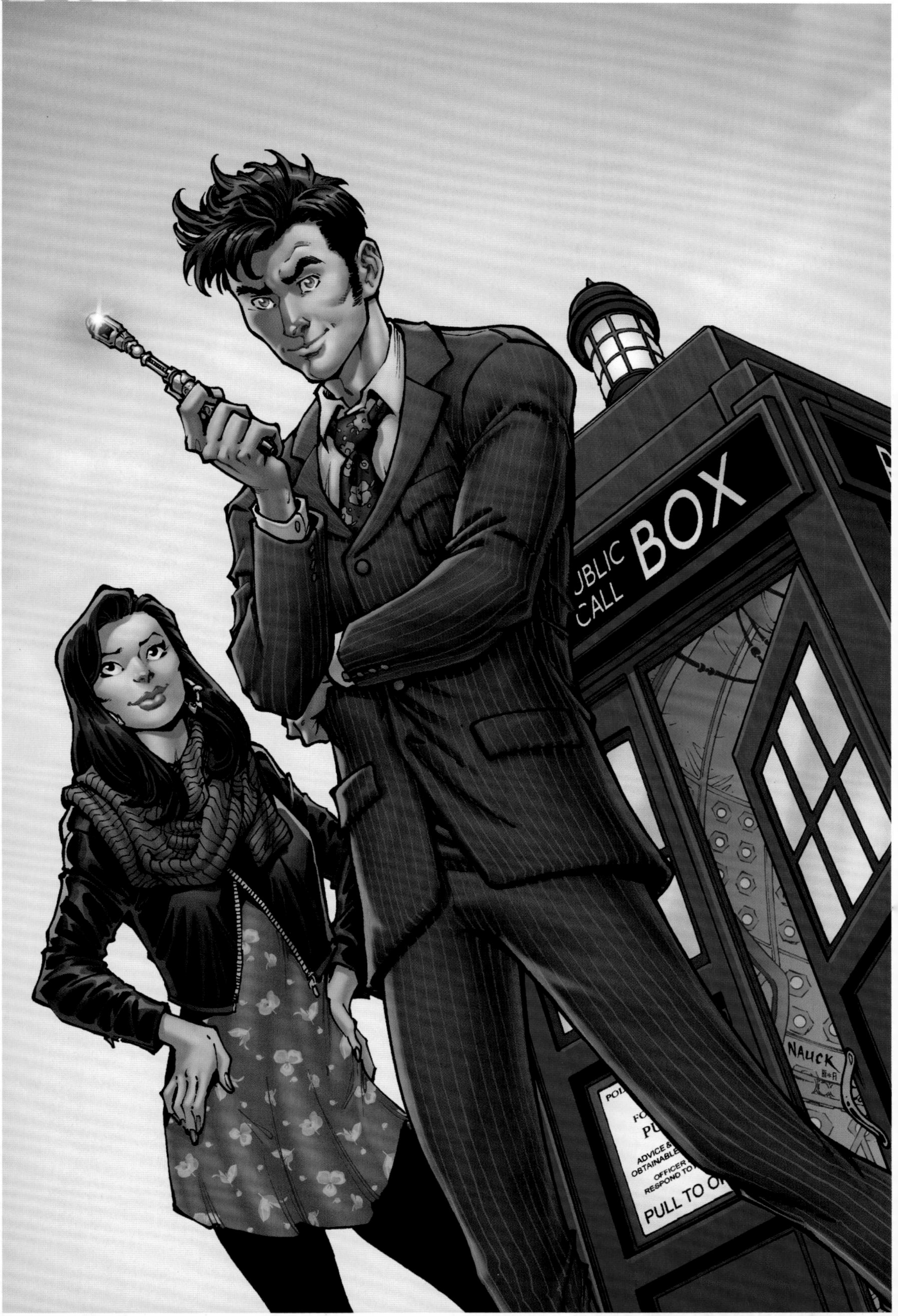

CALL BOX
NAUCK

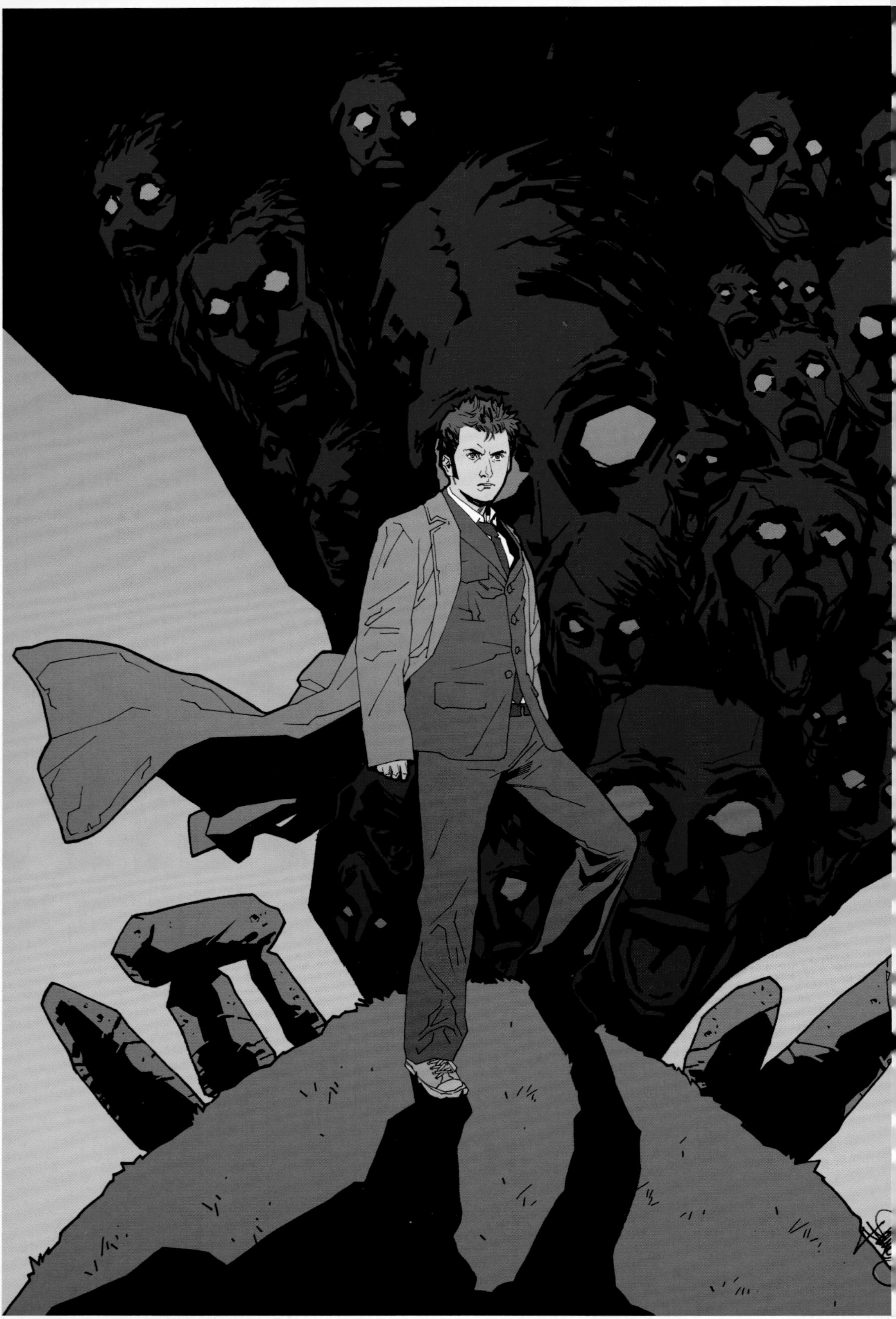

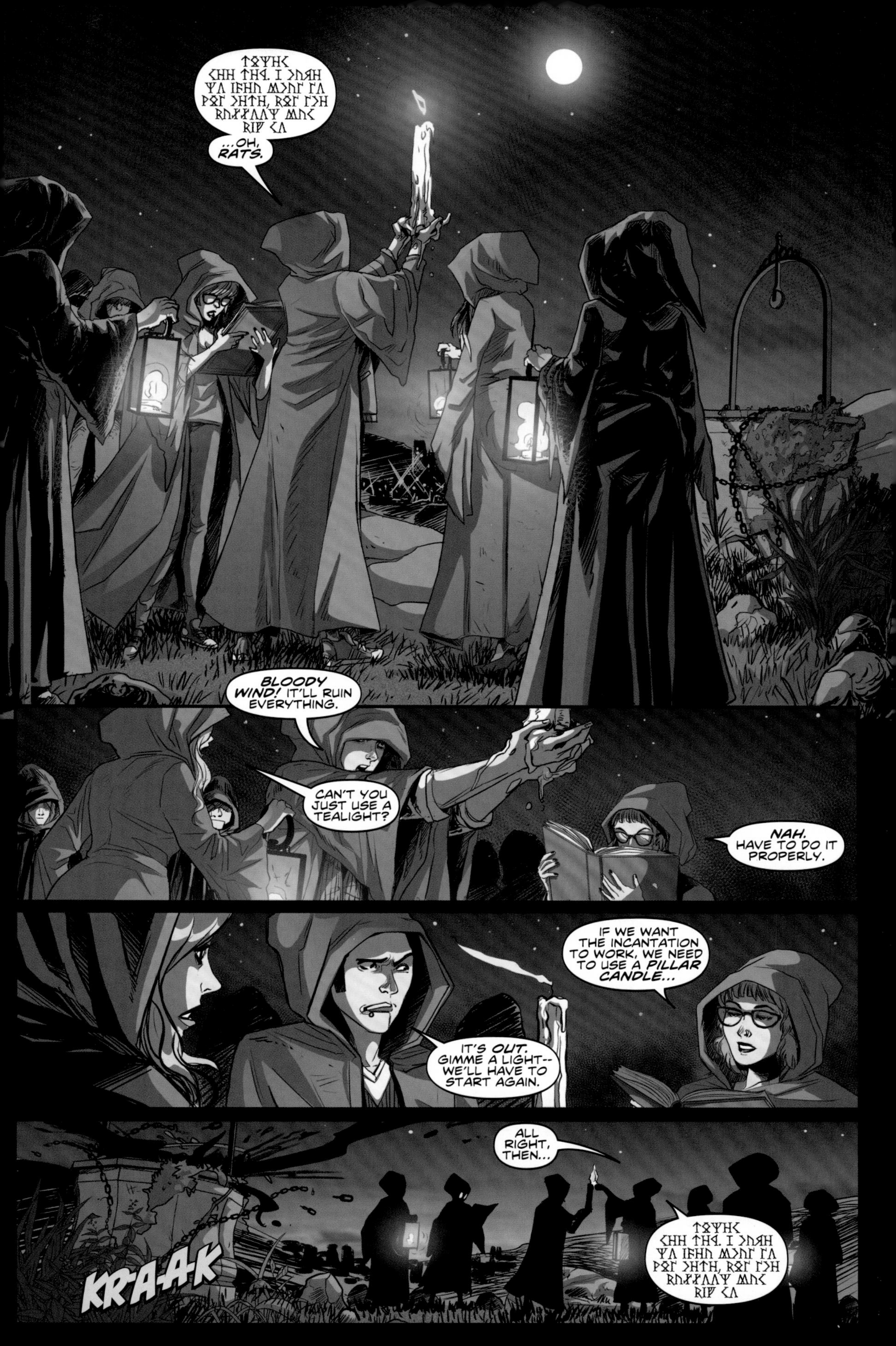
...OH, RATS.
BLOODY WIND! IT'LL RUIN EVERYTHING.
CAN'T YOU JUST USE A TEALIGHT?
NAH. HAVE TO DO IT PROPERLY.
IF WE WANT THE INCANTATION TO WORK, WE NEED TO USE A PILLAR CANDLE...
IT'S OUT. GIMME A LIGHT-- WE'LL HAVE TO START AGAIN.
ALL RIGHT, THEN...
KRAAK

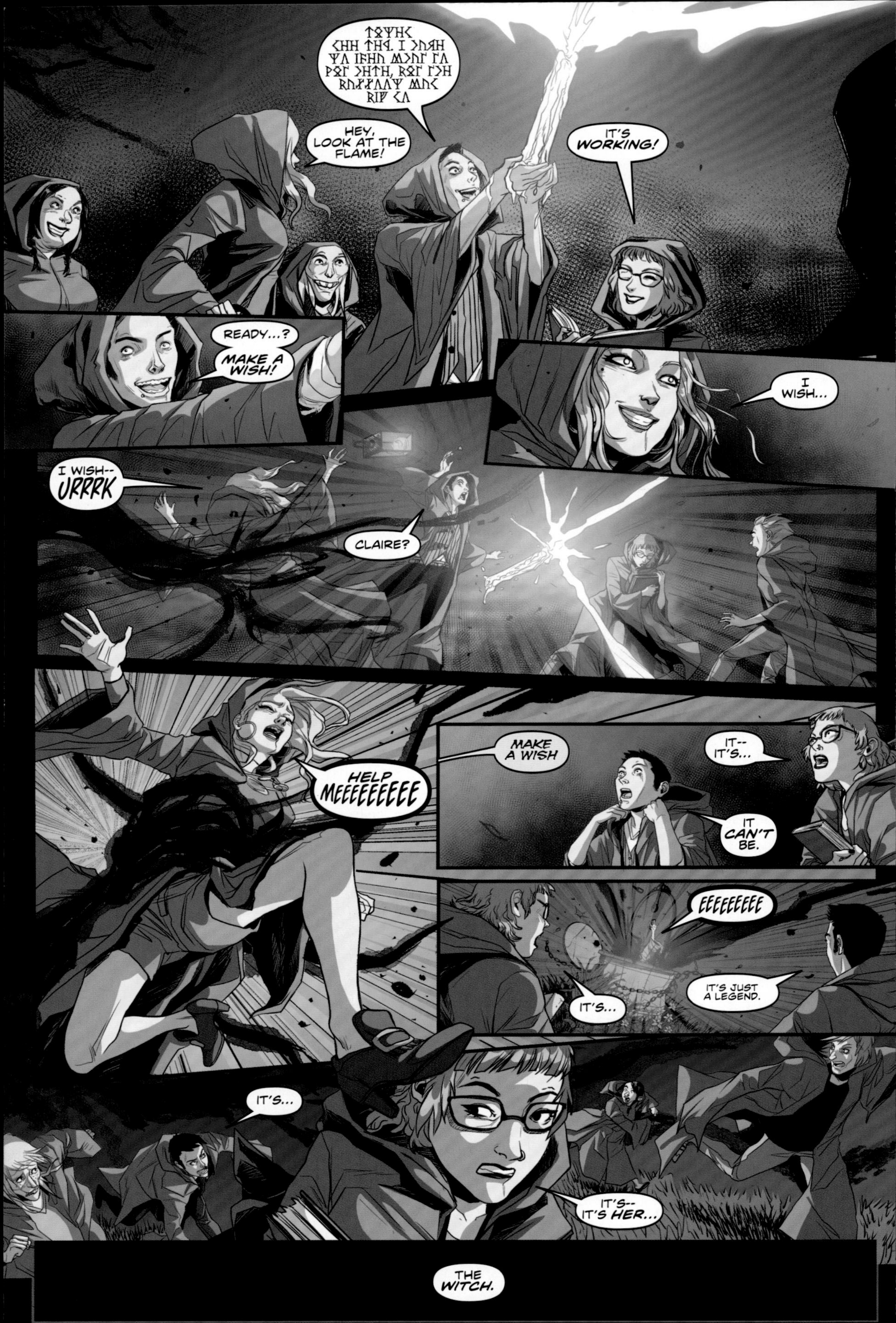
HEY, LOOK AT THE FLAME!
IT'S WORKING!
READY...?
MAKE A WISH!
I WISH...
I WISH-- URRRK
CLAIRE?
HELP MEEEEEEEEE
MAKE A WISH
IT-- IT'S...
IT CAN'T BE.
EEEEEEEEE
IT'S...
IT'S JUST A LEGEND.
IT'S...
IT'S-- IT'S HER...
THE WITCH.

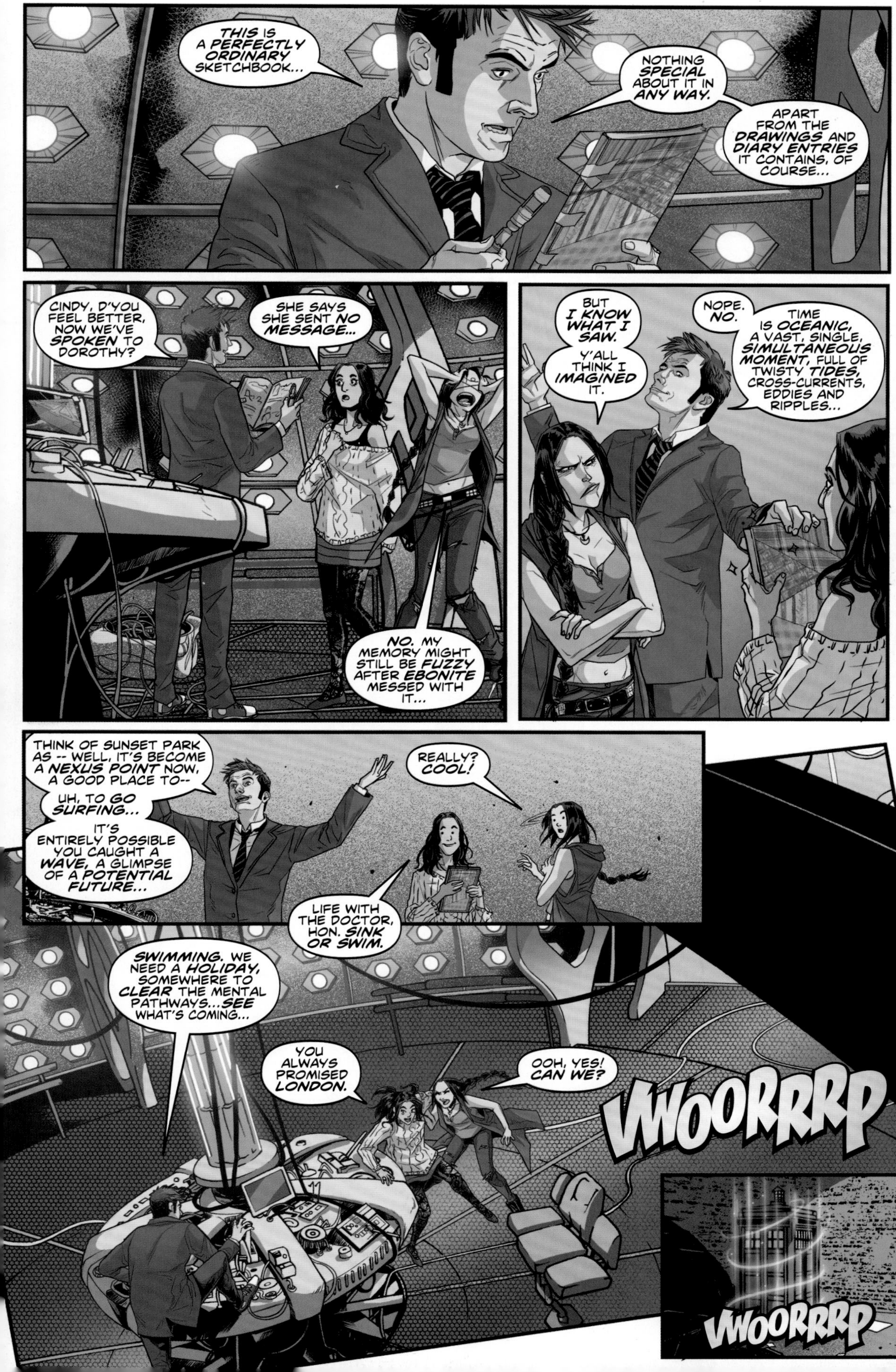
THIS IS A PERFECTLY ORDINARY SKETCHBOOK...
NOTHING SPECIAL ABOUT IT IN ANY WAY.
APART FROM THE DRAWINGS AND DIARY ENTRIES IT CONTAINS, OF COURSE...
CINDY, D'YOU FEEL BETTER, NOW WE'VE SPOKEN TO DOROTHY?
SHE SAYS SHE SENT NO MESSAGE...
NO. MY MEMORY MIGHT STILL BE FUZZY AFTER EBONITE MESSED WITH IT...
BUT I KNOW WHAT I SAW.
Y'ALL THINK I IMAGINED IT.
NOPE. NO.
TIME IS OCEANIC, A VAST, SINGLE, SIMULTANEOUS MOMENT, FULL OF TWISTY TIDES, CROSS-CURRENTS, EDDIES AND RIPPLES...
THINK OF SUNSET PARK AS -- WELL, IT'S BECOME A NEXUS POINT NOW, A GOOD PLACE TO--
UH, TO GO SURFING...
IT'S ENTIRELY POSSIBLE YOU CAUGHT A WAVE, A GLIMPSE OF A POTENTIAL FUTURE...
REALLY? COOL!
LIFE WITH THE DOCTOR, HON. SINK OR SWIM.
SWIMMING. WE NEED A HOLIDAY, SOMEWHERE TO CLEAR THE MENTAL PATHWAYS...SEE WHAT'S COMING...
YOU ALWAYS PROMISED LONDON.
OOH, YES! CAN WE?
VWOORRRP
VWOORRRP

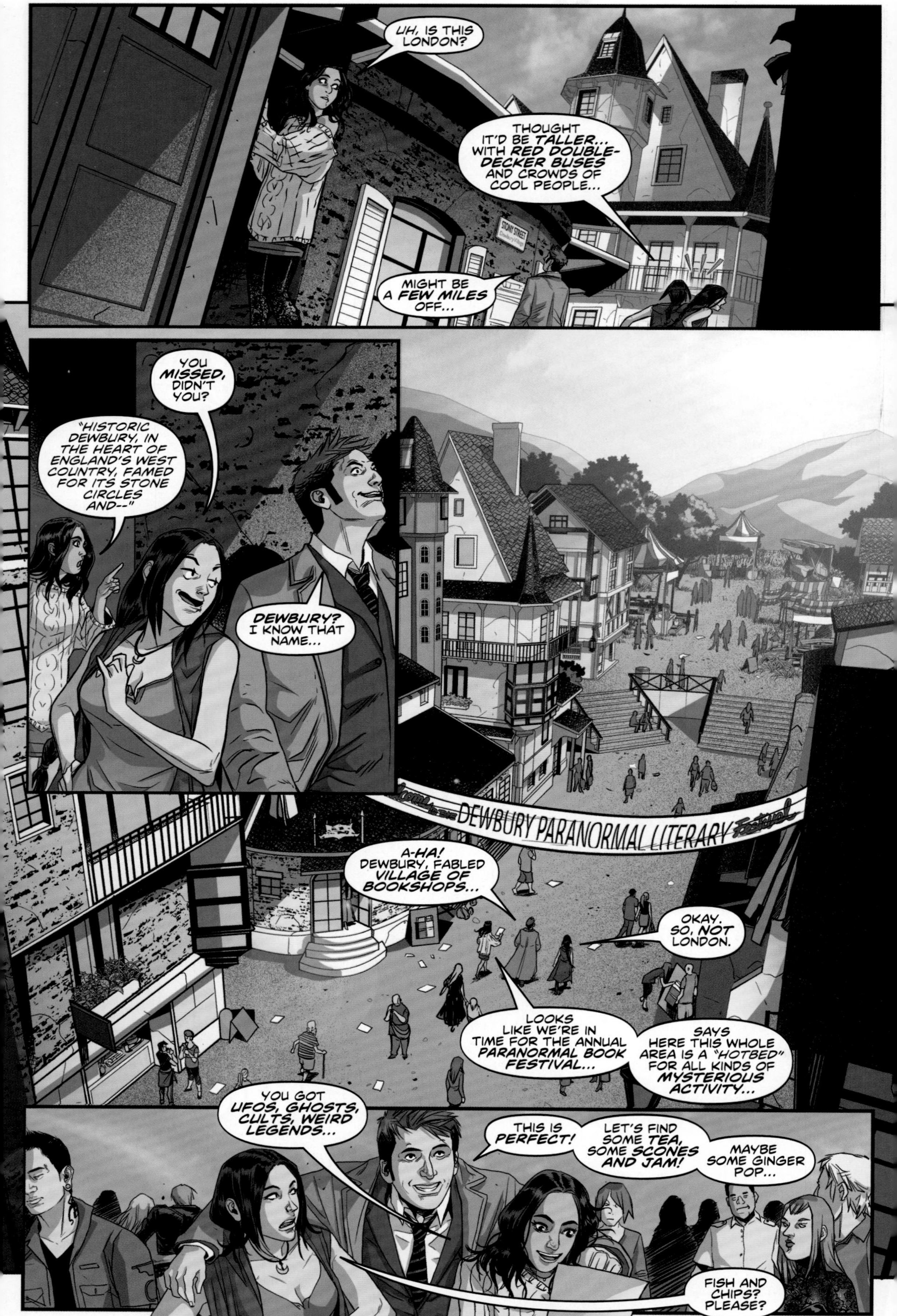
UH, IS THIS LONDON?
THOUGHT IT'D BE TALLER... WITH RED DOUBLE-DECKER BUSES AND CROWDS OF COOL PEOPLE...
STONY STREET
MIGHT BE A FEW MILES OFF...
YOU MISSED, DIDN'T YOU?
"HISTORIC DEWBURY, IN THE HEART OF ENGLAND'S WEST COUNTRY, FAMED FOR ITS STONE CIRCLES AND--"
DEWBURY? I KNOW THAT NAME...
DEWBURY PARANORMAL LITERARY Festival
A-HA! DEWBURY, FABLED VILLAGE OF BOOKSHOPS...
OKAY. SO, NOT LONDON.
LOOKS LIKE WE'RE IN TIME FOR THE ANNUAL PARANORMAL BOOK FESTIVAL...
SAYS HERE THIS WHOLE AREA IS A "HOTBED" FOR ALL KINDS OF MYSTERIOUS ACTIVITY...
YOU GOT UFOS, GHOSTS, CULTS, WEIRD LEGENDS...
THIS IS PERFECT!
LET'S FIND SOME TEA, SOME SCONES AND JAM!
MAYBE SOME GINGER POP...
FISH AND CHIPS? PLEASE?

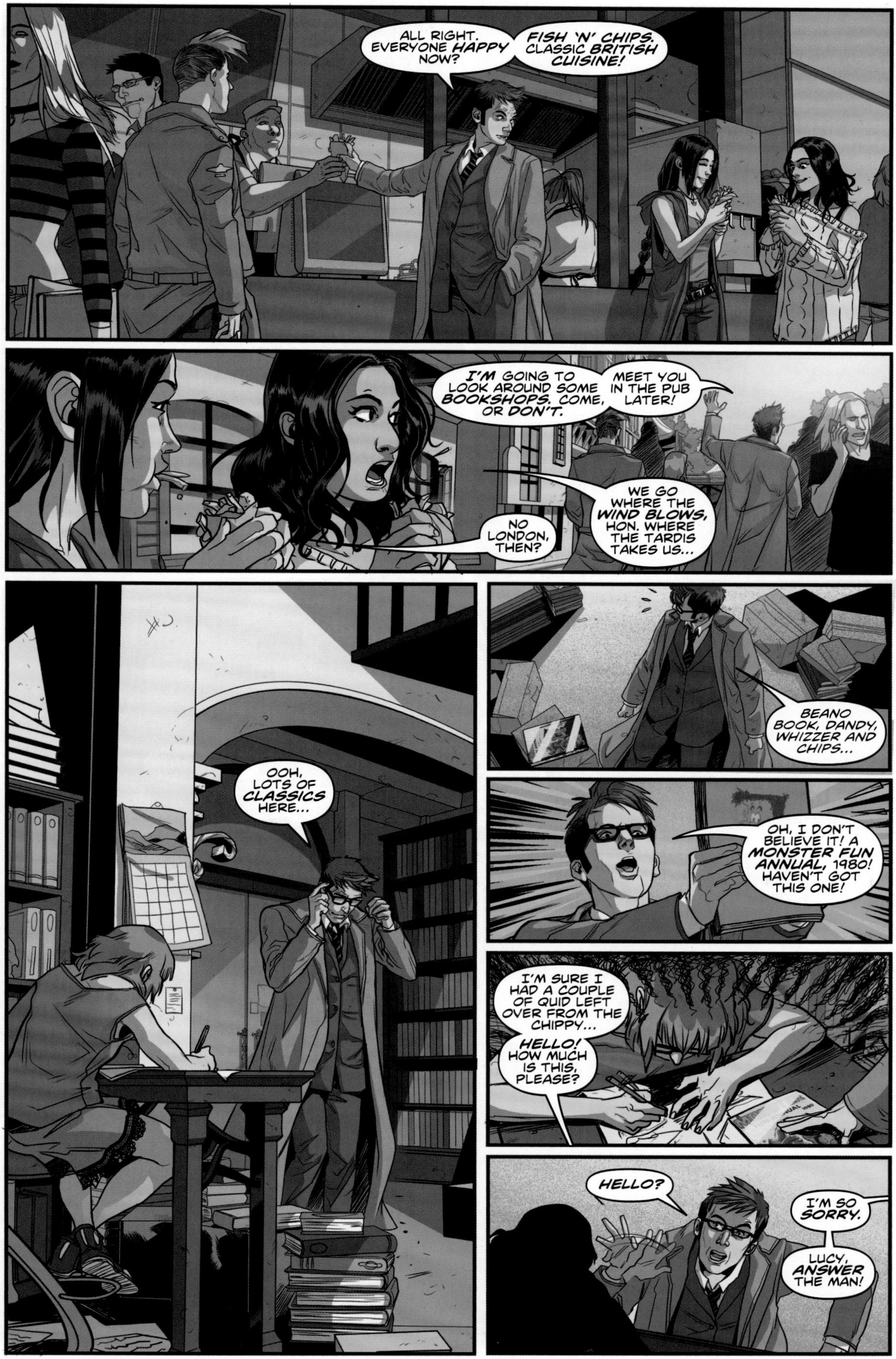

ALL RIGHT. EVERYONE HAPPY NOW?
FISH 'N' CHIPS. CLASSIC BRITISH CUISINE!
I'M GOING TO LOOK AROUND SOME BOOKSHOPS. COME, OR DON'T.
MEET YOU IN THE PUB LATER!
NO LONDON, THEN?
WE GO WHERE THE WIND BLOWS, HON. WHERE THE TARDIS TAKES US...
OOH, LOTS OF CLASSICS HERE...
BEANO BOOK, DANDY, WHIZZER AND CHIPS...
OH, I DON'T BELIEVE IT! A MONSTER FUN ANNUAL, 1980! HAVEN'T GOT THIS ONE!
I'M SURE I HAD A COUPLE OF QUID LEFT OVER FROM THE CHIPPY...
HELLO! HOW MUCH IS THIS, PLEASE?
HELLO?
I'M SO SORRY.
LUCY, ANSWER THE MAN!

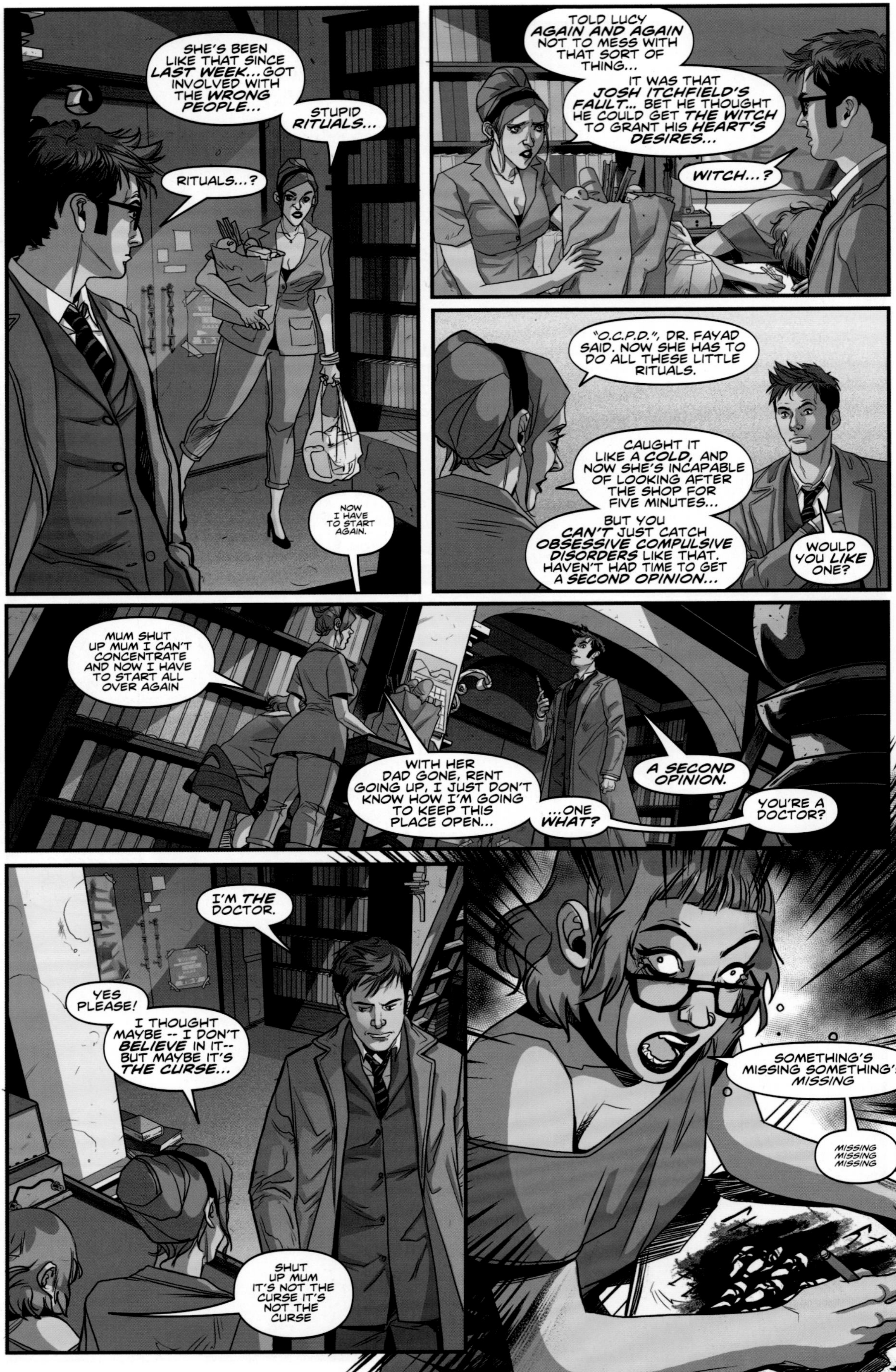
SHE'S BEEN LIKE THAT SINCE LAST WEEK... GOT INVOLVED WITH THE WRONG PEOPLE...
STUPID RITUALS...
RITUALS...?
NOW I HAVE TO START AGAIN.
TOLD LUCY AGAIN AND AGAIN NOT TO MESS WITH THAT SORT OF THING...
IT WAS THAT JOSH ITCHFIELD'S FAULT... BET HE THOUGHT HE COULD GET THE WITCH TO GRANT HIS HEART'S DESIRES...
WITCH...?
"O.C.P.D.", DR. FAYAD SAID. NOW SHE HAS TO DO ALL THESE LITTLE RITUALS.
CAUGHT IT LIKE A COLD, AND NOW SHE'S INCAPABLE OF LOOKING AFTER THE SHOP FOR FIVE MINUTES...
BUT YOU CAN'T JUST CATCH OBSESSIVE COMPULSIVE DISORDERS LIKE THAT. HAVEN'T HAD TIME TO GET A SECOND OPINION...
WOULD YOU LIKE ONE?
MUM SHUT UP MUM I CAN'T CONCENTRATE AND NOW I HAVE TO START ALL OVER AGAIN
WITH HER DAD GONE, RENT GOING UP, I JUST DON'T KNOW HOW I'M GOING TO KEEP THIS PLACE OPEN...
A SECOND OPINION.
...ONE WHAT?
YOU'RE A DOCTOR?
I'M THE DOCTOR.
YES PLEASE!
I THOUGHT MAYBE -- I DON'T BELIEVE IN IT-- BUT MAYBE IT'S THE CURSE...
SHUT UP MUM IT'S NOT THE CURSE IT'S NOT THE CURSE
SOMETHING'S MISSING SOMETHING'S MISSING
MISSING MISSING MISSING

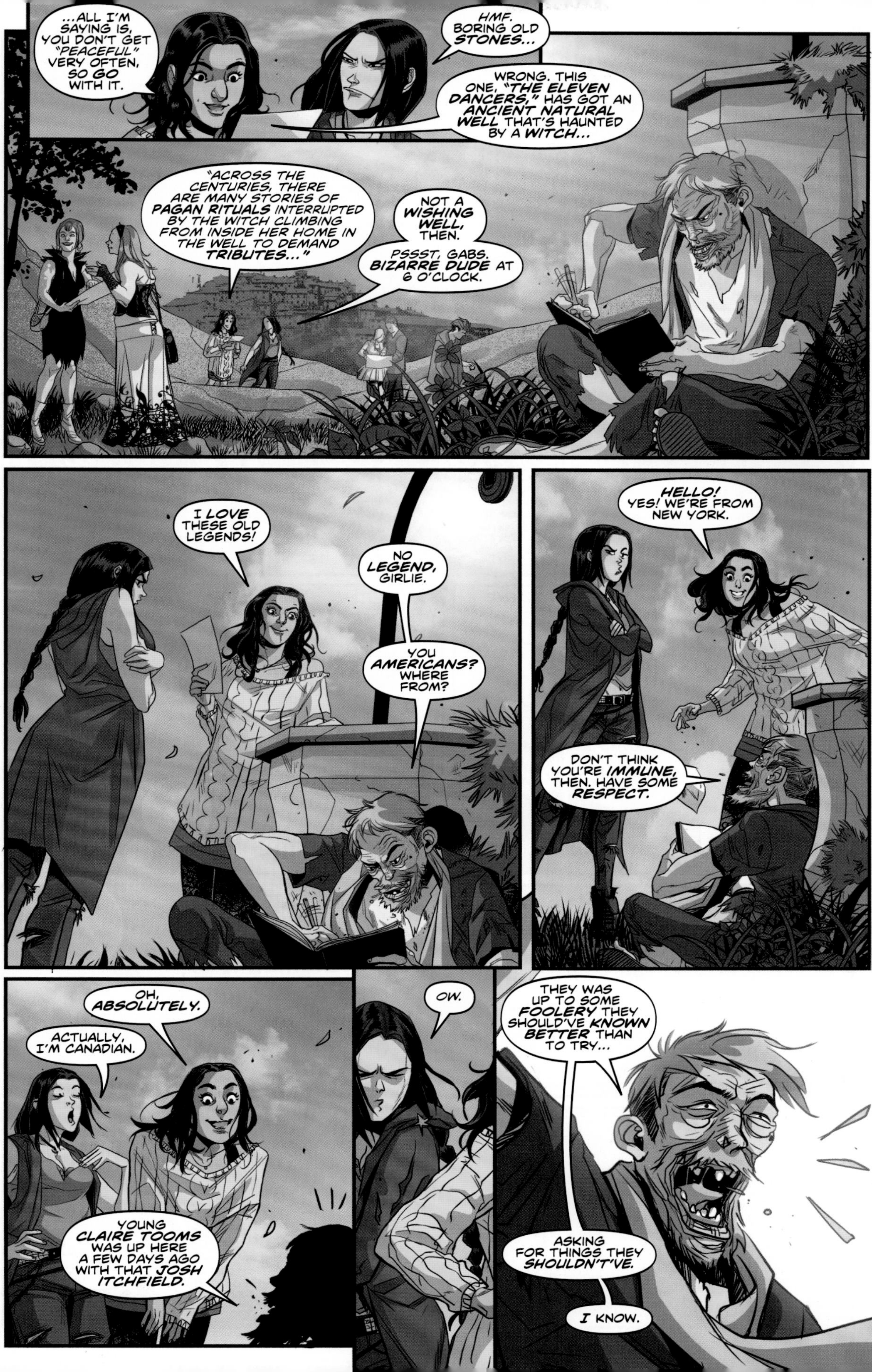
...ALL I'M SAYING IS, YOU DON'T GET "PEACEFUL" VERY OFTEN, SO GO WITH IT.
HMF. BORING OLD STONES...
WRONG. THIS ONE, "THE ELEVEN DANCERS," HAS GOT AN ANCIENT NATURAL WELL THAT'S HAUNTED BY A WITCH...
"ACROSS THE CENTURIES, THERE ARE MANY STORIES OF PAGAN RITUALS INTERRUPTED BY THE WITCH CLIMBING FROM INSIDE HER HOME IN THE WELL TO DEMAND TRIBUTES..."
NOT A WISHING WELL, THEN.
PSSST, GABS. BIZARRE DUDE AT 6 O'CLOCK.
I LOVE THESE OLD LEGENDS!
NO LEGEND, GIRLIE.
YOU AMERICANS? WHERE FROM?
HELLO! YES! WE'RE FROM NEW YORK.
DON'T THINK YOU'RE IMMUNE, THEN. HAVE SOME RESPECT.
OH, ABSOLUTELY.
ACTUALLY, I'M CANADIAN.
YOUNG CLAIRE TOOMS WAS UP HERE A FEW DAYS AGO WITH THAT JOSH ITCHFIELD.
OW.
THEY WAS UP TO SOME FOOLERY THEY SHOULD'VE KNOWN BETTER THAN TO TRY...
ASKING FOR THINGS THEY SHOULDN'T'VE.
I KNOW.

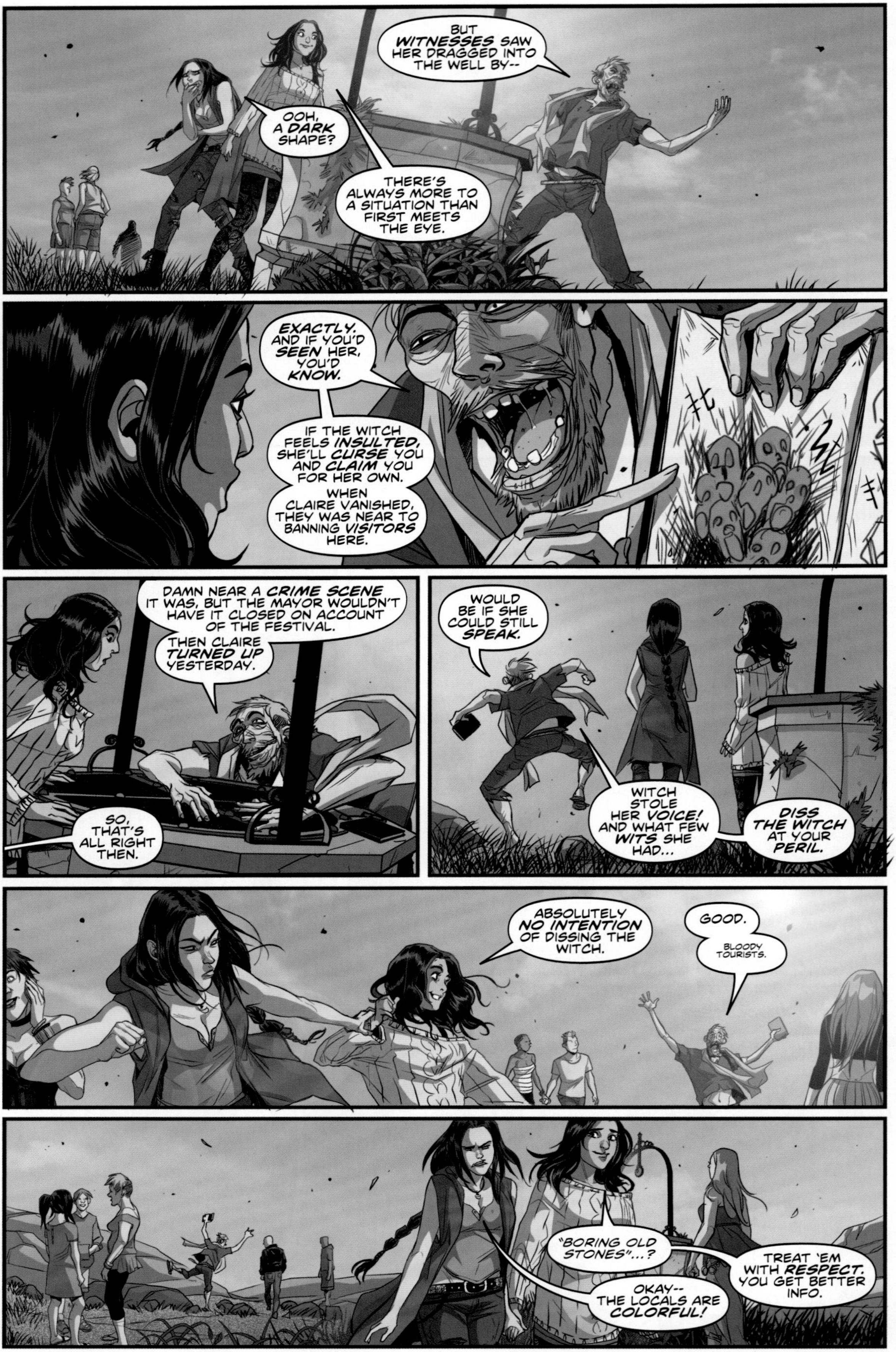

BUT WITNESSES SAW HER DRAGGED INTO THE WELL BY--
OOH, A DARK SHAPE?
THERE'S ALWAYS MORE TO A SITUATION THAN FIRST MEETS THE EYE.
EXACTLY. AND IF YOU'D SEEN HER, YOU'D KNOW.
IF THE WITCH FEELS INSULTED, SHE'LL CURSE YOU AND CLAIM YOU FOR HER OWN.
WHEN CLAIRE VANISHED, THEY WAS NEAR TO BANNING VISITORS HERE.
DAMN NEAR A CRIME SCENE IT WAS, BUT THE MAYOR WOULDN'T HAVE IT CLOSED ON ACCOUNT OF THE FESTIVAL.
THEN CLAIRE TURNED UP YESTERDAY.
SO, THAT'S ALL RIGHT THEN.
WOULD BE IF SHE COULD STILL SPEAK.
WITCH STOLE HER VOICE! AND WHAT FEW WITS SHE HAD...
DISS THE WITCH AT YOUR PERIL.
ABSOLUTELY NO INTENTION OF DISSING THE WITCH.
GOOD.
BLOODY TOURISTS.
"BORING OLD STONES"...?
OKAY-- THE LOCALS ARE COLORFUL!
TREAT 'EM WITH RESPECT. YOU GET BETTER INFO.

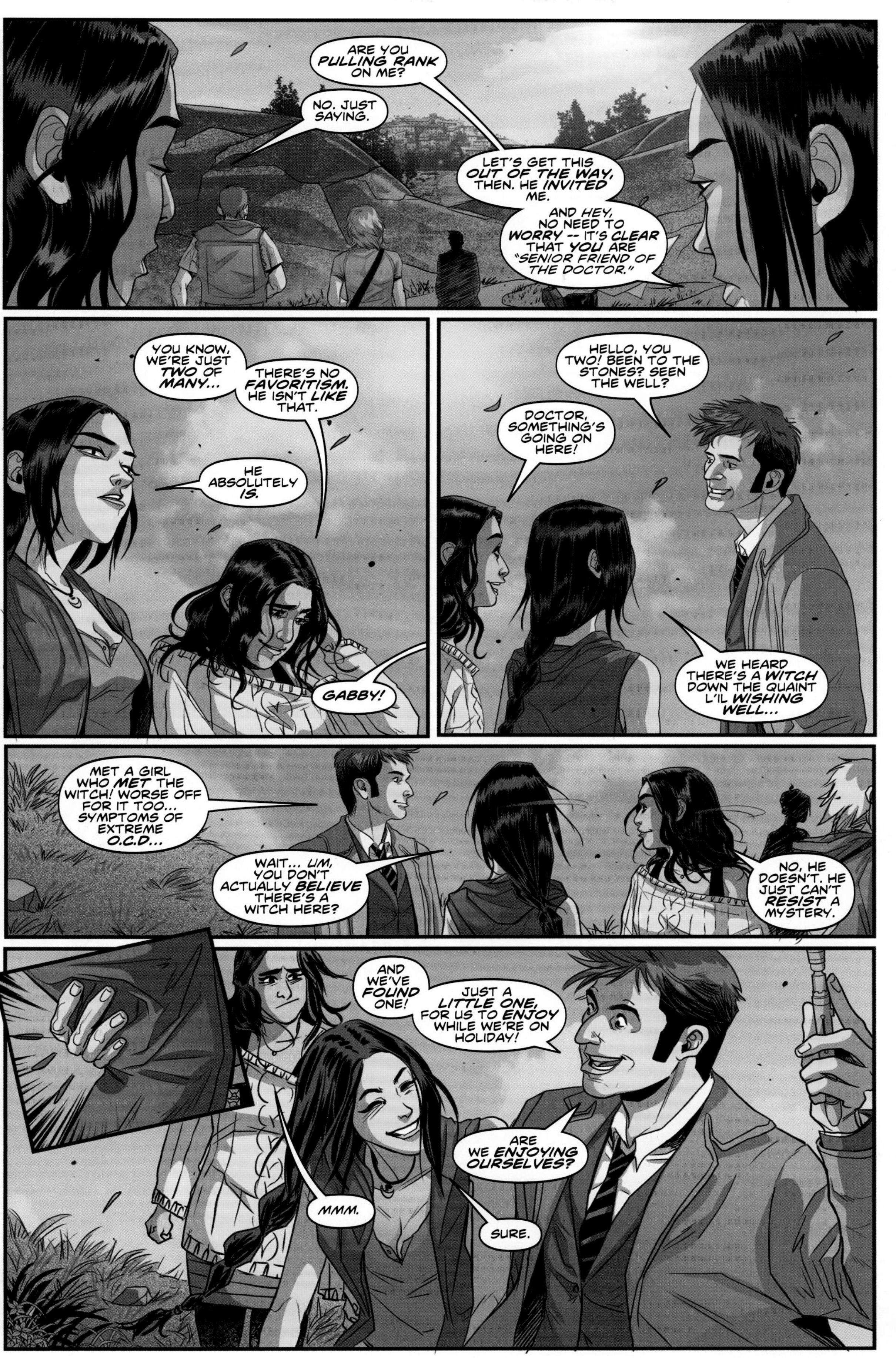

ARE YOU PULLING RANK ON ME?
NO. JUST SAYING.
LET'S GET THIS OUT OF THE WAY, THEN. HE INVITED ME.
AND HEY, NO NEED TO WORRY -- IT'S CLEAR THAT YOU ARE "SENIOR FRIEND OF THE DOCTOR."
YOU KNOW, WE'RE JUST TWO OF MANY...
THERE'S NO FAVORITISM. HE ISN'T LIKE THAT.
HE ABSOLUTELY IS.
GABBY!
HELLO, YOU TWO! BEEN TO THE STONES? SEEN THE WELL?
DOCTOR, SOMETHING'S GOING ON HERE!
WE HEARD THERE'S A WITCH DOWN THE QUAINT L'IL WISHING WELL...
MET A GIRL WHO MET THE WITCH! WORSE OFF FOR IT TOO... SYMPTOMS OF EXTREME O.C.D...
WAIT... UM, YOU DON'T ACTUALLY BELIEVE THERE'S A WITCH HERE?
NO, HE DOESN'T. HE JUST CAN'T RESIST A MYSTERY.
AND WE'VE FOUND ONE!
JUST A LITTLE ONE, FOR US TO ENJOY WHILE WE'RE ON HOLIDAY!
ARE WE ENJOYING OURSELVES?
MMM.
SURE.

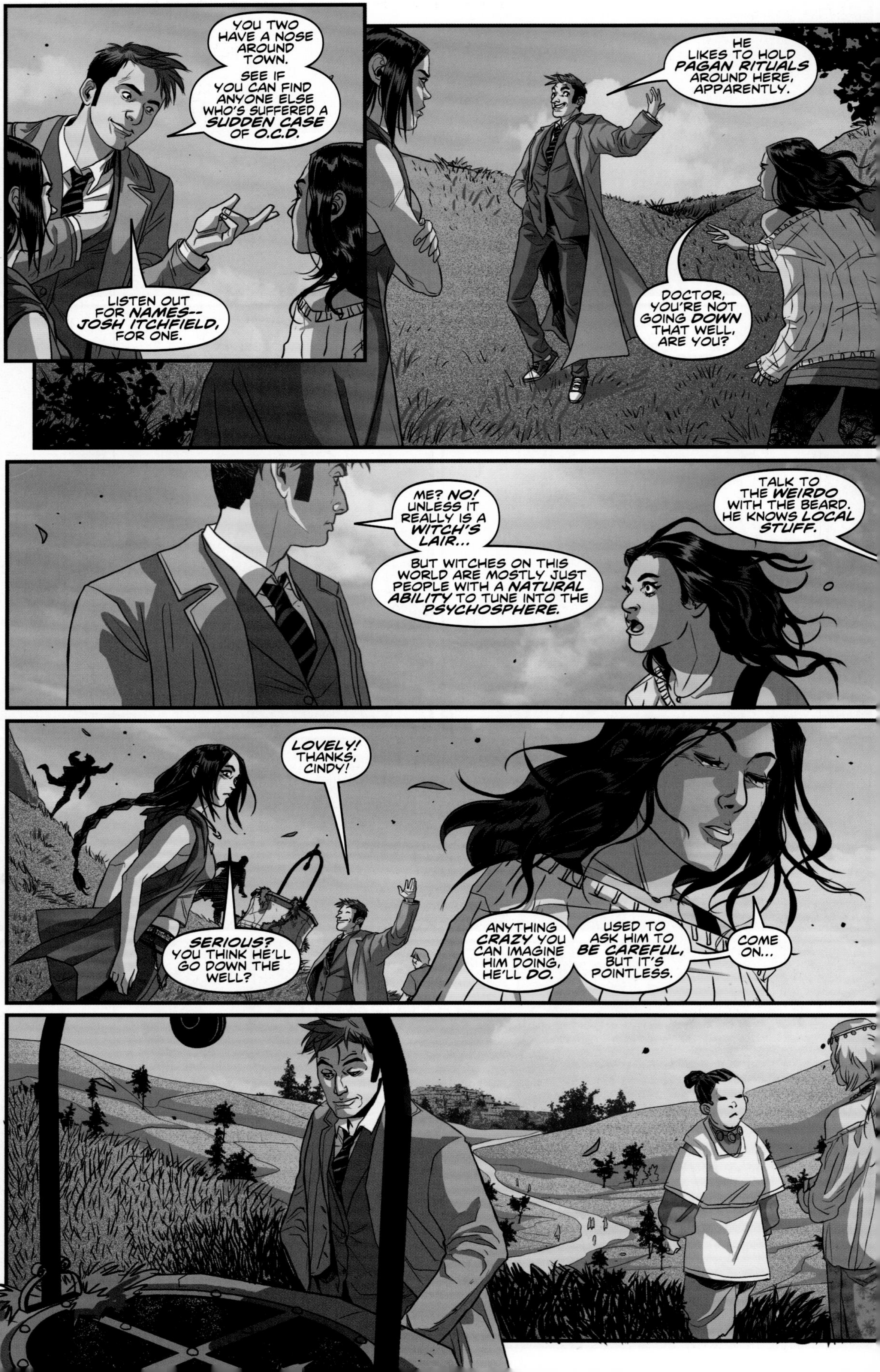
YOU TWO HAVE A NOSE AROUND TOWN.
SEE IF YOU CAN FIND ANYONE ELSE WHO'S SUFFERED A SUDDEN CASE OF O.C.D.
LISTEN OUT FOR NAMES-- JOSH ITCHFIELD, FOR ONE.
HE LIKES TO HOLD PAGAN RITUALS AROUND HERE, APPARENTLY.
DOCTOR, YOU'RE NOT GOING DOWN THAT WELL, ARE YOU?
ME? NO! UNLESS IT REALLY IS A WITCH'S LAIR...
BUT WITCHES ON THIS WORLD ARE MOSTLY JUST PEOPLE WITH A NATURAL ABILITY TO TUNE INTO THE PSYCHOSPHERE.
TALK TO THE WEIRDO WITH THE BEARD. HE KNOWS LOCAL STUFF.
LOVELY! THANKS, CINDY!
SERIOUS? YOU THINK HE'LL GO DOWN THE WELL?
ANYTHING CRAZY YOU CAN IMAGINE HIM DOING, HE'LL DO.
USED TO ASK HIM TO BE CAREFUL, BUT IT'S POINTLESS.
COME ON...

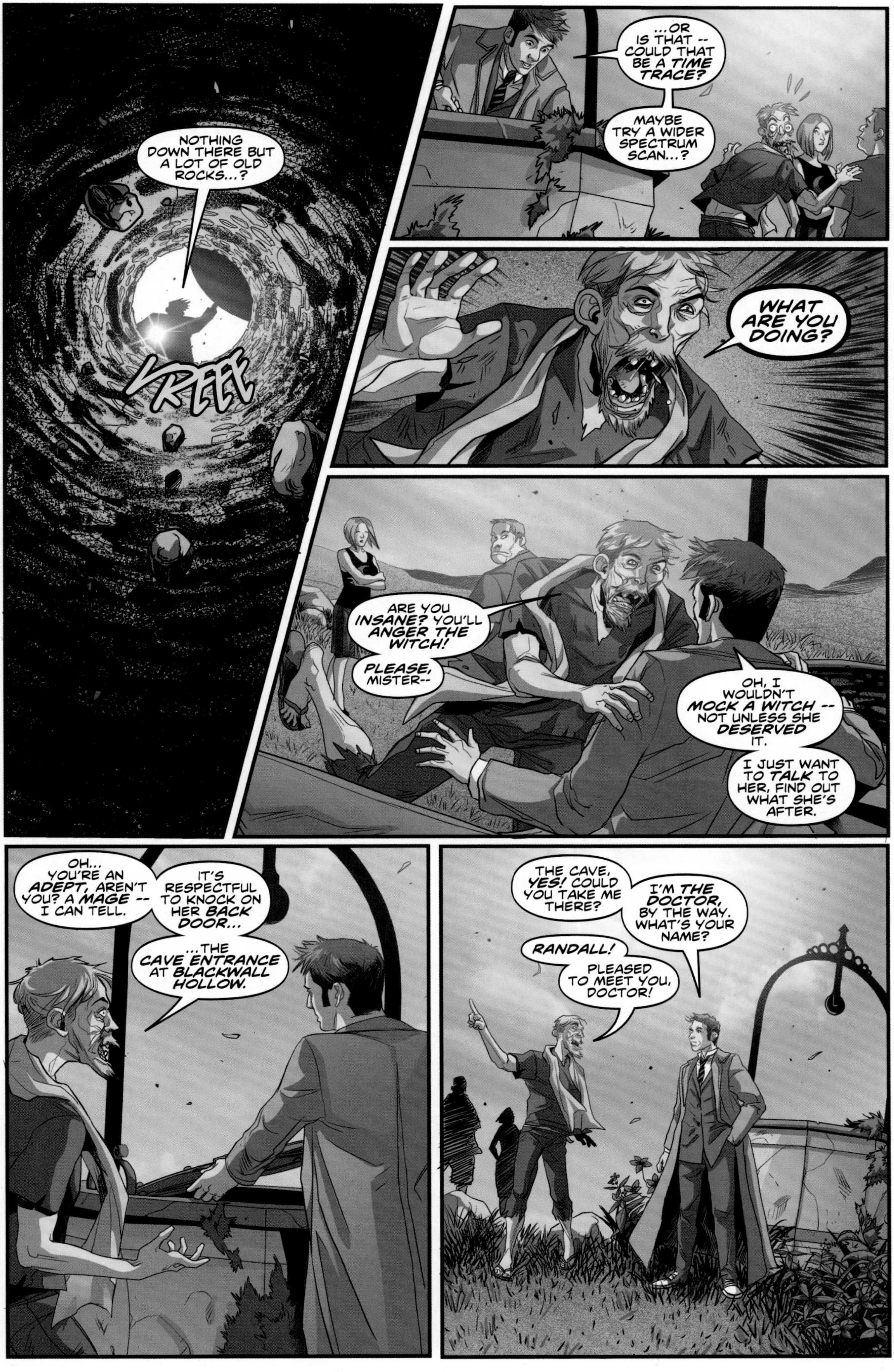

NOTHING DOWN THERE BUT A LOT OF OLD ROCKS...?
VREEE
...OR IS THAT -- COULD THAT BE A TIME TRACE?
MAYBE TRY A WIDER SPECTRUM SCAN...?
WHAT ARE YOU DOING?
ARE YOU INSANE? YOU'LL ANGER THE WITCH!
PLEASE, MISTER--
OH, I WOULDN'T MOCK A WITCH -- NOT UNLESS SHE DESERVED IT.
I JUST WANT TO TALK TO HER, FIND OUT WHAT SHE'S AFTER.
OH... YOU'RE AN ADEPT, AREN'T YOU? A MAGE -- I CAN TELL.
IT'S RESPECTFUL TO KNOCK ON HER BACK DOOR...
...THE CAVE ENTRANCE AT BLACKWALL HOLLOW.
THE CAVE, YES! COULD YOU TAKE ME THERE?
I'M THE DOCTOR, BY THE WAY. WHAT'S YOUR NAME?
RANDALL!
PLEASED TO MEET YOU, DOCTOR!

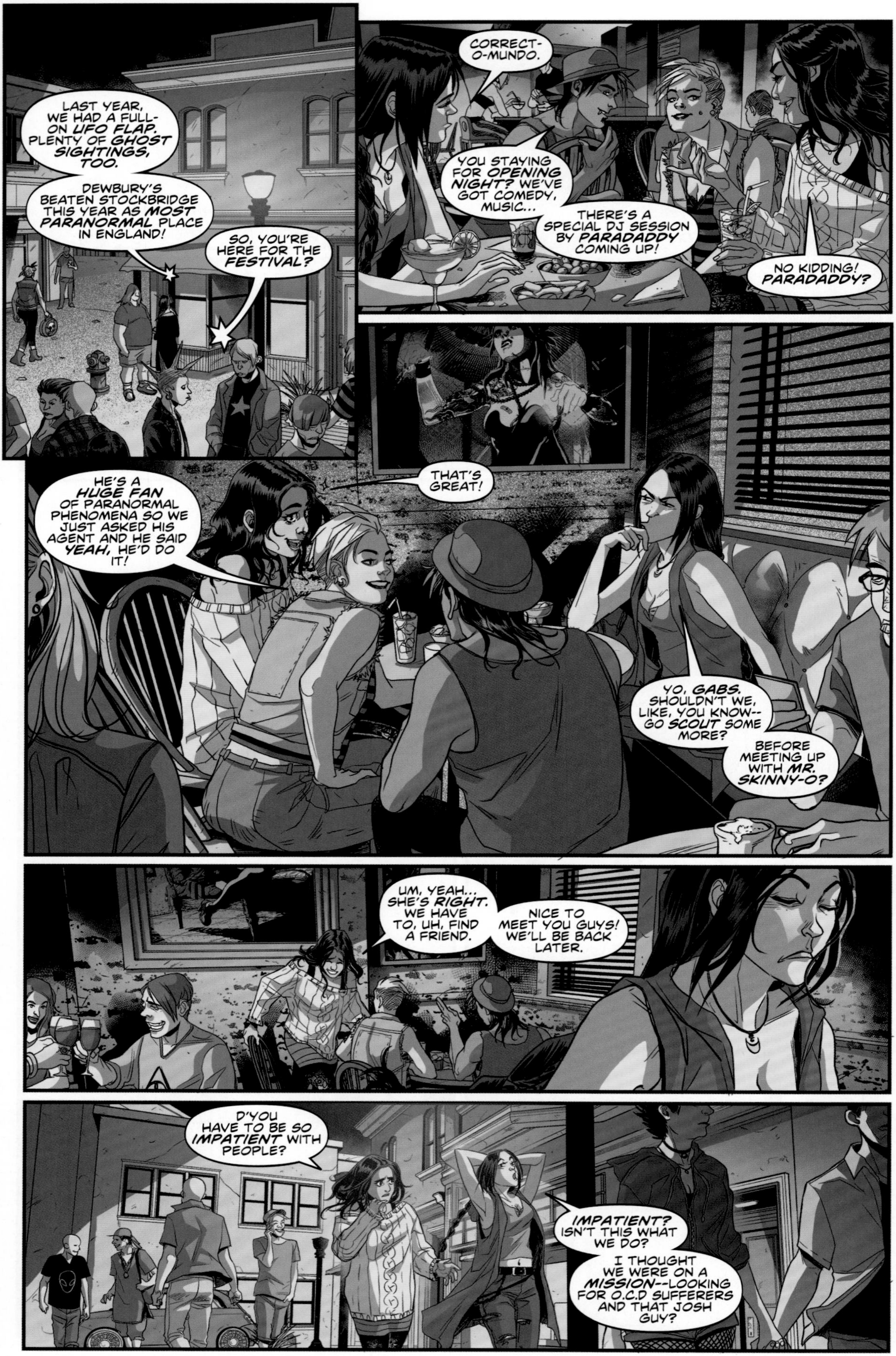
LAST YEAR, WE HAD A FULL-ON UFO FLAP. PLENTY OF GHOST SIGHTINGS, TOO.
DEWBURY'S BEATEN STOCKBRIDGE THIS YEAR AS MOST PARANORMAL PLACE IN ENGLAND!
SO, YOU'RE HERE FOR THE FESTIVAL?
CORRECT-O-MUNDO.
YOU STAYING FOR OPENING NIGHT? WE'VE GOT COMEDY, MUSIC...
THERE'S A SPECIAL DJ SESSION BY PARADADDY COMING UP!
NO KIDDING! PARADADDY?
HE'S A HUGE FAN OF PARANORMAL PHENOMENA SO WE JUST ASKED HIS AGENT AND HE SAID YEAH, HE'D DO IT!
THAT'S GREAT!
YO, GABS. SHOULDN'T WE, LIKE, YOU KNOW--GO SCOUT SOME MORE?
BEFORE MEETING UP WITH MR. SKINNY-O?
UM, YEAH... SHE'S RIGHT. WE HAVE TO, UH, FIND A FRIEND.
NICE TO MEET YOU GUYS! WE'LL BE BACK LATER.
D'YOU HAVE TO BE SO IMPATIENT WITH PEOPLE?
IMPATIENT? ISN'T THIS WHAT WE DO?
I THOUGHT WE WERE ON A MISSION--LOOKING FOR O.C.D SUFFERERS AND THAT JOSH GUY?

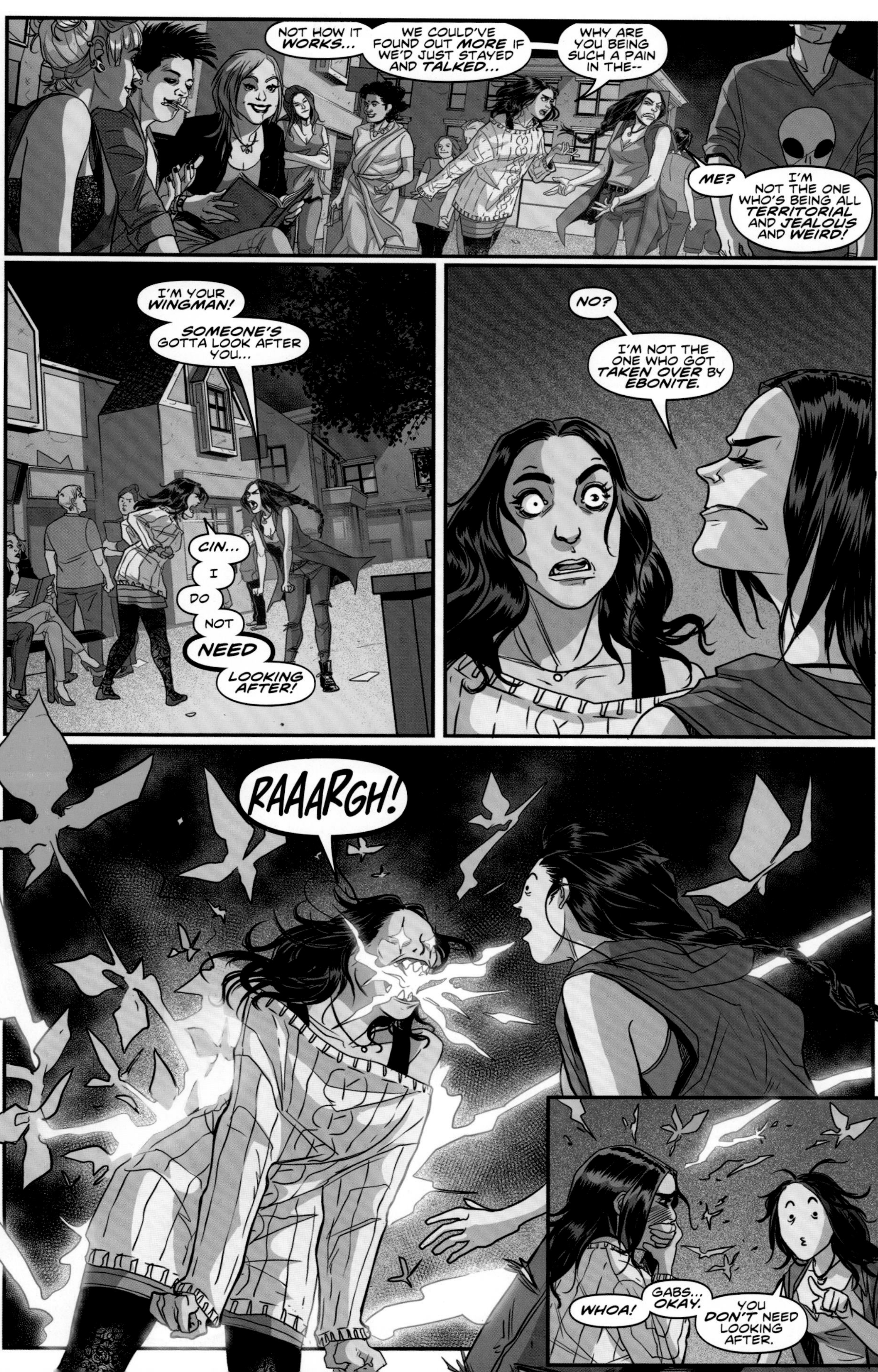

NOT HOW IT WORKS...
WE COULD'VE FOUND OUT MORE IF WE'D JUST STAYED AND TALKED...
WHY ARE YOU BEING SUCH A PAIN IN THE--
ME?
I'M NOT THE ONE WHO'S BEING ALL TERRITORIAL AND JEALOUS AND WEIRD!
I'M YOUR WINGMAN!
SOMEONE'S GOTTA LOOK AFTER YOU...
CIN...
I
DO
NOT
NEED
LOOKING AFTER!
NO?
I'M NOT THE ONE WHO GOT TAKEN OVER BY EBONITE.
RAAARGH!
WHOA!
GABS... OKAY.
YOU DON'T NEED LOOKING AFTER.

GABS, I'M SORRY!

I'M SORRY!

I'M SO STUPID...

WERE YOU ALWAYS INTERESTED IN THE *ARCANE* AND THE *OCCULT*, RANDALL?

SHE DID?

NOT 'TIL THE WITCH HERSELF *VISITED* ME, DOCTOR.

MM. ONE NIGHT, SOMETHING LIKE A *BIG BLACK DOG* WITH *RED EYES* FOLLOWED ME HOME.

WELL, I *THOUGHT* IT WAS A *GHOST DOG*, BUT IT WAS ONE OF THE WITCHES' *FACES.*

SHE'S GOT MORE THAN *ONE?*

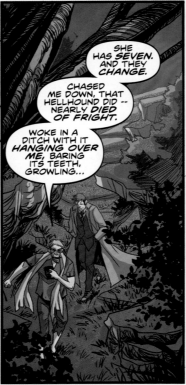

SHE HAS *SEVEN.* AND THEY *CHANGE.*

CHASED ME DOWN, THAT *HELLHOUND* DID -- NEARLY *DIED OF FRIGHT.*

WOKE IN A DITCH WITH IT *HANGING OVER ME,* BARING ITS TEETH, GROWLING...

THEN SUDDENLY, IT WASN'T *A BEAST* NO MORE BUT A *CHILD,* A BEAUTIFUL, TERRIFIED LITTLE KID...

BEEN TRYING TO 'MEMBER THE *OTHER FACES* EVER SINCE.

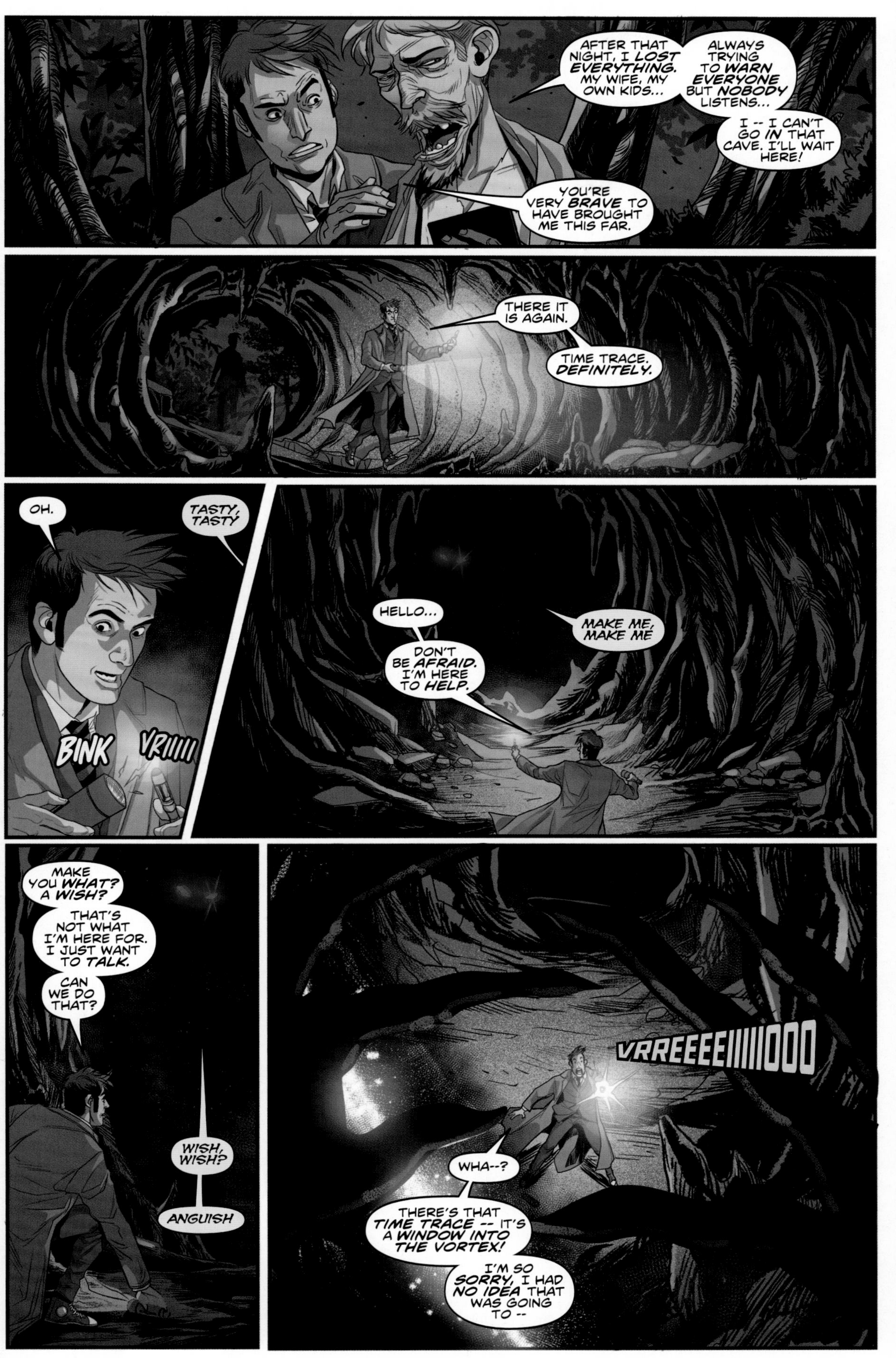
AFTER THAT NIGHT, I LOST EVERYTHING. MY WIFE, MY OWN KIDS...
ALWAYS TRYING TO WARN EVERYONE BUT NOBODY LISTENS...
I -- I CAN'T GO IN THAT CAVE. I'LL WAIT HERE!
YOU'RE VERY BRAVE TO HAVE BROUGHT ME THIS FAR.
THERE IT IS AGAIN.
TIME TRACE. DEFINITELY.
OH.
TASTY, TASTY
BINK
VRIIIII
HELLO...
DON'T BE AFRAID. I'M HERE TO HELP.
MAKE ME, MAKE ME
MAKE YOU WHAT? A WISH?
THAT'S NOT WHAT I'M HERE FOR. I JUST WANT TO TALK.
CAN WE DO THAT?
WISH, WISH?
ANGUISH
VRREEEEIIIIIOOO
WHA--?
THERE'S THAT TIME TRACE -- IT'S A WINDOW INTO THE VORTEX!
I'M SO SORRY, I HAD NO IDEA THAT WAS GOING TO --

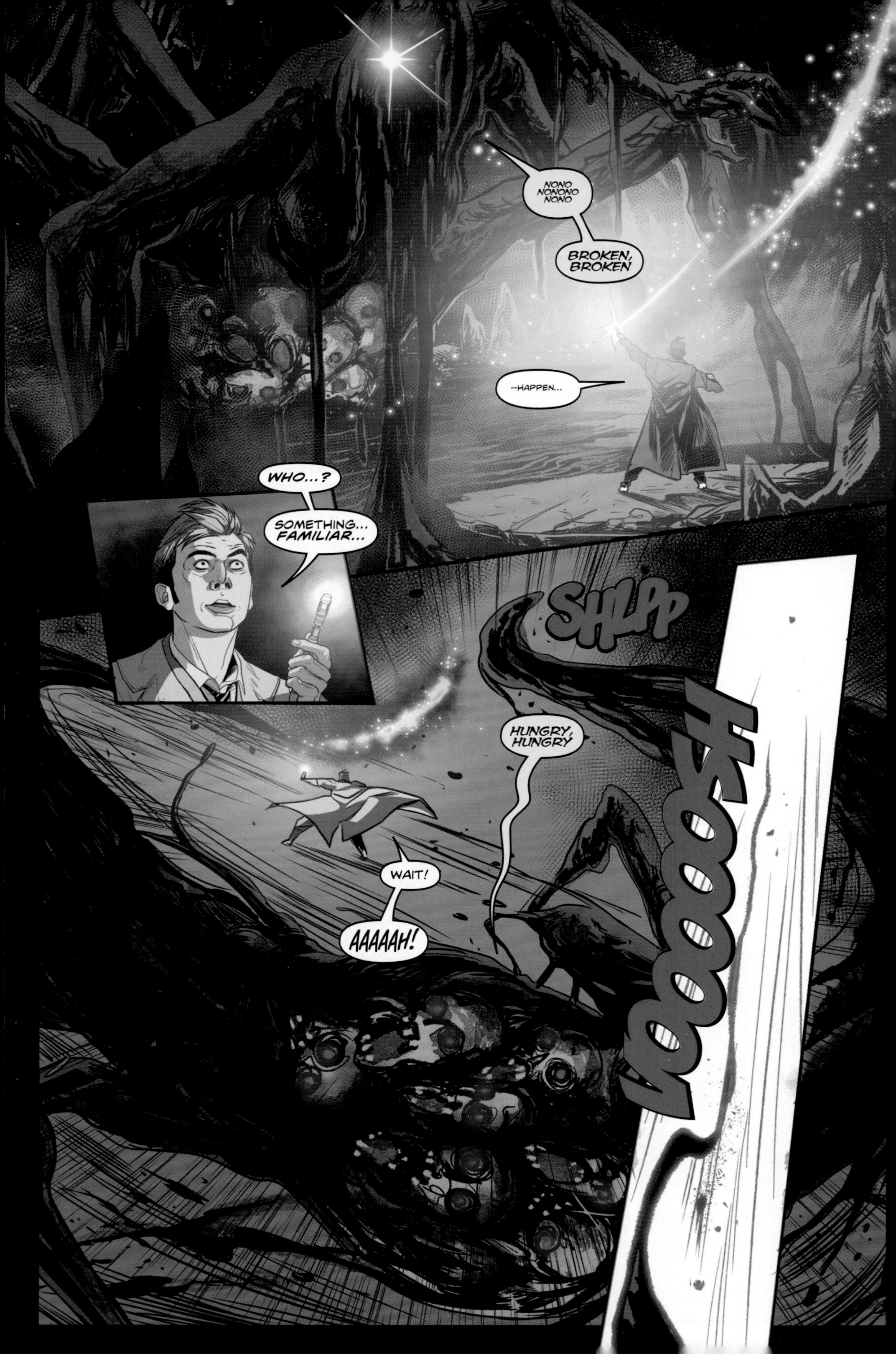
NONO NONONO NONO
BROKEN, BROKEN
--HAPPEN...
WHO...?
SOMETHING... FAMILIAR...
SHLPP
HUNGRY, HUNGRY
WAIT!
AAAAAH!
VOOOOOSH

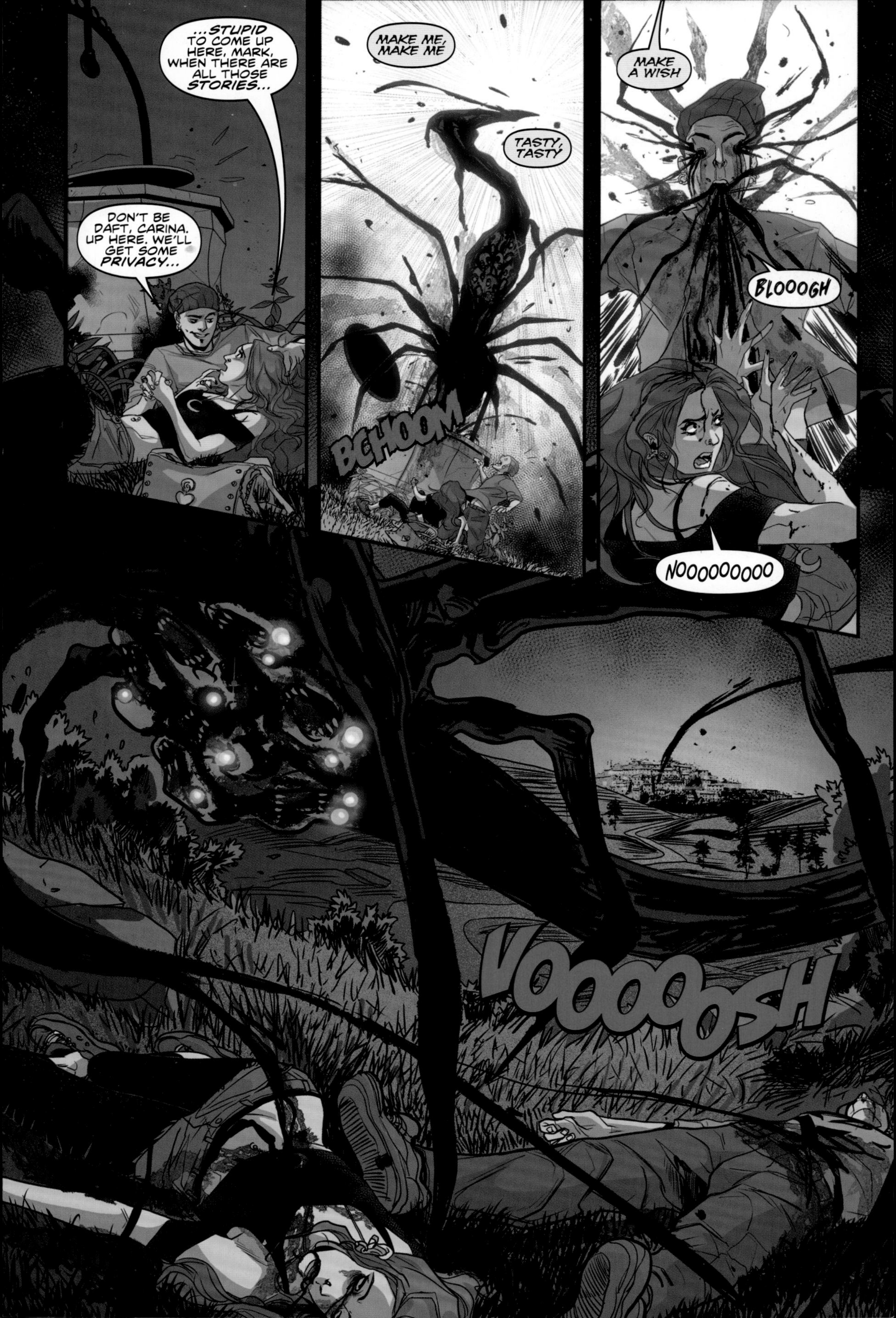

...STUPID TO COME UP HERE, MARK, WHEN THERE ARE ALL THOSE STORIES...
DON'T BE DAFT, CARINA. UP HERE. WE'LL GET SOME PRIVACY...
MAKE ME, MAKE ME
TASTY, TASTY
BCHOOM
MAKE A WISH
BLOOOGH
NOOOOOOOOO
VOOOOOSH

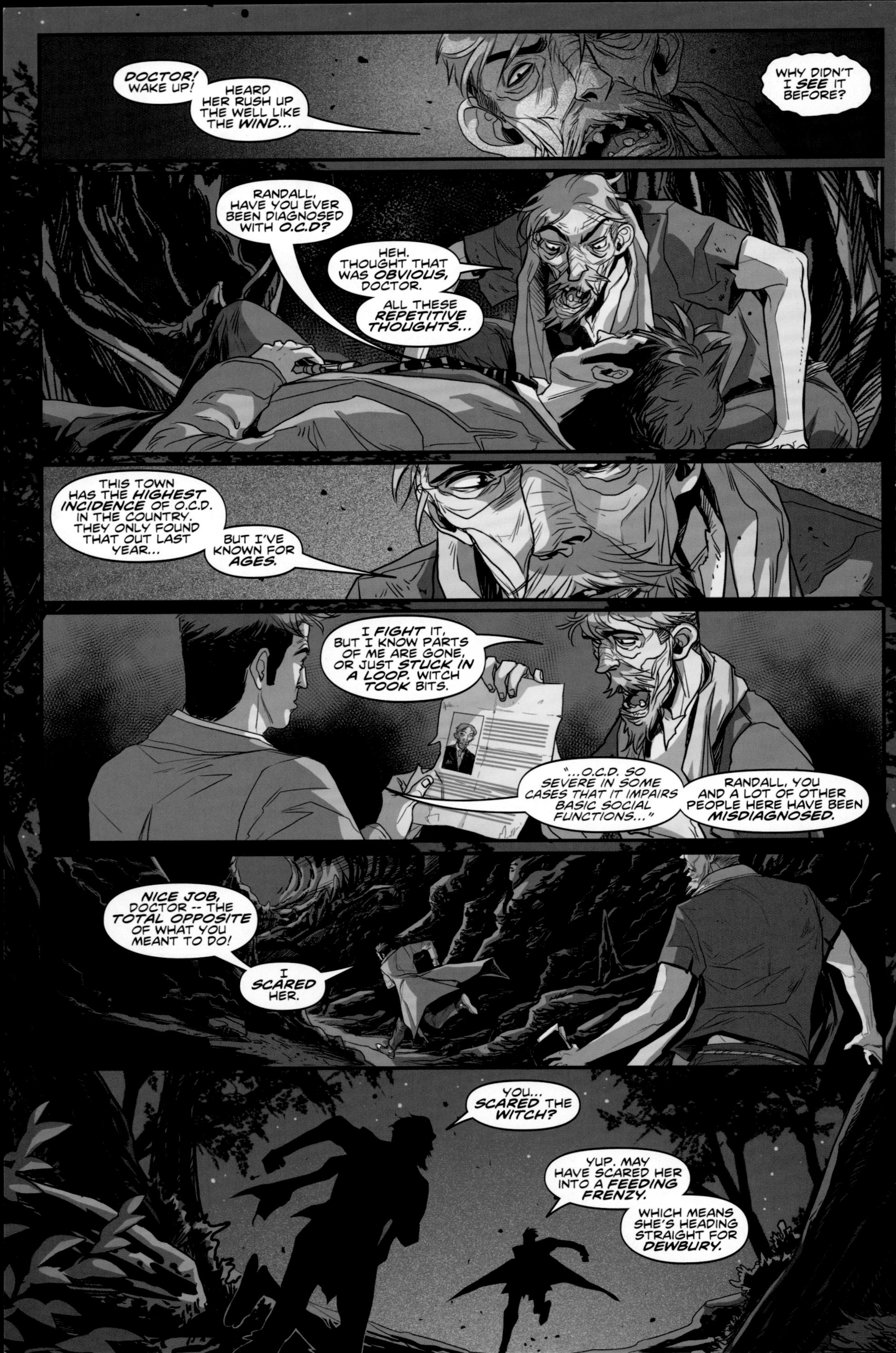
DOCTOR! WAKE UP!
HEARD HER RUSH UP THE WELL LIKE THE WIND...
WHY DIDN'T I SEE IT BEFORE?
RANDALL, HAVE YOU EVER BEEN DIAGNOSED WITH O.C.D?
HEH. THOUGHT THAT WAS OBVIOUS, DOCTOR.
ALL THESE REPETITIVE THOUGHTS...
THIS TOWN HAS THE HIGHEST INCIDENCE OF O.C.D. IN THE COUNTRY. THEY ONLY FOUND THAT OUT LAST YEAR...
BUT I'VE KNOWN FOR AGES.
I FIGHT IT, BUT I KNOW PARTS OF ME ARE GONE, OR JUST STUCK IN A LOOP. WITCH TOOK BITS.
"...O.C.D. SO SEVERE IN SOME CASES THAT IT IMPAIRS BASIC SOCIAL FUNCTIONS..."
RANDALL, YOU AND A LOT OF OTHER PEOPLE HERE HAVE BEEN MISDIAGNOSED.
NICE JOB, DOCTOR -- THE TOTAL OPPOSITE OF WHAT YOU MEANT TO DO!
I SCARED HER.
YOU... SCARED THE WITCH?
YUP. MAY HAVE SCARED HER INTO A FEEDING FRENZY.
WHICH MEANS SHE'S HEADING STRAIGHT FOR DEWBURY.

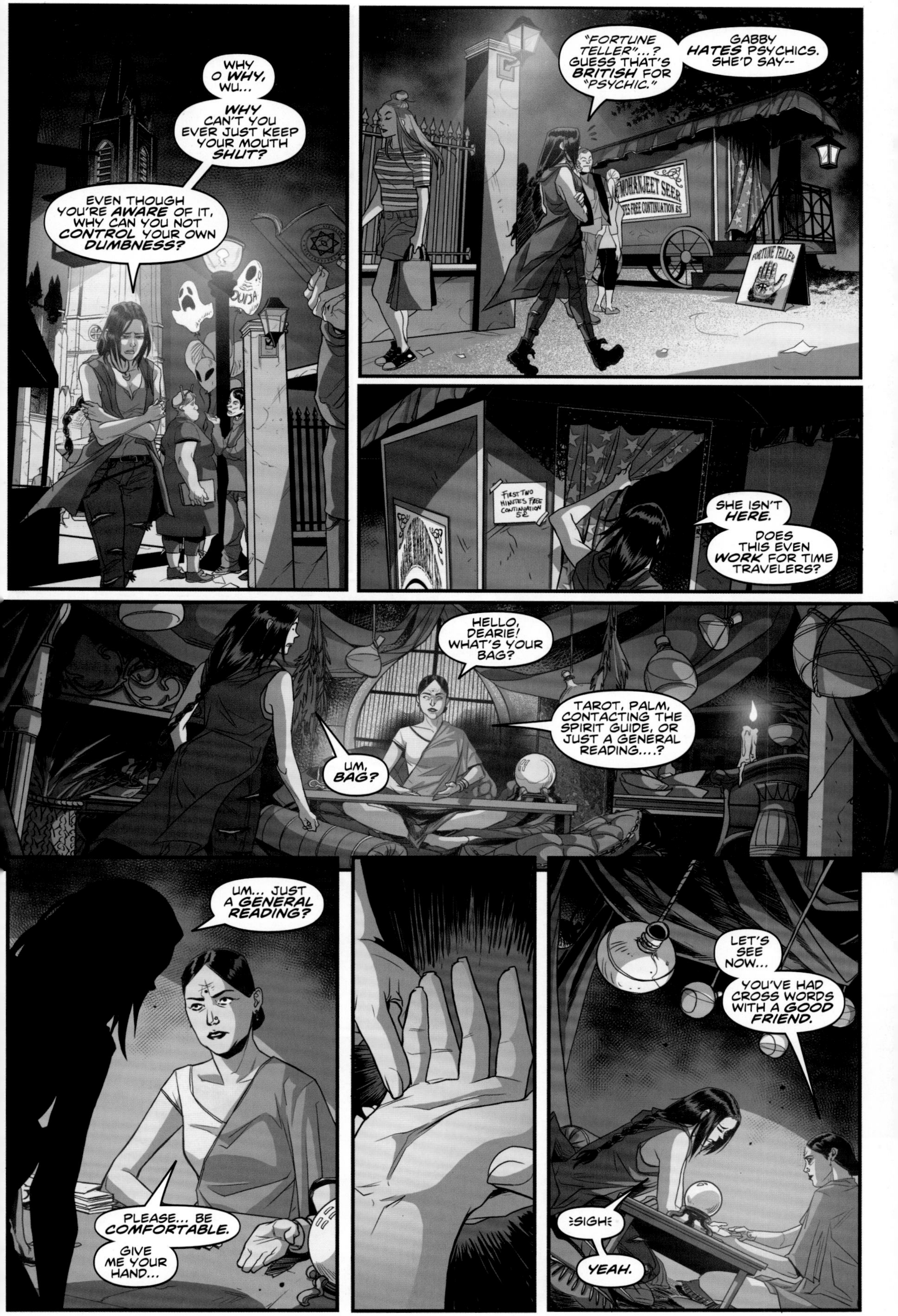

WHY O WHY, WU...
WHY CAN'T YOU EVER JUST KEEP YOUR MOUTH SHUT?
EVEN THOUGH YOU'RE AWARE OF IT, WHY CAN YOU NOT CONTROL YOUR OWN DUMBNESS?
OUIJA
"FORTUNE TELLER"...? GUESS THAT'S BRITISH FOR "PSYCHIC."
GABBY HATES PSYCHICS. SHE'D SAY--
MOHANJEET SEER
FORTUNE TELLER
FIRST TWO MINUTES FREE CONTINUATION 5£
SHE ISN'T HERE.
DOES THIS EVEN WORK FOR TIME TRAVELERS?
HELLO, DEARIE! WHAT'S YOUR BAG?
TAROT, PALM, CONTACTING THE SPIRIT GUIDE, OR JUST A GENERAL READING....?
UM, BAG?
UM... JUST A GENERAL READING?
PLEASE... BE COMFORTABLE.
GIVE ME YOUR HAND...
LET'S SEE NOW...
YOU'VE HAD CROSS WORDS WITH A GOOD FRIEND.
SIGH
YEAH.

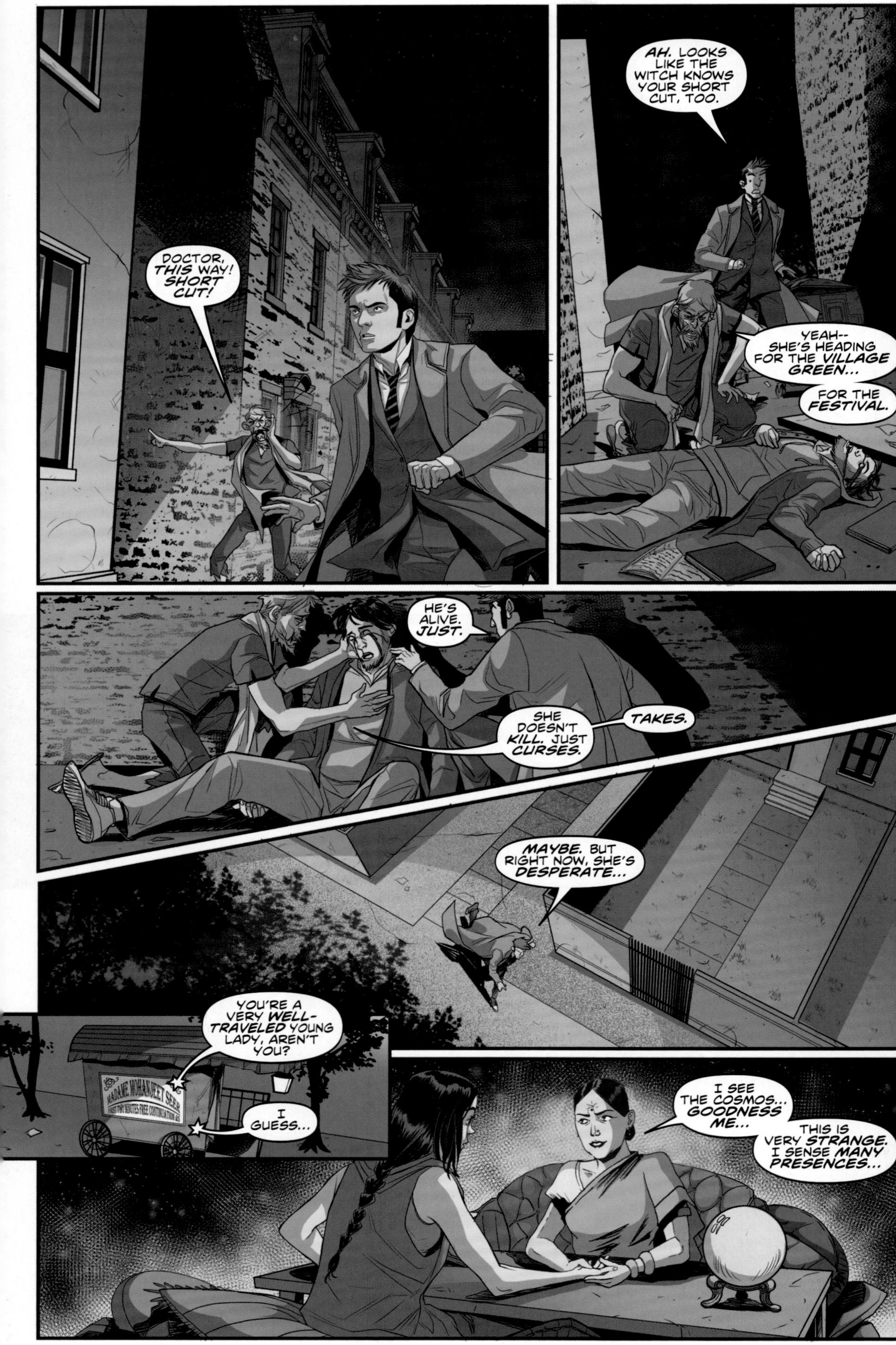
DOCTOR, THIS WAY! SHORT CUT!
AH. LOOKS LIKE THE WITCH KNOWS YOUR SHORT CUT, TOO.
YEAH-- SHE'S HEADING FOR THE VILLAGE GREEN...
FOR THE FESTIVAL.
HE'S ALIVE. JUST.
SHE DOESN'T KILL. JUST CURSES.
TAKES.
MAYBE. BUT RIGHT NOW, SHE'S DESPERATE...
YOU'RE A VERY WELL-TRAVELED YOUNG LADY, AREN'T YOU?
MADAME MOHANJEET SEER
I GUESS...
I SEE THE COSMOS... GOODNESS ME...
THIS IS VERY STRANGE. I SENSE MANY PRESENCES...

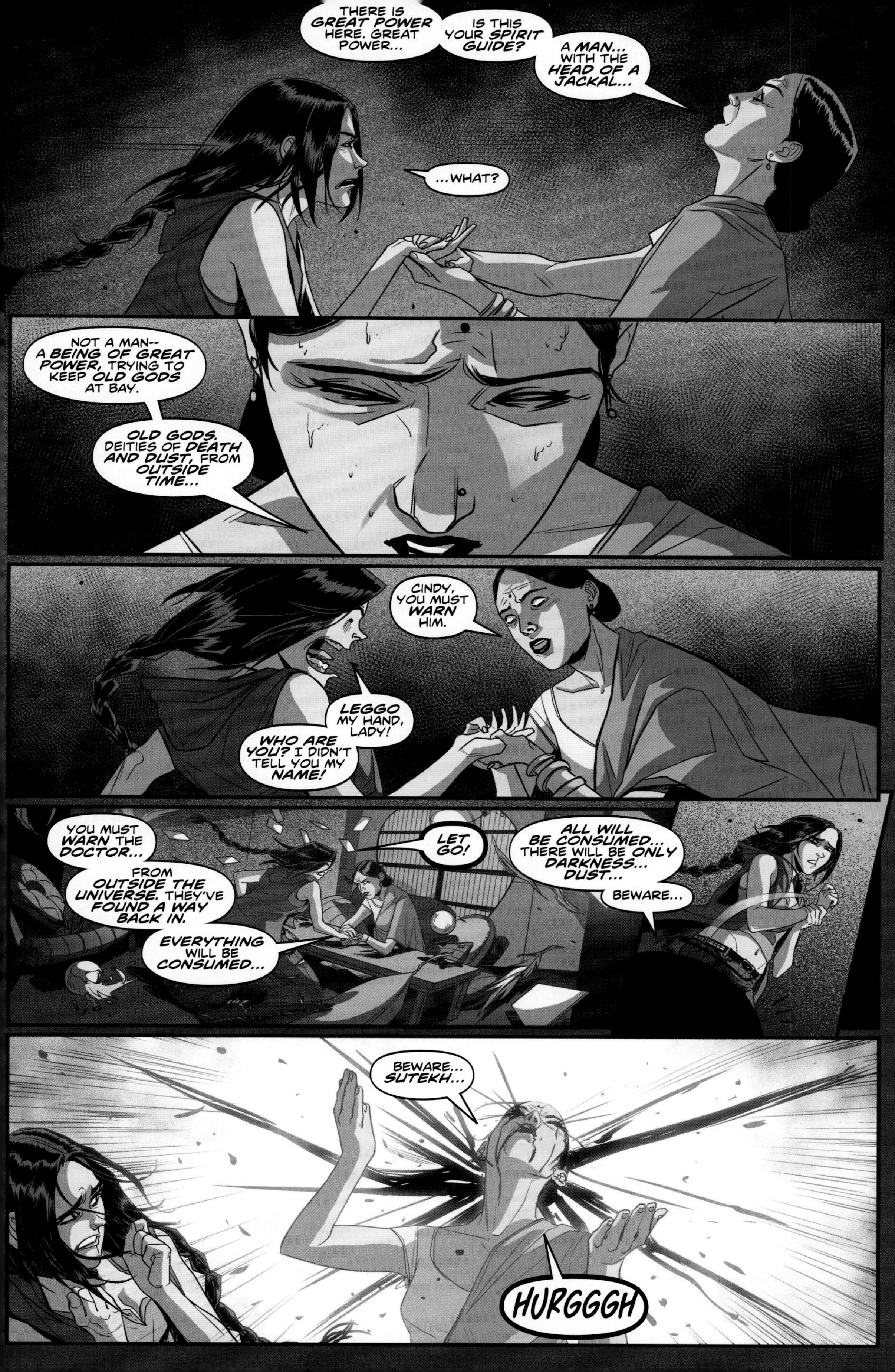
THERE IS GREAT POWER HERE. GREAT POWER...
IS THIS YOUR SPIRIT GUIDE?
A MAN... WITH THE HEAD OF A JACKAL...
...WHAT?
NOT A MAN-- A BEING OF GREAT POWER, TRYING TO KEEP OLD GODS AT BAY.
OLD GODS. DEITIES OF DEATH AND DUST, FROM OUTSIDE TIME...
CINDY, YOU MUST WARN HIM.
LEGGO MY HAND, LADY!
WHO ARE YOU? I DIDN'T TELL YOU MY NAME!
YOU MUST WARN THE DOCTOR...
FROM OUTSIDE THE UNIVERSE. THEY'VE FOUND A WAY BACK IN.
EVERYTHING WILL BE CONSUMED...
LET GO!
ALL WILL BE CONSUMED... THERE WILL BE ONLY DARKNESS... DUST...
BEWARE...
BEWARE... SUTEKH...
HURGGGH

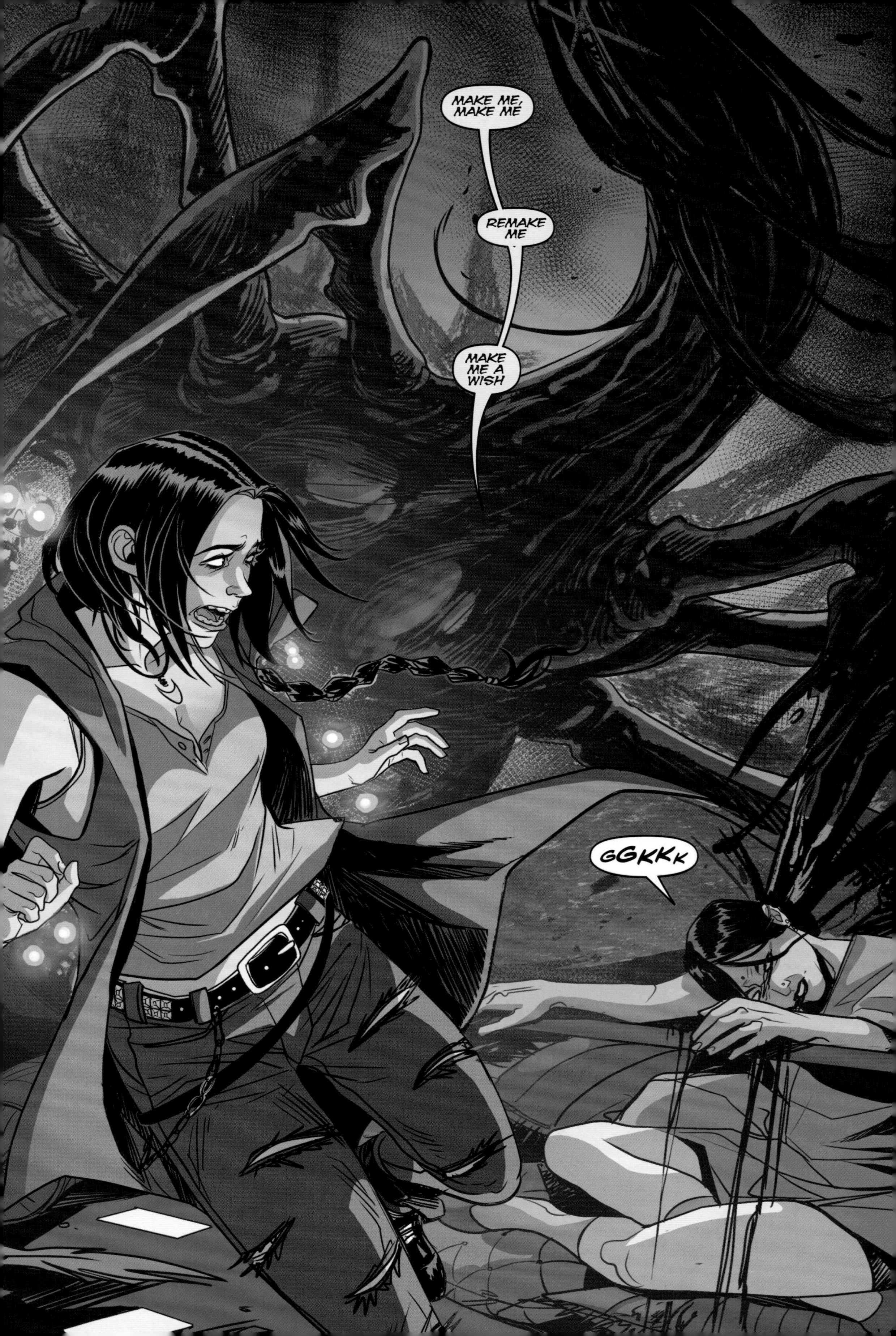
MAKE ME, MAKE ME
REMAKE ME
MAKE ME A WISH
GGKKK

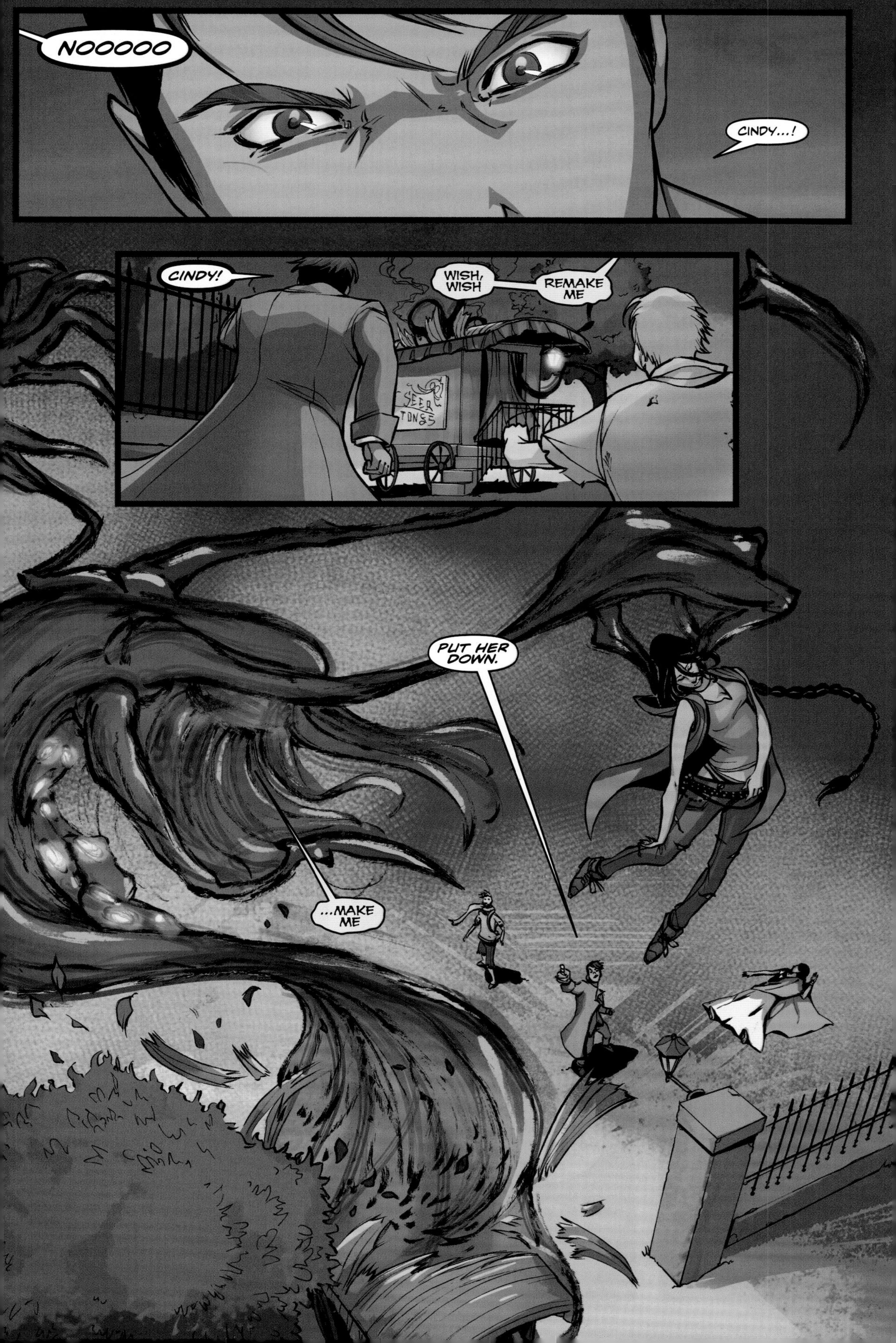
NOOOOO
CINDY...!
CINDY!
WISH, WISH
REMAKE ME
SEER TONGS
PUT HER DOWN.
...MAKE ME

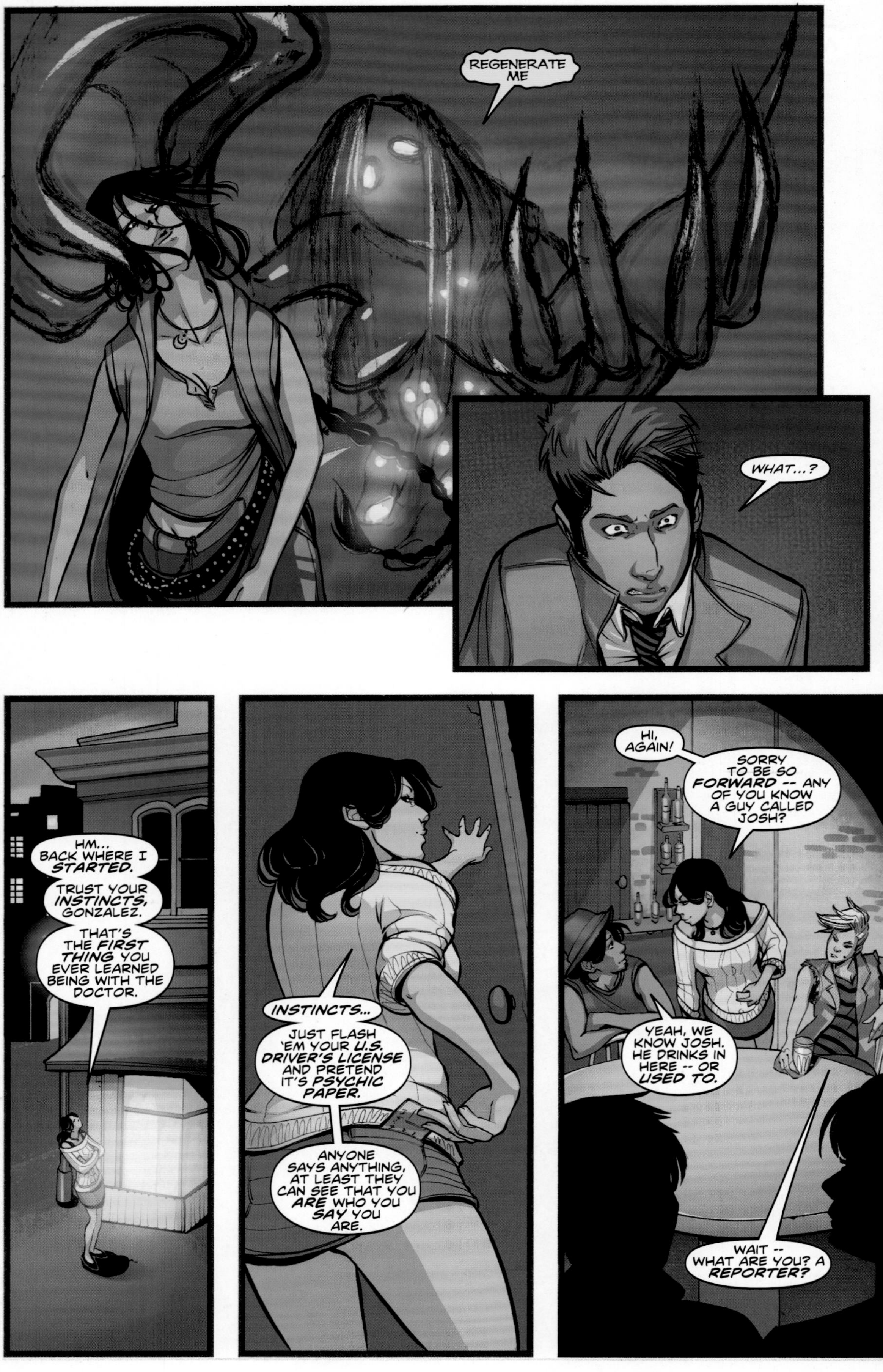
REGENERATE ME
WHAT...?
HM... BACK WHERE I STARTED.
TRUST YOUR INSTINCTS, GONZALEZ.
THAT'S THE FIRST THING YOU EVER LEARNED BEING WITH THE DOCTOR.
INSTINCTS...
JUST FLASH 'EM YOUR U.S. DRIVER'S LICENSE AND PRETEND IT'S PSYCHIC PAPER.
ANYONE SAYS ANYTHING, AT LEAST THEY CAN SEE THAT YOU ARE WHO YOU SAY YOU ARE.
HI, AGAIN!
SORRY TO BE SO FORWARD -- ANY OF YOU KNOW A GUY CALLED JOSH?
YEAH, WE KNOW JOSH. HE DRINKS IN HERE -- OR USED TO.
WAIT -- WHAT ARE YOU? A REPORTER?

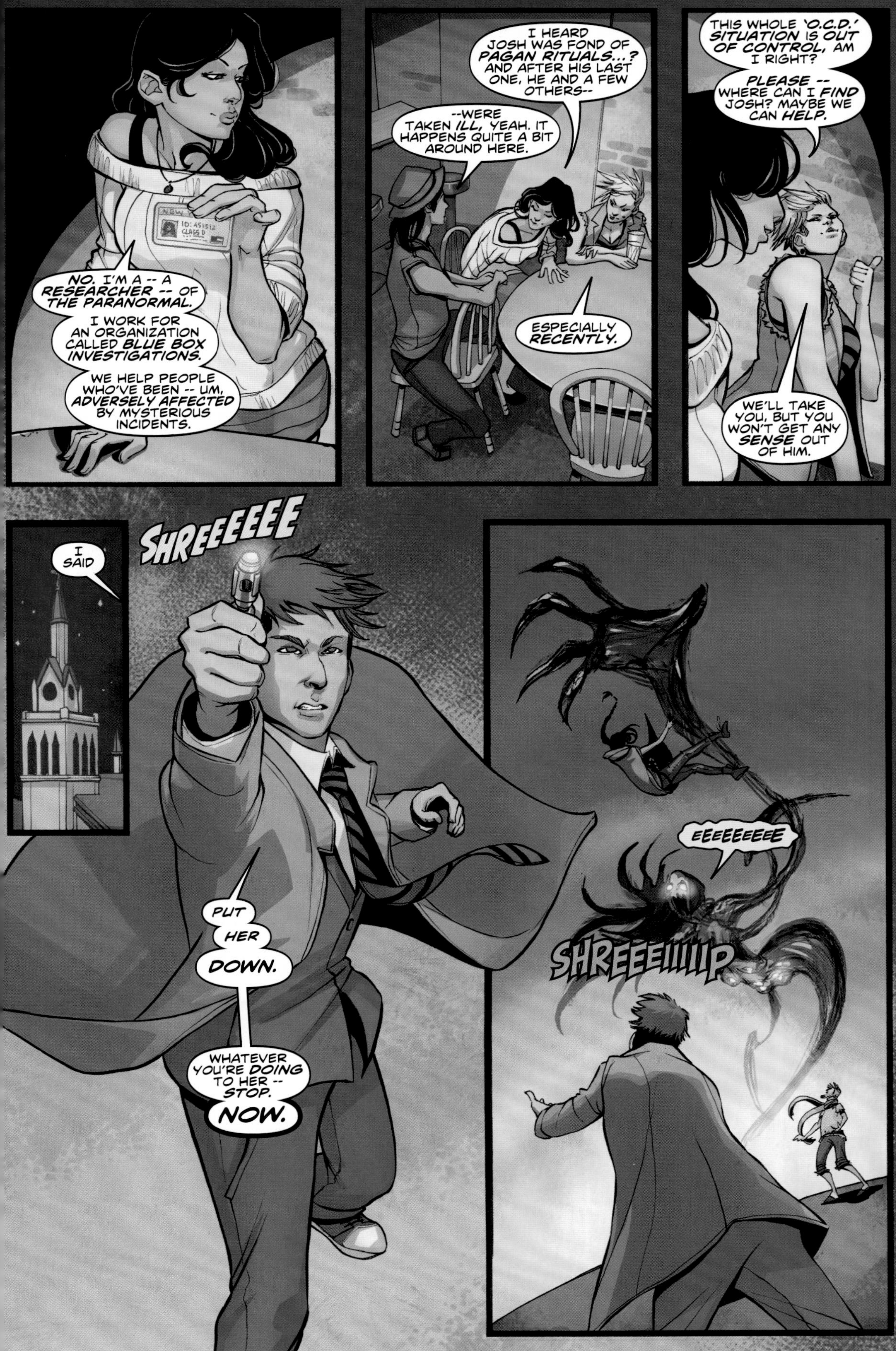
NO. I'M A -- A RESEARCHER -- OF THE PARANORMAL.
I WORK FOR AN ORGANIZATION CALLED BLUE BOX INVESTIGATIONS.
WE HELP PEOPLE WHO'VE BEEN -- UM, ADVERSELY AFFECTED BY MYSTERIOUS INCIDENTS.
I HEARD JOSH WAS FOND OF PAGAN RITUALS...? AND AFTER HIS LAST ONE, HE AND A FEW OTHERS--
--WERE TAKEN ILL, YEAH. IT HAPPENS QUITE A BIT AROUND HERE.
ESPECIALLY RECENTLY.
THIS WHOLE 'O.C.D.' SITUATION IS OUT OF CONTROL, AM I RIGHT?
PLEASE -- WHERE CAN I FIND JOSH? MAYBE WE CAN HELP.
WE'LL TAKE YOU, BUT YOU WON'T GET ANY SENSE OUT OF HIM.
I SAID
SHREEEEEEE
PUT HER DOWN.
WHATEVER YOU'RE DOING TO HER -- STOP. NOW.
EEEEEEEEE
SHREEEIIIIIP

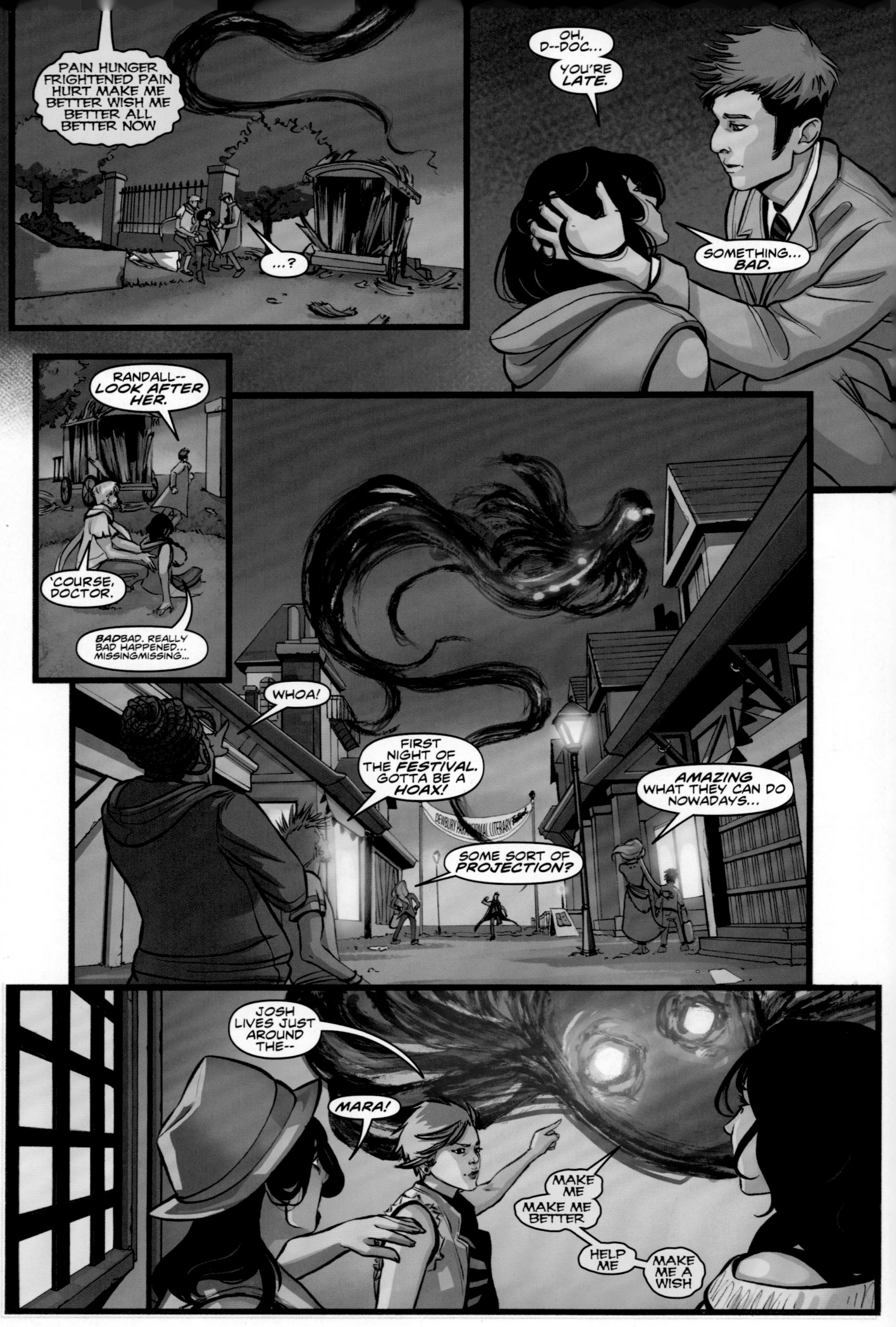
PAIN HUNGER FRIGHTENED PAIN HURT MAKE ME BETTER WISH ME BETTER ALL BETTER NOW
...?
OH, D--DOC...
YOU'RE *LATE.*
SOMETHING... *BAD.*
RANDALL-- *LOOK AFTER HER.*
'COURSE, DOCTOR.
BADBAD. REALLY BAD HAPPENED... MISSINGMISSING...
WHOA!
FIRST NIGHT OF THE *FESTIVAL.* GOTTA BE A *HOAX!*
AMAZING WHAT THEY CAN DO NOWADAYS...
SOME SORT OF *PROJECTION?*
JOSH LIVES JUST AROUND THE--
MARA!
MAKE ME
MAKE ME BETTER
HELP ME
MAKE ME A WISH

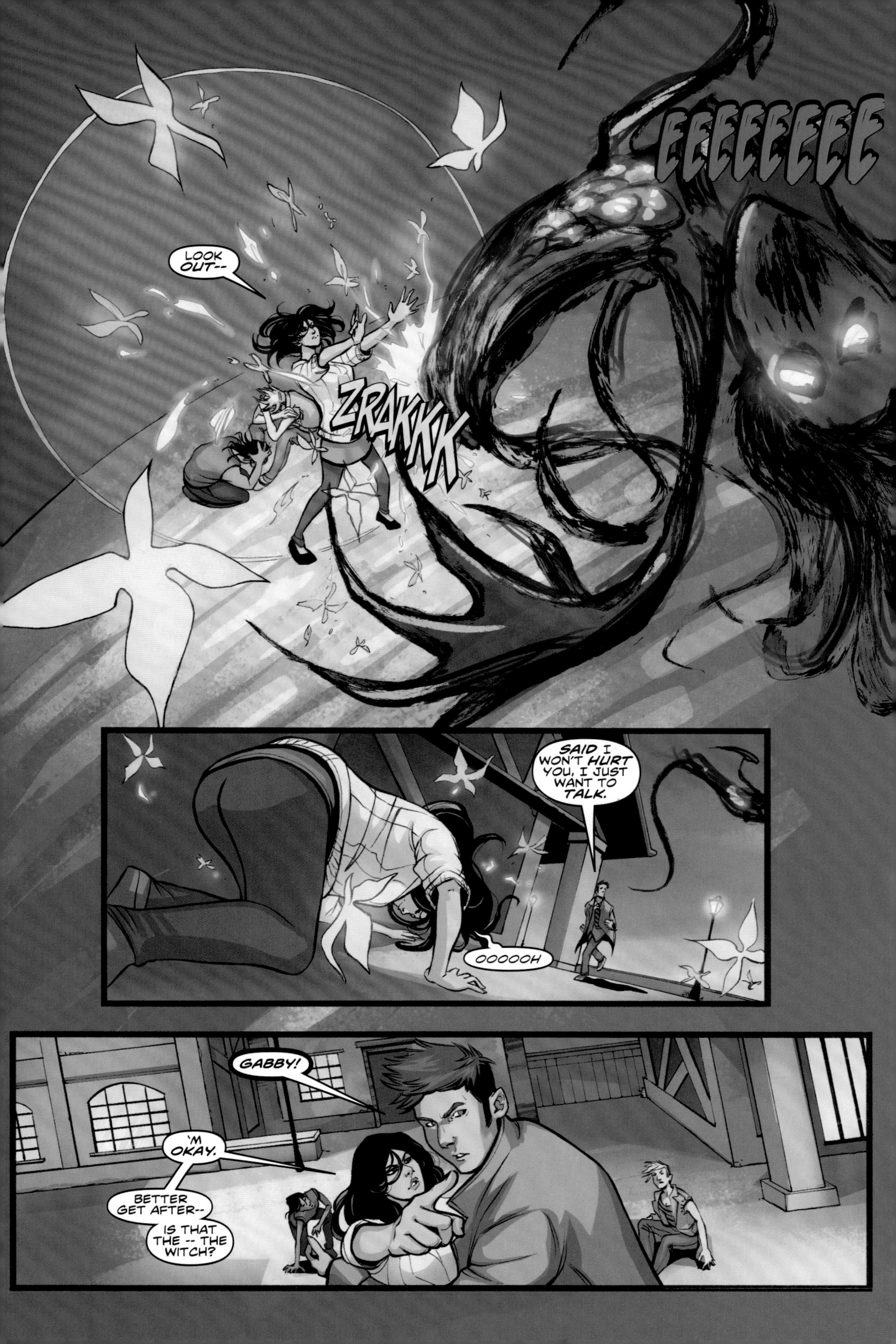
EEEEEEEE
LOOK OUT--
ZRAKKK
SAID I WON'T HURT YOU, I JUST WANT TO TALK.
OOOOOH
GABBY!
'M OKAY.
BETTER GET AFTER--
IS THAT THE -- THE WITCH?

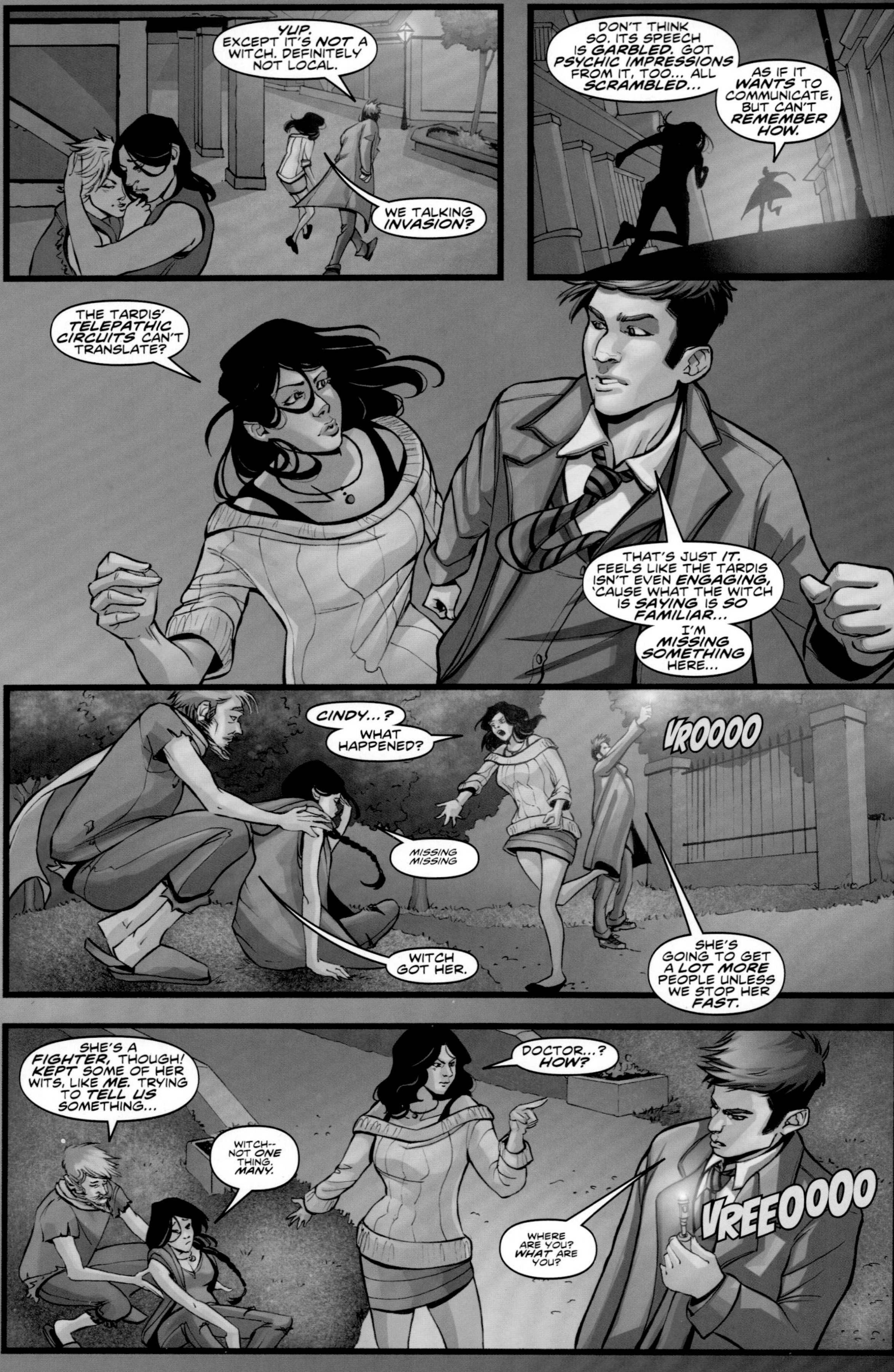

YUP. EXCEPT IT'S NOT A WITCH. DEFINITELY NOT LOCAL.
WE TALKING INVASION?
DON'T THINK SO. ITS SPEECH IS GARBLED. GOT PSYCHIC IMPRESSIONS FROM IT, TOO... ALL SCRAMBLED...
AS IF IT WANTS TO COMMUNICATE, BUT CAN'T REMEMBER HOW.
THE TARDIS' TELEPATHIC CIRCUITS CAN'T TRANSLATE?
THAT'S JUST IT. FEELS LIKE THE TARDIS ISN'T EVEN ENGAGING, 'CAUSE WHAT THE WITCH IS SAYING IS SO FAMILIAR...
I'M MISSING SOMETHING HERE...
CINDY...?
WHAT HAPPENED?
MISSING MISSING
WITCH GOT HER.
VROOOO
SHE'S GOING TO GET A LOT MORE PEOPLE UNLESS WE STOP HER FAST.
SHE'S A FIGHTER, THOUGH! KEPT SOME OF HER WITS, LIKE ME. TRYING TO TELL US SOMETHING...
WITCH-- NOT ONE THING. MANY.
DOCTOR...? HOW?
VREEOOOO
WHERE ARE YOU? WHAT ARE YOU?

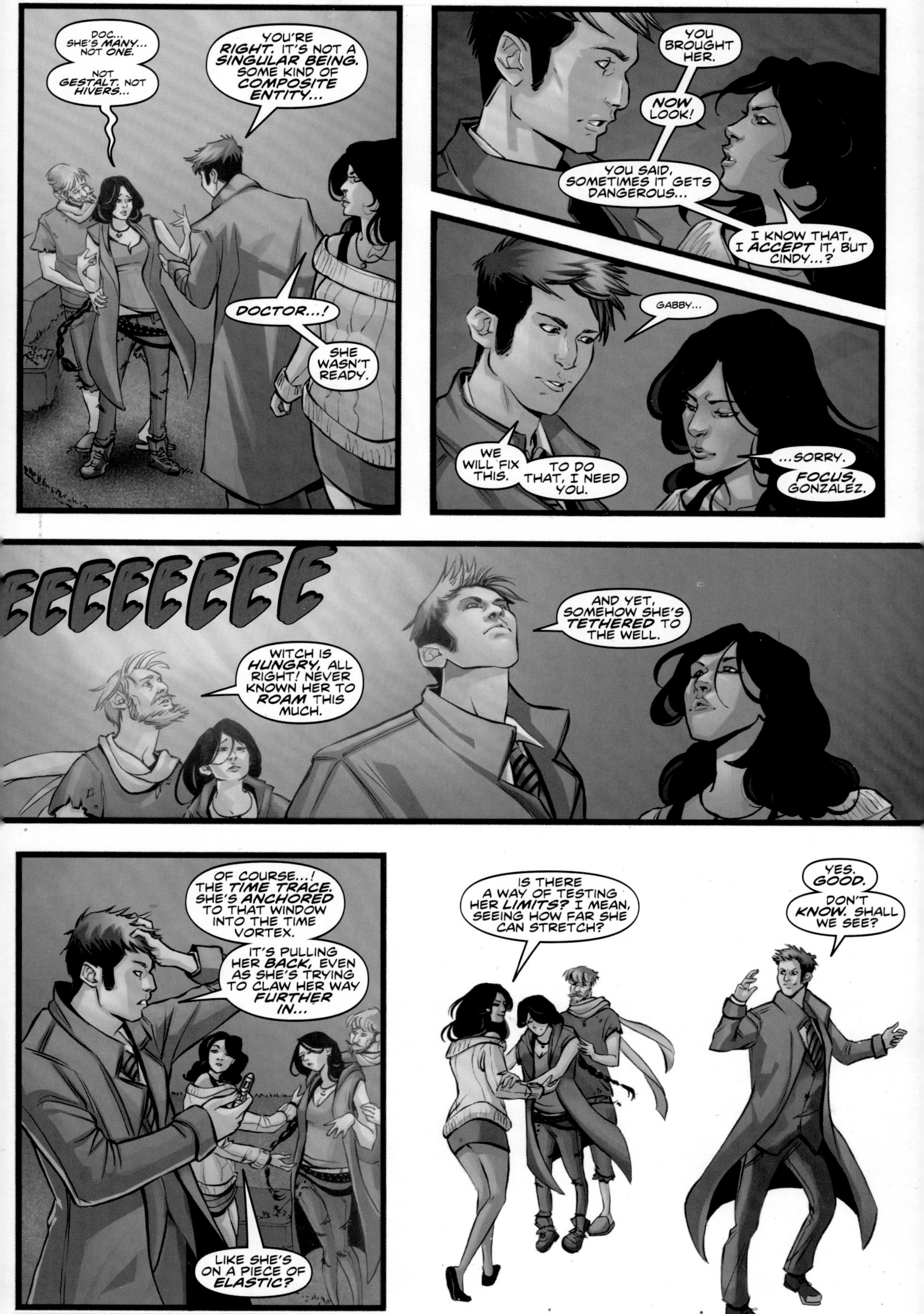
DOC... SHE'S MANY... NOT ONE.
NOT GESTALT. NOT HIVERS...
YOU'RE RIGHT. IT'S NOT A SINGULAR BEING. SOME KIND OF COMPOSITE ENTITY...
DOCTOR...!
SHE WASN'T READY.
YOU BROUGHT HER.
NOW LOOK!
YOU SAID, SOMETIMES IT GETS DANGEROUS...
I KNOW THAT, I ACCEPT IT, BUT CINDY...?
GABBY...
WE WILL FIX THIS.
TO DO THAT, I NEED YOU.
...SORRY. FOCUS, GONZALEZ.
EEEEEEEE
WITCH IS HUNGRY, ALL RIGHT! NEVER KNOWN HER TO ROAM THIS MUCH.
AND YET, SOMEHOW SHE'S TETHERED TO THE WELL.
OF COURSE...! THE TIME TRACE. SHE'S ANCHORED TO THAT WINDOW INTO THE TIME VORTEX.
IT'S PULLING HER BACK, EVEN AS SHE'S TRYING TO CLAW HER WAY FURTHER IN...
LIKE SHE'S ON A PIECE OF ELASTIC?
IS THERE A WAY OF TESTING HER LIMITS? I MEAN, SEEING HOW FAR SHE CAN STRETCH?
YES. GOOD.
DON'T KNOW. SHALL WE SEE?

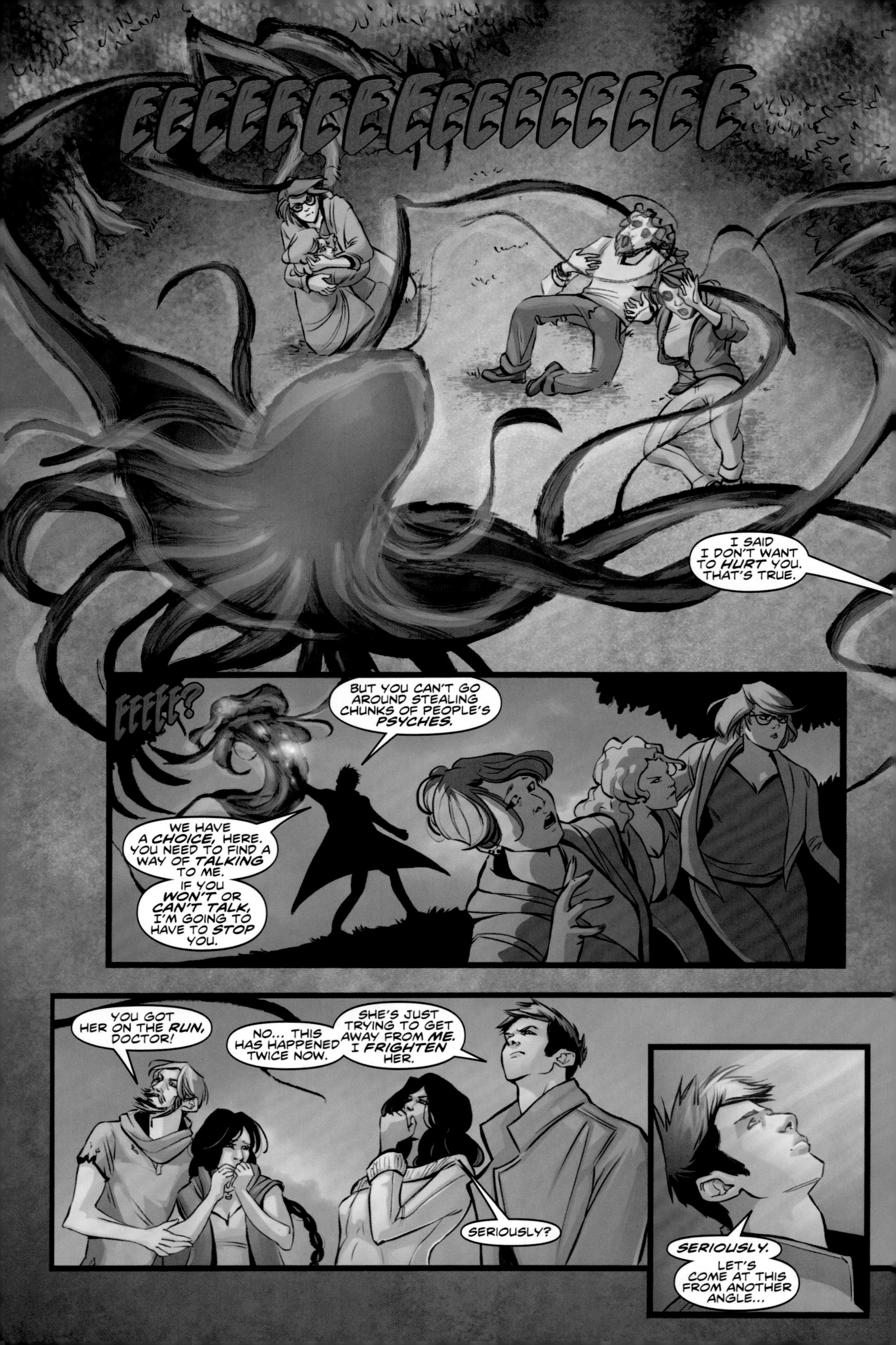
EEEEEEEEEEEEEEEEE
I SAID I DON'T WANT TO HURT YOU. THAT'S TRUE.
EEEEE?
BUT YOU CAN'T GO AROUND STEALING CHUNKS OF PEOPLE'S PSYCHES.
WE HAVE A CHOICE, HERE. YOU NEED TO FIND A WAY OF TALKING TO ME.
IF YOU WON'T OR CAN'T TALK, I'M GOING TO HAVE TO STOP YOU.
YOU GOT HER ON THE RUN, DOCTOR!
NO... THIS HAS HAPPENED TWICE NOW.
SHE'S JUST TRYING TO GET AWAY FROM ME. I FRIGHTEN HER.
SERIOUSLY?
SERIOUSLY.
LET'S COME AT THIS FROM ANOTHER ANGLE...

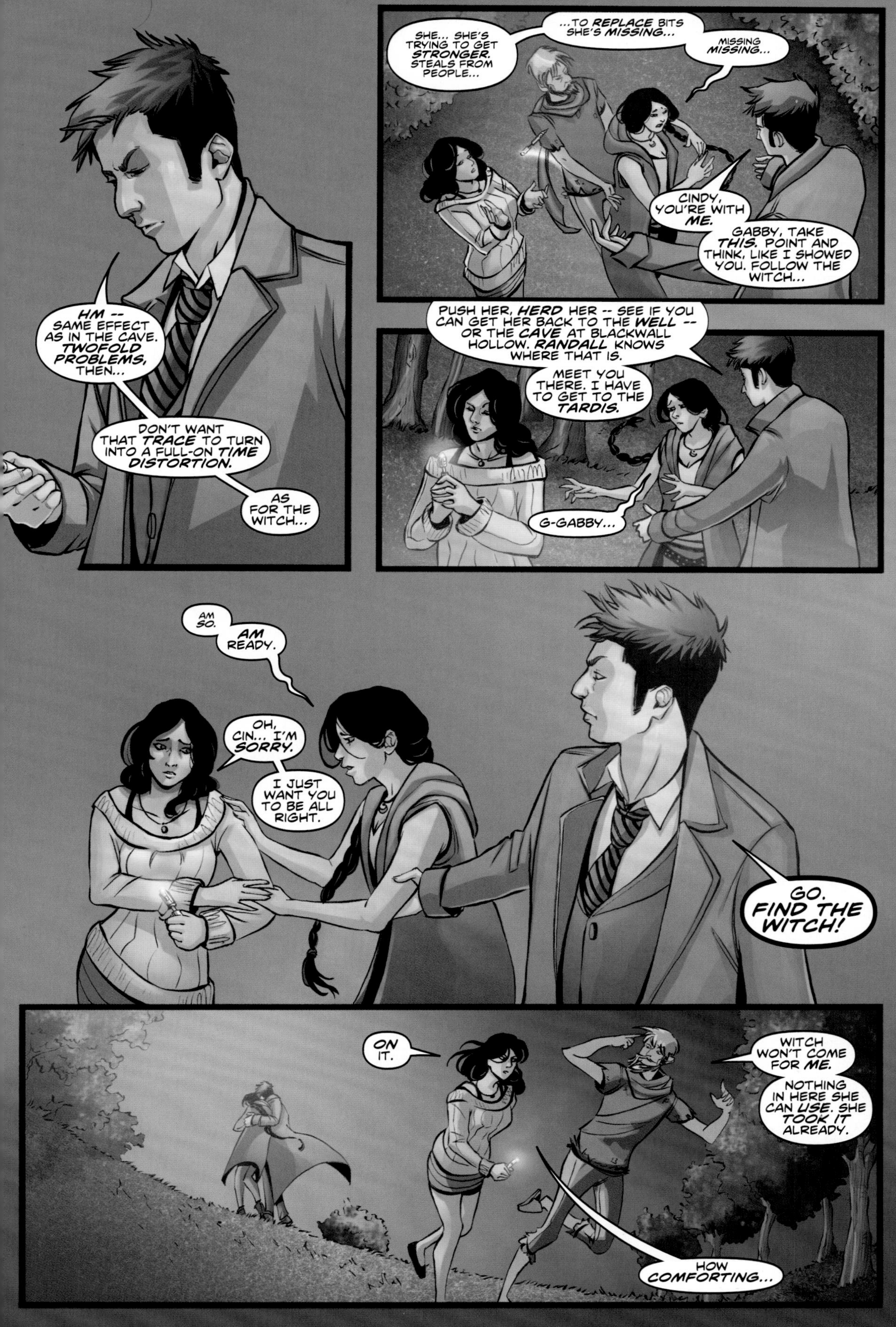
HM -- SAME EFFECT AS IN THE CAVE. TWOFOLD PROBLEMS, THEN...
DON'T WANT THAT TRACE TO TURN INTO A FULL-ON TIME DISTORTION.
AS FOR THE WITCH...
SHE... SHE'S TRYING TO GET STRONGER. STEALS FROM PEOPLE...
...TO REPLACE BITS SHE'S MISSING...
MISSING MISSING...
CINDY, YOU'RE WITH ME.
GABBY, TAKE THIS. POINT AND THINK, LIKE I SHOWED YOU. FOLLOW THE WITCH...
PUSH HER, HERD HER -- SEE IF YOU CAN GET HER BACK TO THE WELL -- OR THE CAVE AT BLACKWALL HOLLOW. RANDALL KNOWS WHERE THAT IS.
MEET YOU THERE. I HAVE TO GET TO THE TARDIS.
G-GABBY...
AM SO. AM READY.
OH, CIN... I'M SORRY.
I JUST WANT YOU TO BE ALL RIGHT.
GO. FIND THE WITCH!
ON IT.
WITCH WON'T COME FOR ME.
NOTHING IN HERE SHE CAN USE. SHE TOOK IT ALREADY.
HOW COMFORTING...

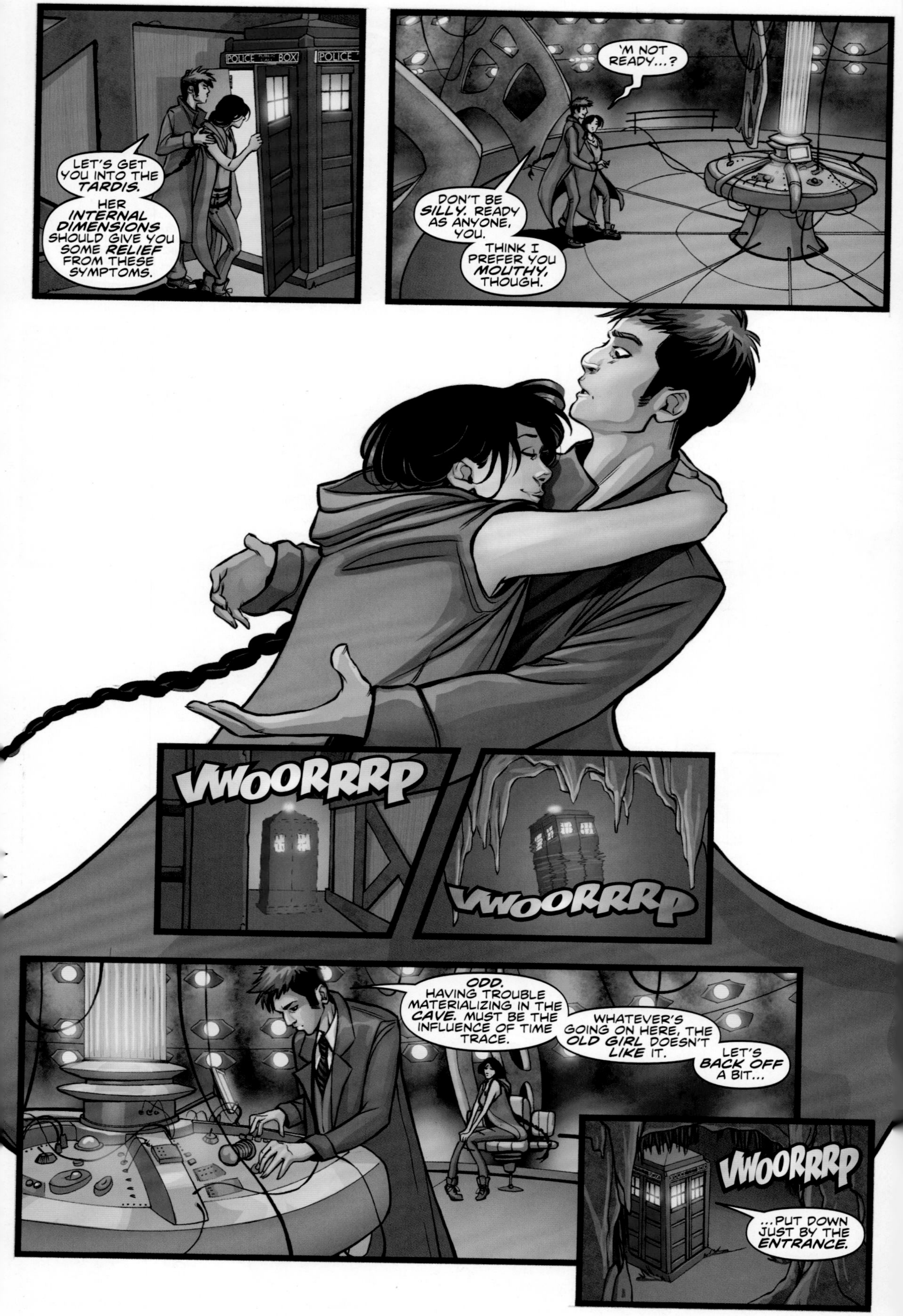
LET'S GET YOU INTO THE TARDIS.
HER INTERNAL DIMENSIONS SHOULD GIVE YOU SOME RELIEF FROM THESE SYMPTOMS.
POLICE PUBLIC CALL BOX
POLICE
'M NOT READY...?
DON'T BE SILLY. READY AS ANYONE, YOU.
THINK I PREFER YOU MOUTHY, THOUGH.
VWOORRRP
VWOORRRP
ODD. HAVING TROUBLE MATERIALIZING IN THE CAVE. MUST BE THE INFLUENCE OF TIME TRACE.
WHATEVER'S GOING ON HERE, THE OLD GIRL DOESN'T LIKE IT.
LET'S BACK OFF A BIT...
VWOORRRP
...PUT DOWN JUST BY THE ENTRANCE.

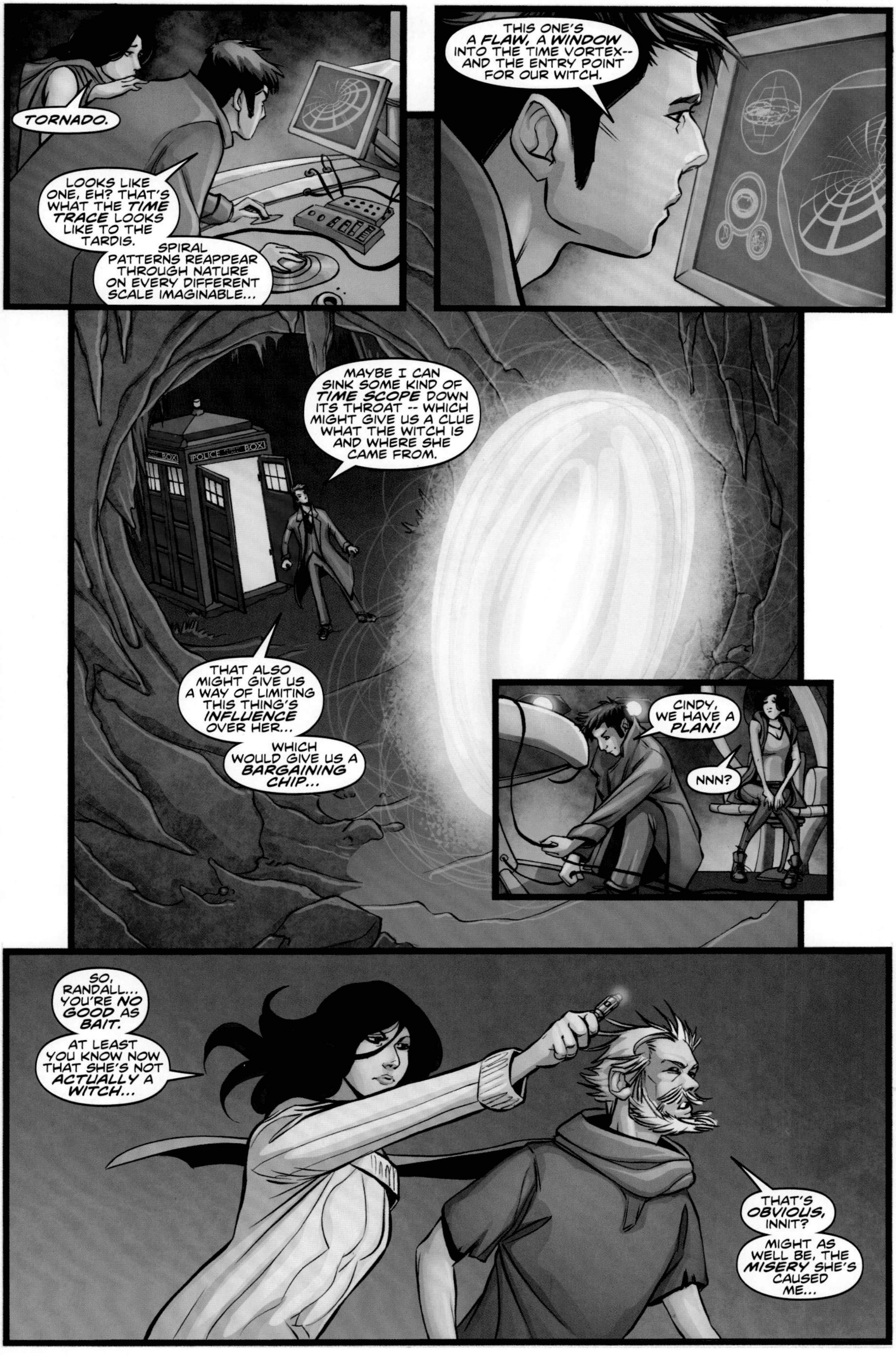
TORNADO.
LOOKS LIKE ONE, EH? THAT'S WHAT THE TIME TRACE LOOKS LIKE TO THE TARDIS.
SPIRAL PATTERNS REAPPEAR THROUGH NATURE ON EVERY DIFFERENT SCALE IMAGINABLE...
THIS ONE'S A FLAW, A WINDOW INTO THE TIME VORTEX-- AND THE ENTRY POINT FOR OUR WITCH.
MAYBE I CAN SINK SOME KIND OF TIME SCOPE DOWN ITS THROAT -- WHICH MIGHT GIVE US A CLUE WHAT THE WITCH IS AND WHERE SHE CAME FROM.
POLICE BOX
THAT ALSO MIGHT GIVE US A WAY OF LIMITING THIS THING'S INFLUENCE OVER HER...
WHICH WOULD GIVE US A BARGAINING CHIP...
CINDY, WE HAVE A PLAN!
NNN?
SO, RANDALL... YOU'RE NO GOOD AS BAIT.
AT LEAST YOU KNOW NOW THAT SHE'S NOT ACTUALLY A WITCH...
THAT'S OBVIOUS, INNIT?
MIGHT AS WELL BE, THE MISERY SHE'S CAUSED ME...

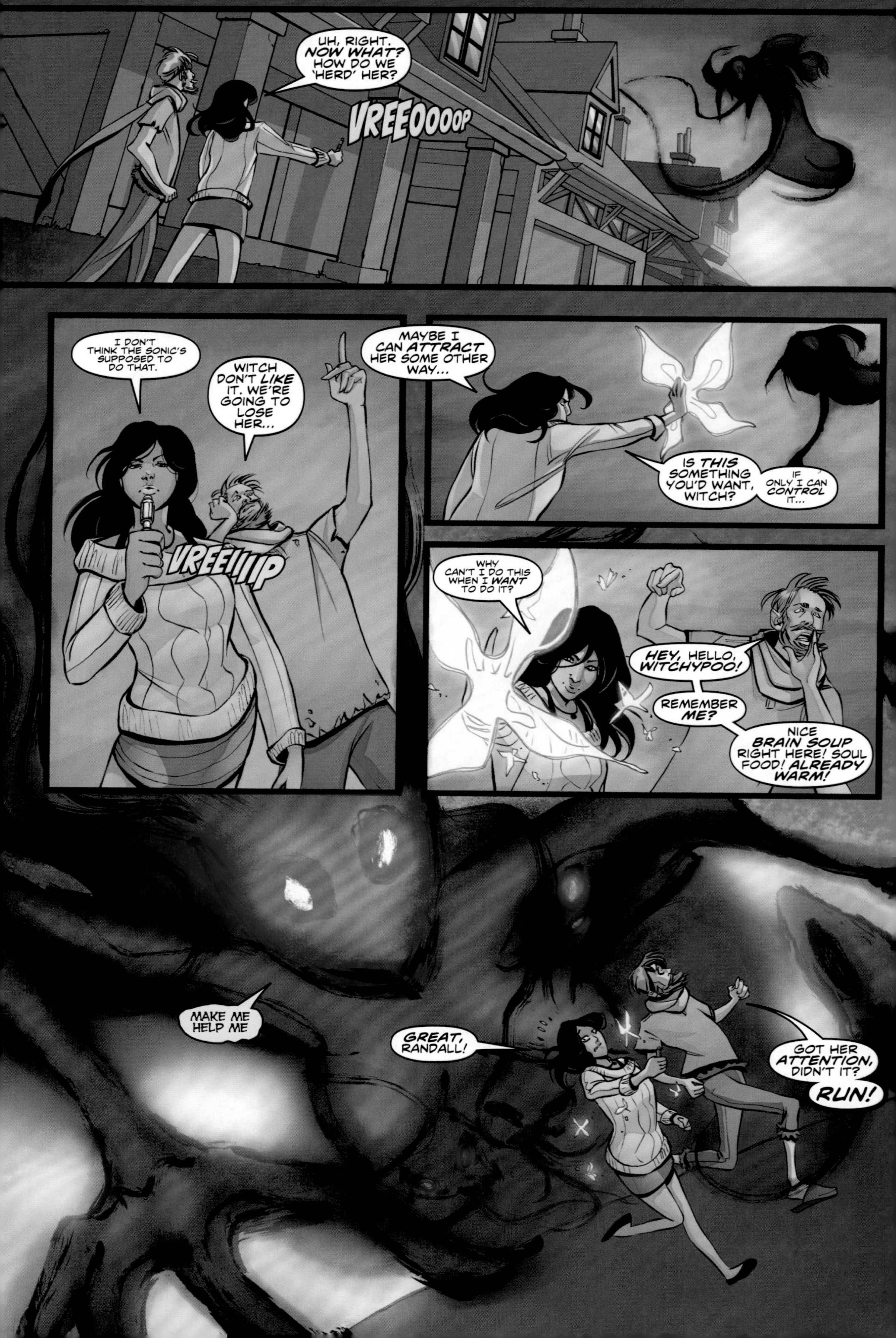

UH, RIGHT. NOW WHAT? HOW DO WE 'HERD' HER?
VREEOOOOP
I DON'T THINK THE SONIC'S SUPPOSED TO DO THAT.
WITCH DON'T LIKE IT. WE'RE GOING TO LOSE HER...
VREEIIIIP
MAYBE I CAN ATTRACT HER SOME OTHER WAY...
IS THIS SOMETHING YOU'D WANT, WITCH?
IF ONLY I CAN CONTROL IT...
WHY CAN'T I DO THIS WHEN I WANT TO DO IT?
HEY, HELLO, WITCHYPOO!
REMEMBER ME?
NICE BRAIN SOUP RIGHT HERE! SOUL FOOD! ALREADY WARM!
MAKE ME HELP ME
GREAT, RANDALL!
GOT HER ATTENTION, DIDN'T IT?
RUN!

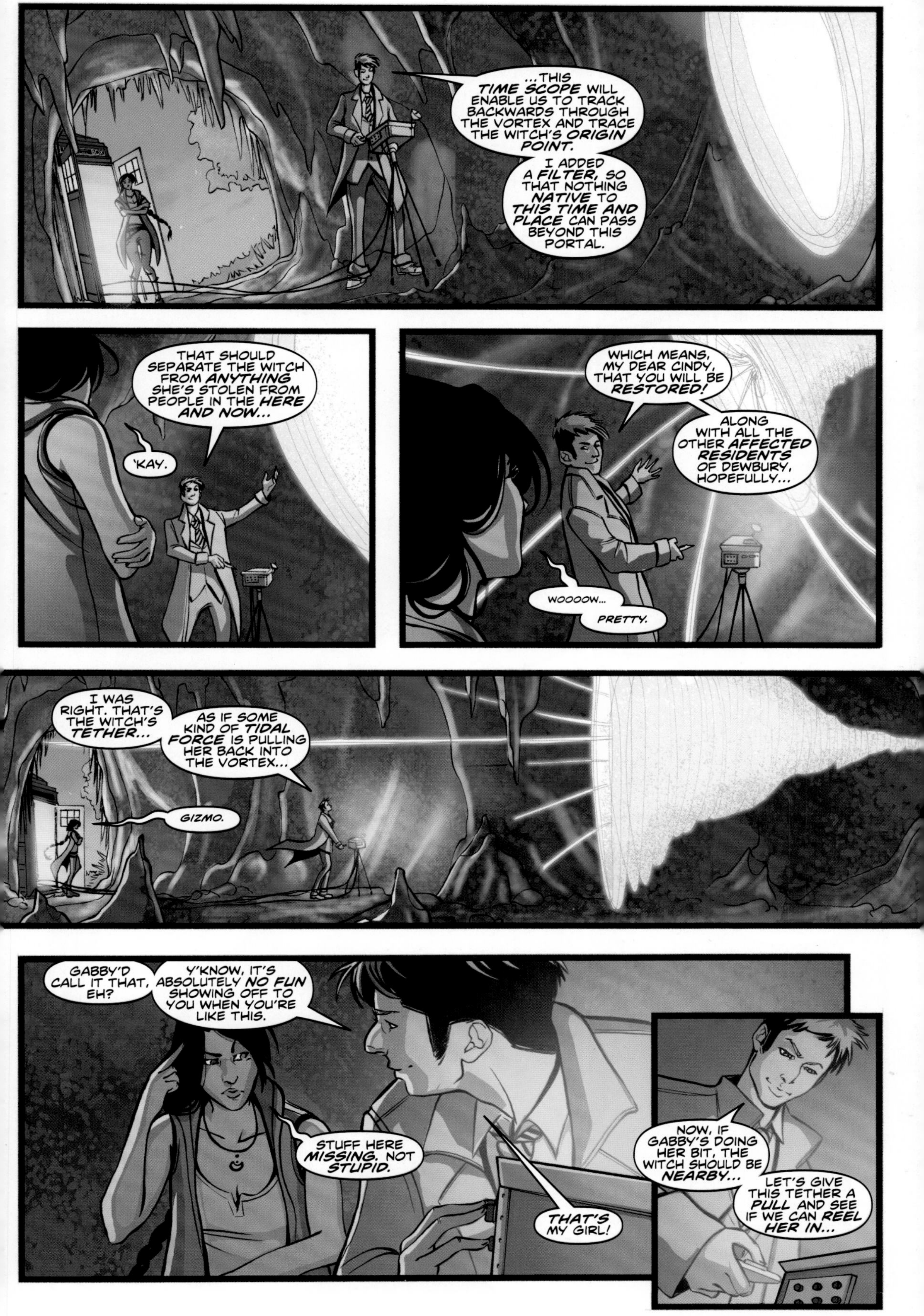
...THIS TIME SCOPE WILL ENABLE US TO TRACK BACKWARDS THROUGH THE VORTEX AND TRACE THE WITCH'S ORIGIN POINT.
I ADDED A FILTER, SO THAT NOTHING NATIVE TO THIS TIME AND PLACE CAN PASS BEYOND THIS PORTAL.
THAT SHOULD SEPARATE THE WITCH FROM ANYTHING SHE'S STOLEN FROM PEOPLE IN THE HERE AND NOW...
'KAY.
WHICH MEANS, MY DEAR CINDY, THAT YOU WILL BE RESTORED!
ALONG WITH ALL THE OTHER AFFECTED RESIDENTS OF DEWBURY, HOPEFULLY...
WOOOOW...
PRETTY.
I WAS RIGHT. THAT'S THE WITCH'S TETHER...
AS IF SOME KIND OF TIDAL FORCE IS PULLING HER BACK INTO THE VORTEX...
GIZMO.
GABBY'D CALL IT THAT, EH?
Y'KNOW, IT'S ABSOLUTELY NO FUN SHOWING OFF TO YOU WHEN YOU'RE LIKE THIS.
STUFF HERE MISSING. NOT STUPID.
THAT'S MY GIRL!
NOW, IF GABBY'S DOING HER BIT, THE WITCH SHOULD BE NEARBY...
LET'S GIVE THIS TETHER A PULL AND SEE IF WE CAN REEL HER IN...

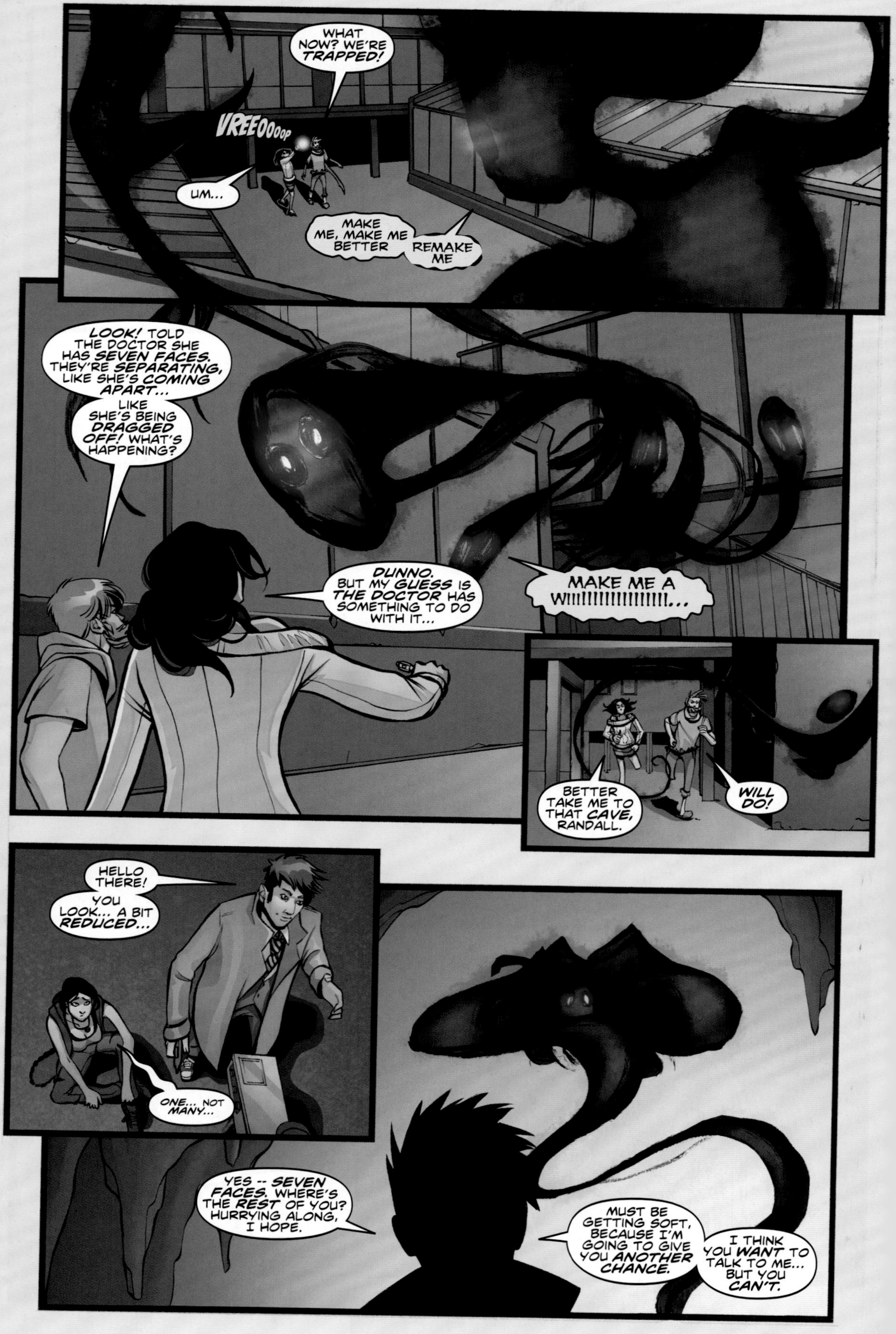
WHAT NOW? WE'RE TRAPPED!
VREEOOOOP
UM...
MAKE ME, MAKE ME BETTER
REMAKE ME
LOOK! TOLD THE DOCTOR SHE HAS SEVEN FACES. THEY'RE SEPARATING, LIKE SHE'S COMING APART...
LIKE SHE'S BEING DRAGGED OFF! WHAT'S HAPPENING?
DUNNO. BUT MY GUESS IS THE DOCTOR HAS SOMETHING TO DO WITH IT...
MAKE ME A WIIIIIIIIIIIIIIIII...
BETTER TAKE ME TO THAT CAVE, RANDALL.
WILL DO!
HELLO THERE!
YOU LOOK... A BIT REDUCED...
ONE... NOT MANY...
YES -- SEVEN FACES. WHERE'S THE REST OF YOU? HURRYING ALONG, I HOPE.
MUST BE GETTING SOFT, BECAUSE I'M GOING TO GIVE YOU ANOTHER CHANCE.
I THINK YOU WANT TO TALK TO ME... BUT YOU CAN'T.

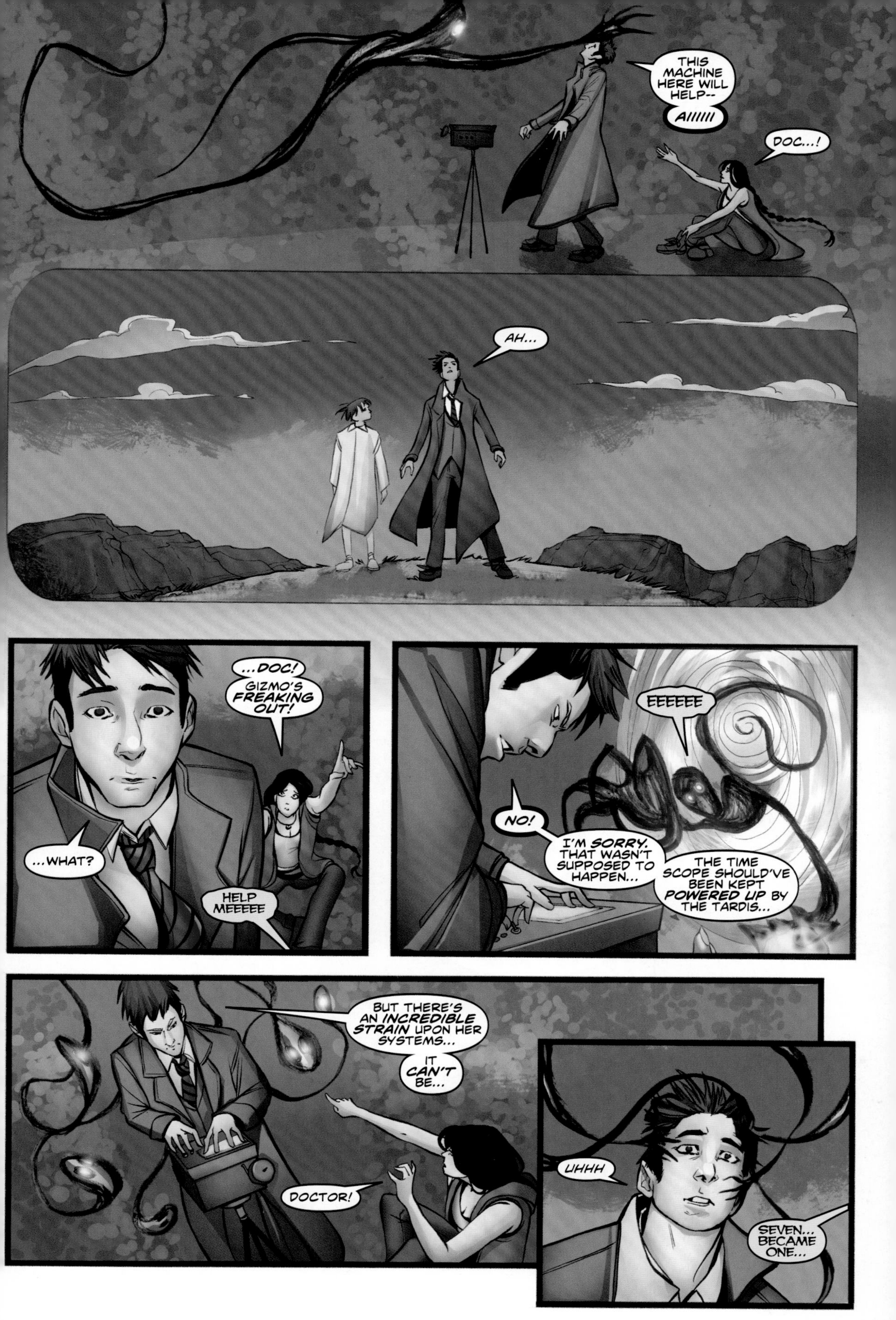
THIS MACHINE HERE WILL HELP--
AIIIIII
DOC...!
AH...
...DOC! GIZMO'S FREAKING OUT!
...WHAT?
HELP MEEEEE
EEEEEE
NO!
I'M SORRY. THAT WASN'T SUPPOSED TO HAPPEN...
THE TIME SCOPE SHOULD'VE BEEN KEPT POWERED UP BY THE TARDIS...
BUT THERE'S AN INCREDIBLE STRAIN UPON HER SYSTEMS...
IT CAN'T BE...
DOCTOR!
UHHH
SEVEN... BECAME ONE...

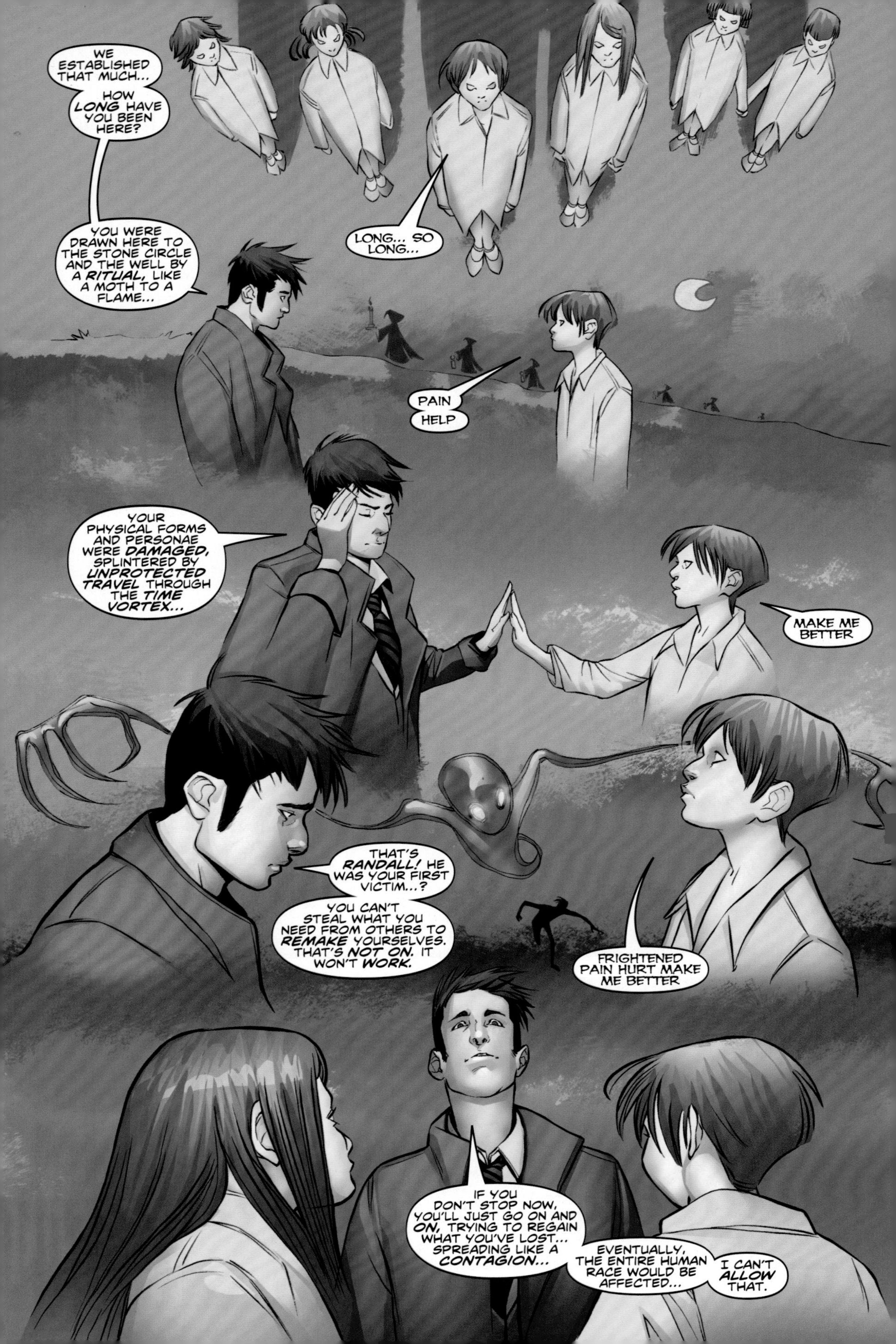
WE ESTABLISHED THAT MUCH...
HOW LONG HAVE YOU BEEN HERE?
LONG... SO LONG...
YOU WERE DRAWN HERE TO THE STONE CIRCLE AND THE WELL BY A RITUAL, LIKE A MOTH TO A FLAME...
PAIN
HELP
YOUR PHYSICAL FORMS AND PERSONAE WERE DAMAGED, SPLINTERED BY UNPROTECTED TRAVEL THROUGH THE TIME VORTEX...
MAKE ME BETTER
THAT'S RANDALL! HE WAS YOUR FIRST VICTIM...?
YOU CAN'T STEAL WHAT YOU NEED FROM OTHERS TO REMAKE YOURSELVES. THAT'S NOT ON. IT WON'T WORK.
FRIGHTENED PAIN HURT MAKE ME BETTER
IF YOU DON'T STOP NOW, YOU'LL JUST GO ON AND ON, TRYING TO REGAIN WHAT YOU'VE LOST... SPREADING LIKE A CONTAGION...
EVENTUALLY, THE ENTIRE HUMAN RACE WOULD BE AFFECTED...
I CAN'T ALLOW THAT.

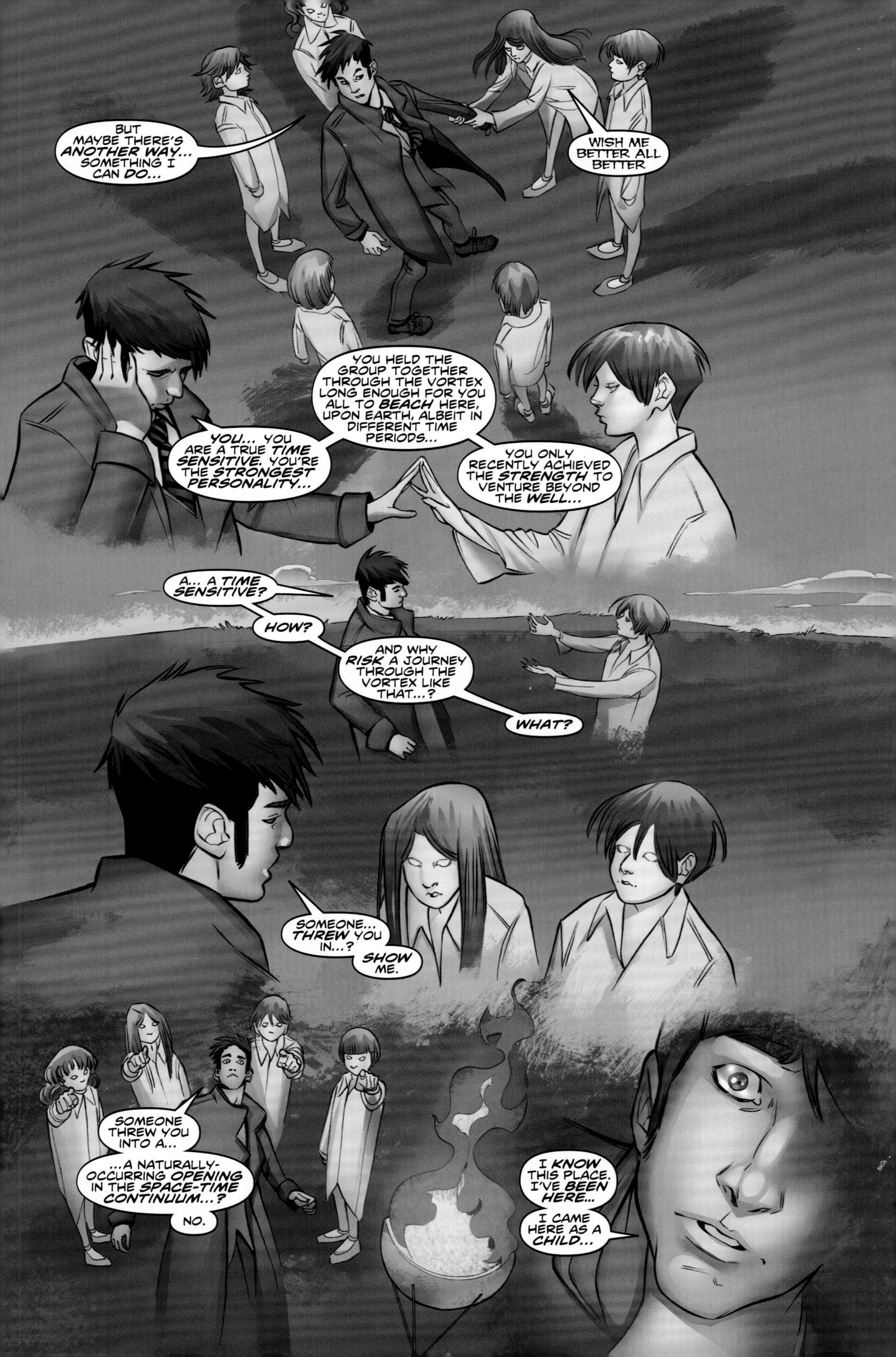

BUT MAYBE THERE'S ANOTHER WAY... SOMETHING I CAN DO...
WISH ME BETTER ALL BETTER
YOU... YOU ARE A TRUE TIME SENSITIVE. YOU'RE THE STRONGEST PERSONALITY...
YOU HELD THE GROUP TOGETHER THROUGH THE VORTEX LONG ENOUGH FOR YOU ALL TO BEACH HERE, UPON EARTH, ALBEIT IN DIFFERENT TIME PERIODS...
YOU ONLY RECENTLY ACHIEVED THE STRENGTH TO VENTURE BEYOND THE WELL...
A... A TIME SENSITIVE?
HOW?
AND WHY RISK A JOURNEY THROUGH THE VORTEX LIKE THAT...?
WHAT?
SOMEONE... THREW YOU IN...?
SHOW ME.
SOMEONE THREW YOU INTO A...
...A NATURALLY-OCCURRING OPENING IN THE SPACE-TIME CONTINUUM...?
NO.
I KNOW THIS PLACE. I'VE BEEN HERE...
I CAME HERE AS A CHILD...

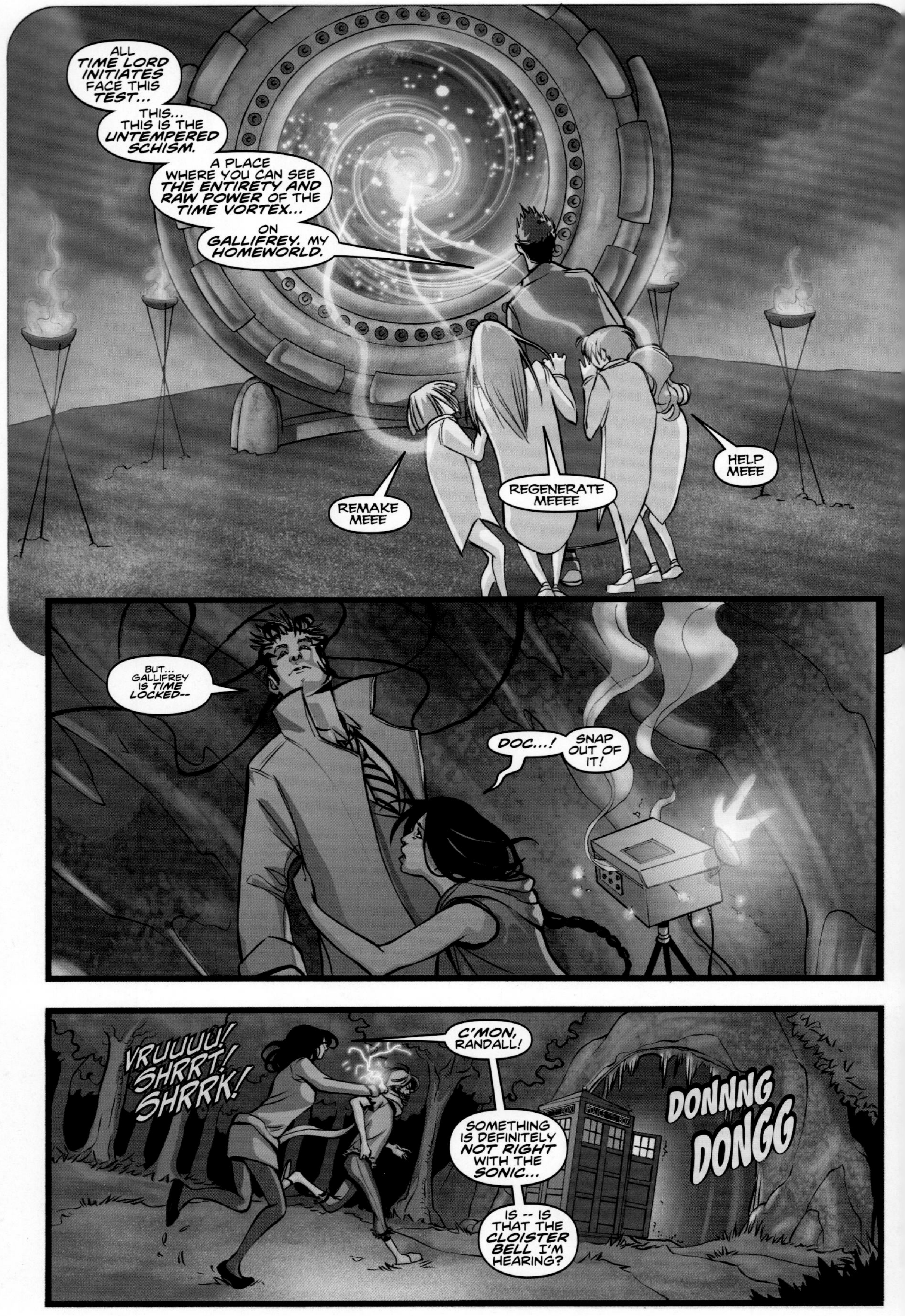
ALL TIME LORD INITIATES FACE THIS TEST...
THIS... THIS IS THE UNTEMPERED SCHISM.
A PLACE WHERE YOU CAN SEE THE ENTIRETY AND RAW POWER OF THE TIME VORTEX...
ON GALLIFREY. MY HOMEWORLD.
REMAKE MEEE
REGENERATE MEEEE
HELP MEEE
BUT... GALLIFREY IS TIME LOCKED--
DOC...!
SNAP OUT OF IT!
VRUUUU! SHRRT! SHRRK!
C'MON, RANDALL!
SOMETHING IS DEFINITELY NOT RIGHT WITH THE SONIC...
IS -- IS THAT THE CLOISTER BELL I'M HEARING?
DONNNG DONGG

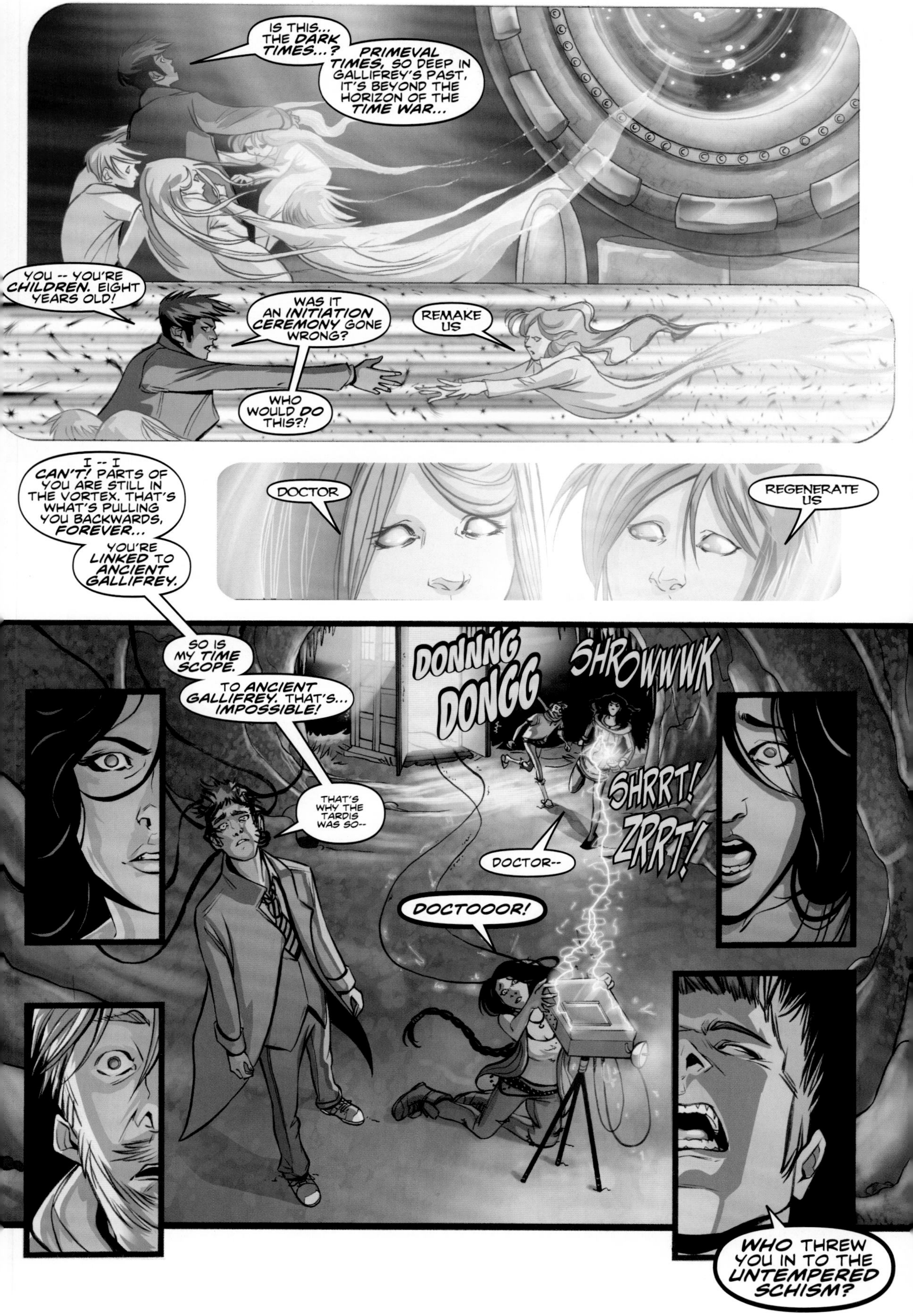
IS THIS... THE DARK TIMES...?
PRIMEVAL TIMES, SO DEEP IN GALLIFREY'S PAST, IT'S BEYOND THE HORIZON OF THE TIME WAR...
YOU -- YOU'RE CHILDREN. EIGHT YEARS OLD!
WAS IT AN INITIATION CEREMONY GONE WRONG?
WHO WOULD DO THIS?!
REMAKE US
I -- I CAN'T! PARTS OF YOU ARE STILL IN THE VORTEX. THAT'S WHAT'S PULLING YOU BACKWARDS, FOREVER...
YOU'RE LINKED TO ANCIENT GALLIFREY.
DOCTOR
REGENERATE US
SO IS MY TIME SCOPE.
TO ANCIENT GALLIFREY. THAT'S... IMPOSSIBLE!
DONNNG DONGG
SHROWWWK
THAT'S WHY THE TARDIS WAS SO--
SHRRT! ZRRT!
DOCTOR--
DOCTOOOR!
WHO THREW YOU IN TO THE UNTEMPERED SCHISM?

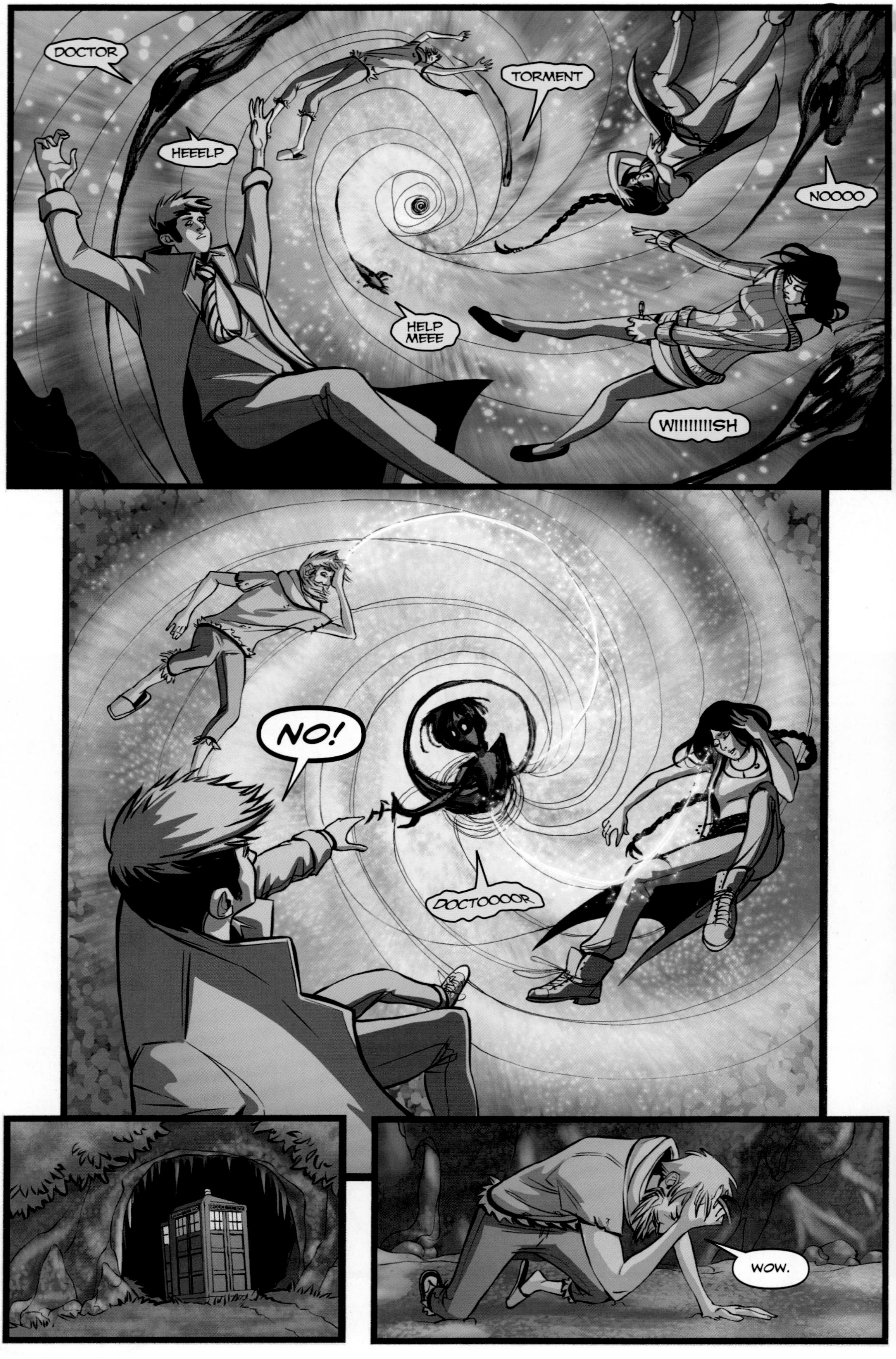
DOCTOR
HEEELP
TORMENT
NOOOO
HELP MEEE
WIIIIIIIISH
NO!
DOCTOOOOR
WOW.

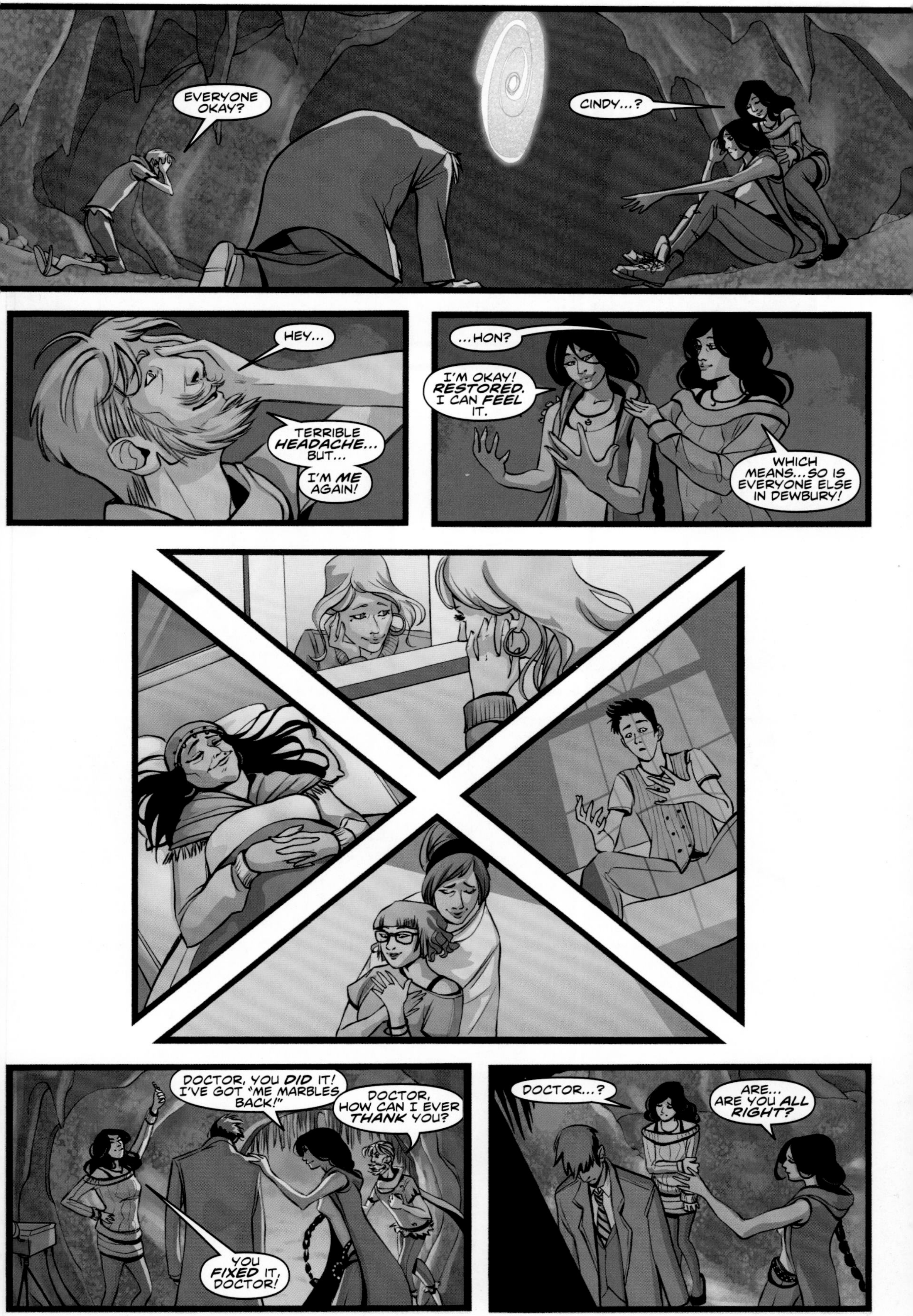
EVERYONE OKAY?
CINDY...?
HEY...
TERRIBLE HEADACHE... BUT...
I'M ME AGAIN!
...HON?
I'M OKAY! RESTORED. I CAN FEEL IT.
WHICH MEANS... SO IS EVERYONE ELSE IN DEWBURY!
DOCTOR, YOU DID IT! I'VE GOT "ME MARBLES BACK!"
DOCTOR, HOW CAN I EVER THANK YOU?
YOU FIXED IT, DOCTOR!
DOCTOR...?
ARE... ARE YOU ALL RIGHT?

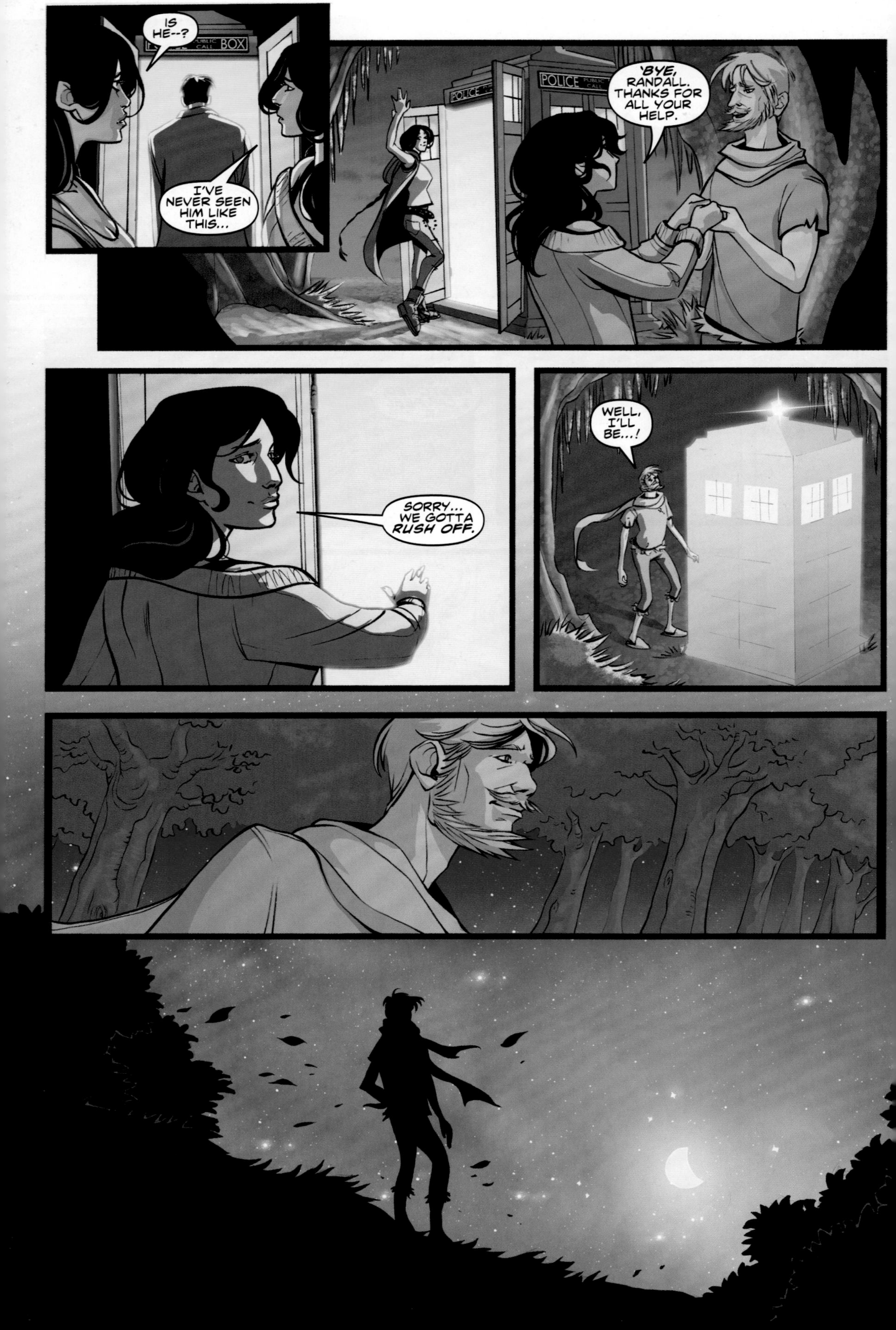
IS HE--?
I'VE NEVER SEEN HIM LIKE THIS...
POLICE PUBLIC CALL BOX
'BYE, RANDALL. THANKS FOR ALL YOUR HELP.
SORRY... WE GOTTA RUSH OFF.
WELL, I'LL BE...!

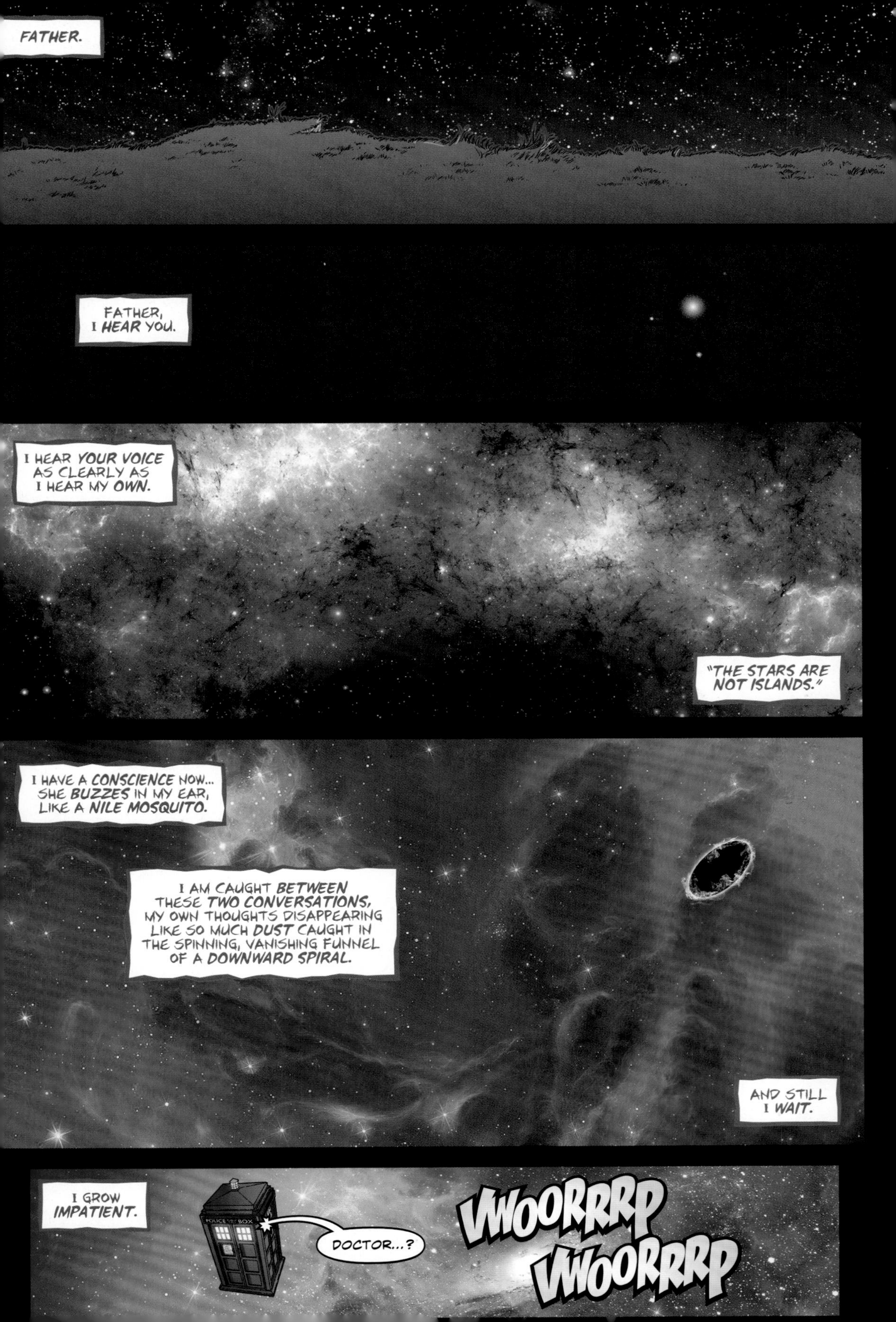
FATHER.
FATHER, I HEAR YOU.
I HEAR YOUR VOICE AS CLEARLY AS I HEAR MY OWN.
"THE STARS ARE NOT ISLANDS."
I HAVE A CONSCIENCE NOW... SHE BUZZES IN MY EAR, LIKE A NILE MOSQUITO.
I AM CAUGHT BETWEEN THESE TWO CONVERSATIONS, MY OWN THOUGHTS DISAPPEARING LIKE SO MUCH DUST CAUGHT IN THE SPINNING, VANISHING FUNNEL OF A DOWNWARD SPIRAL.
AND STILL I WAIT.
I GROW IMPATIENT.
POLICE BOX
DOCTOR...?
VWOORRRP
VWOORRRP

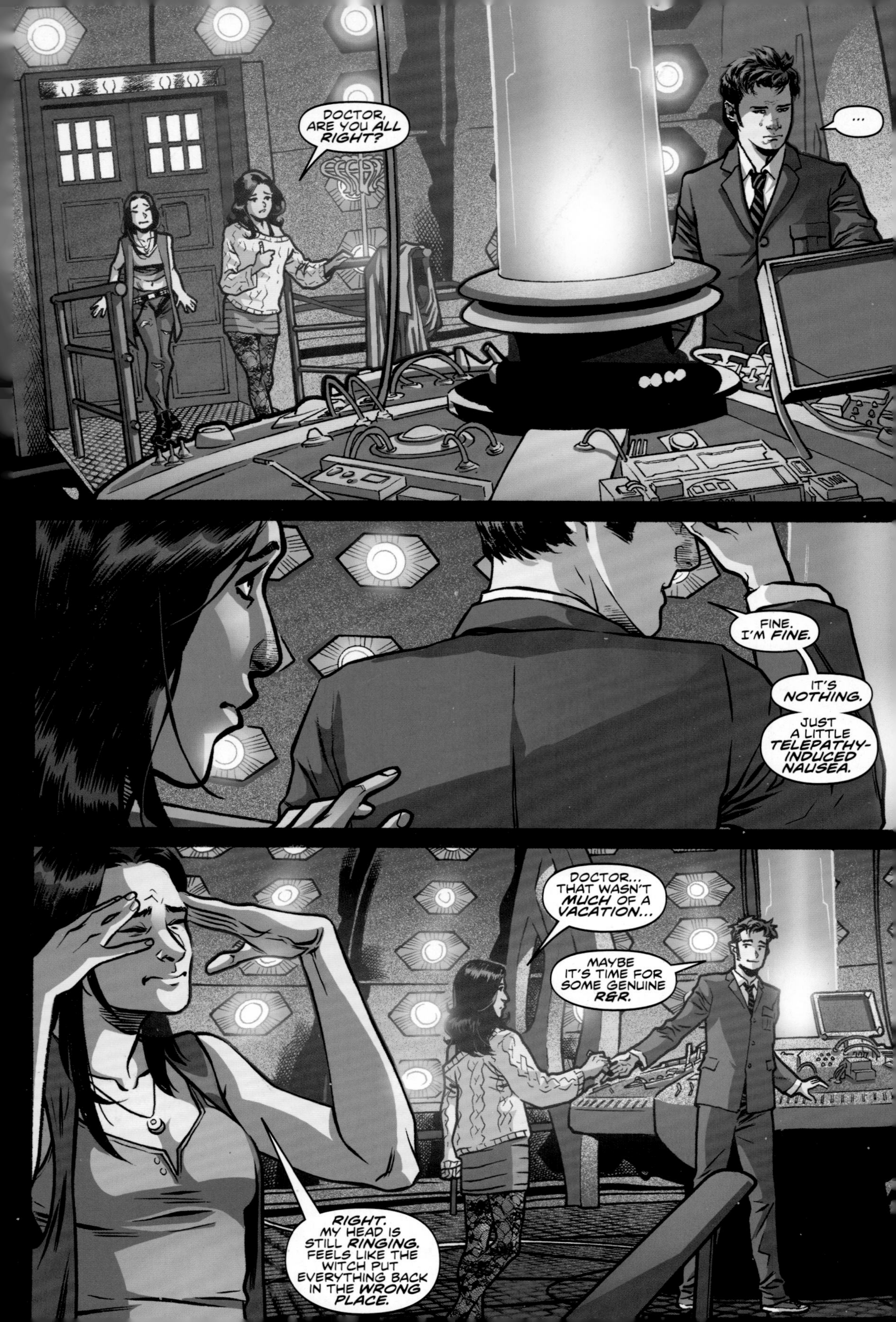
DOCTOR, ARE YOU ALL RIGHT?
...
FINE. I'M FINE.
IT'S NOTHING.
JUST A LITTLE TELEPATHY-INDUCED NAUSEA.
DOCTOR... THAT WASN'T MUCH OF A VACATION...
MAYBE IT'S TIME FOR SOME GENUINE R&R.
RIGHT. MY HEAD IS STILL RINGING. FEELS LIKE THE WITCH PUT EVERYTHING BACK IN THE WRONG PLACE.

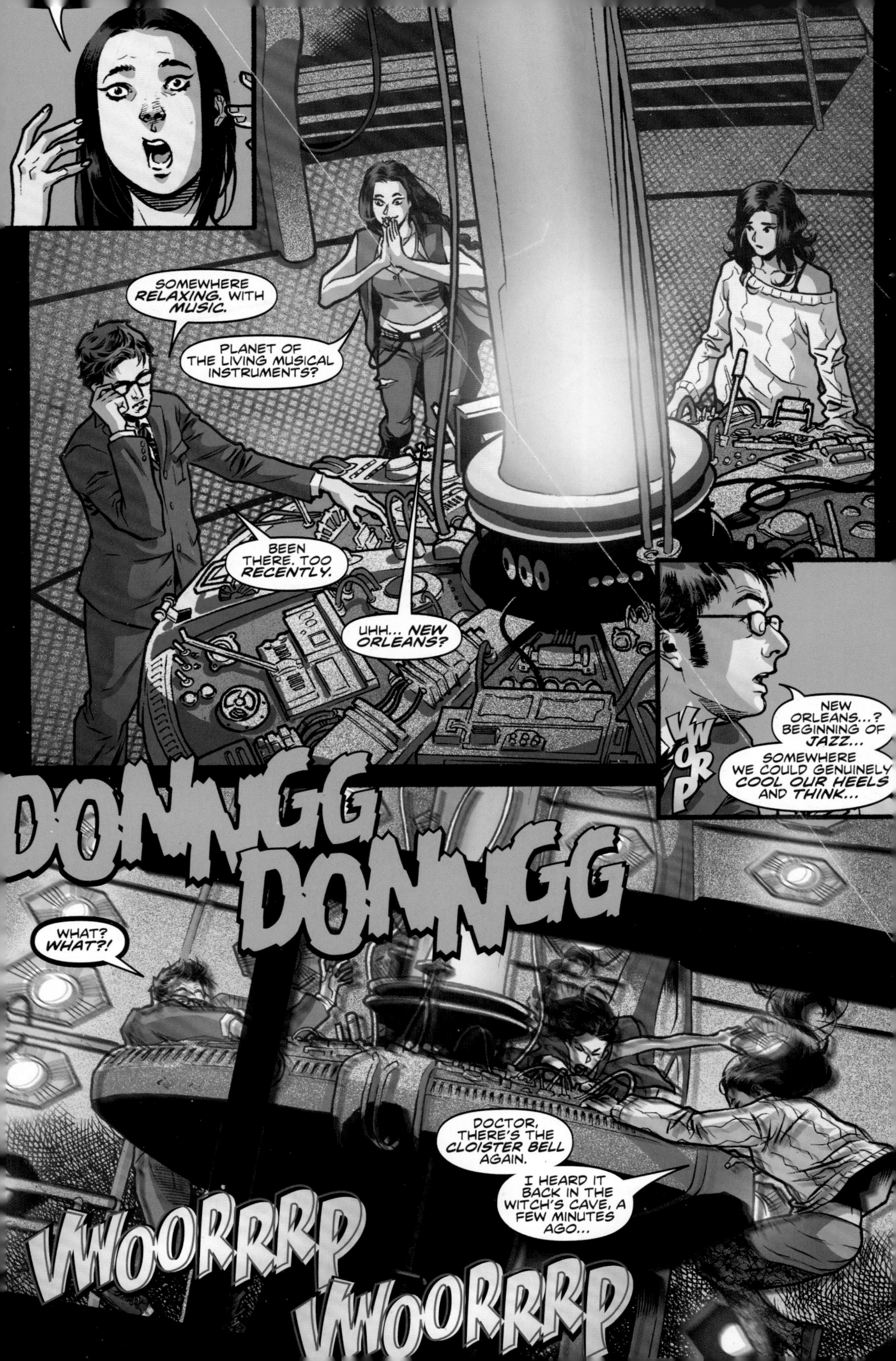
SOMEWHERE RELAXING. WITH MUSIC.
PLANET OF THE LIVING MUSICAL INSTRUMENTS?
BEEN THERE. TOO RECENTLY.
UHH... NEW ORLEANS?
NEW ORLEANS...? BEGINNING OF JAZZ...
SOMEWHERE WE COULD GENUINELY COOL OUR HEELS AND THINK...
VWORP
DONNGG
DONNGG
WHAT? WHAT?!
DOCTOR, THERE'S THE CLOISTER BELL AGAIN.
I HEARD IT BACK IN THE WITCH'S CAVE, A FEW MINUTES AGO...
VWOORRRP
VWOORRRP

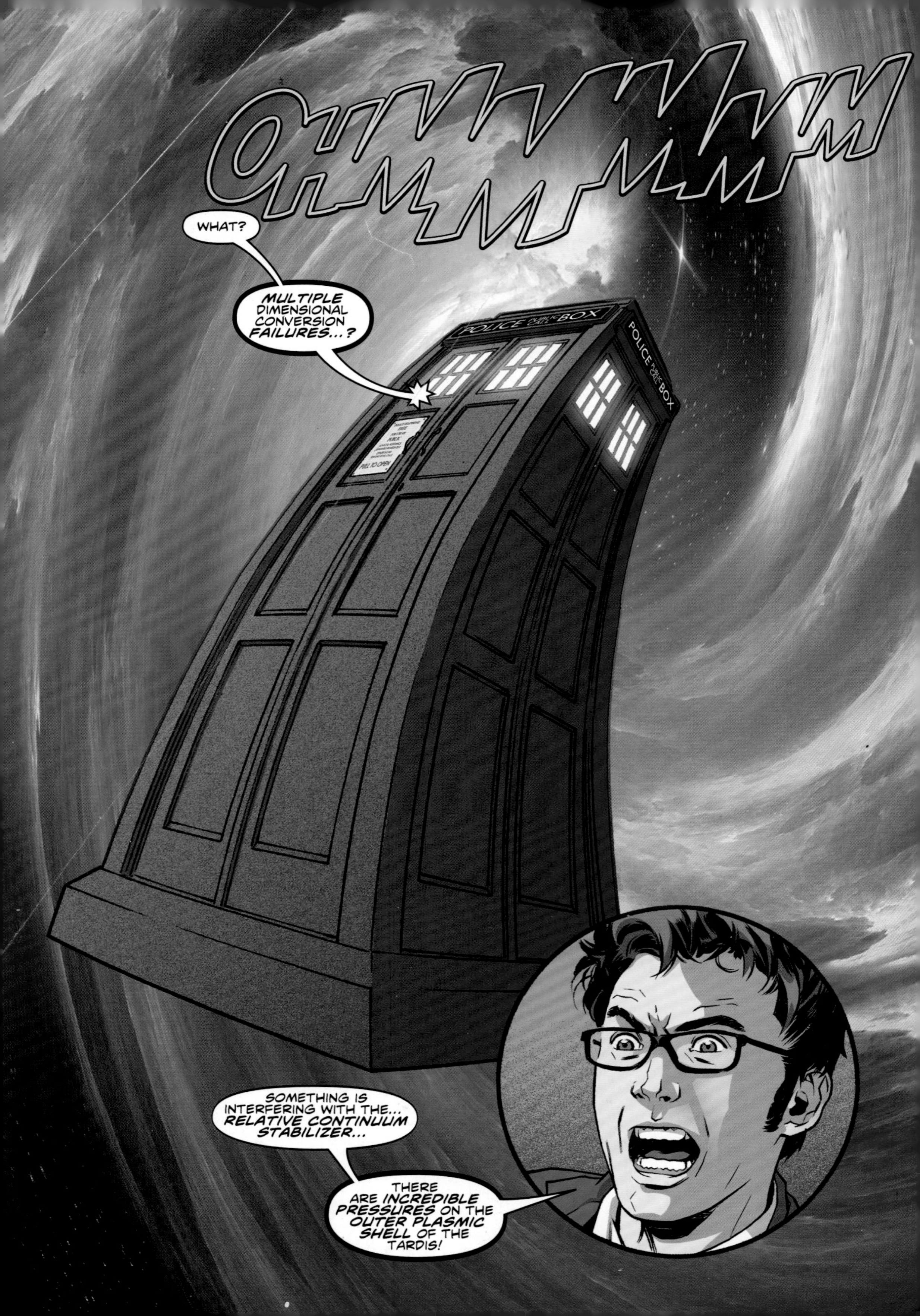
VWORRRMMMM
WHAT?
MULTIPLE DIMENSIONAL CONVERSION FAILURES...?
POLICE PUBLIC CALL BOX
PULL TO OPEN
SOMETHING IS INTERFERING WITH THE... RELATIVE CONTINUUM STABILIZER...
THERE ARE INCREDIBLE PRESSURES ON THE OUTER PLASMIC SHELL OF THE TARDIS!

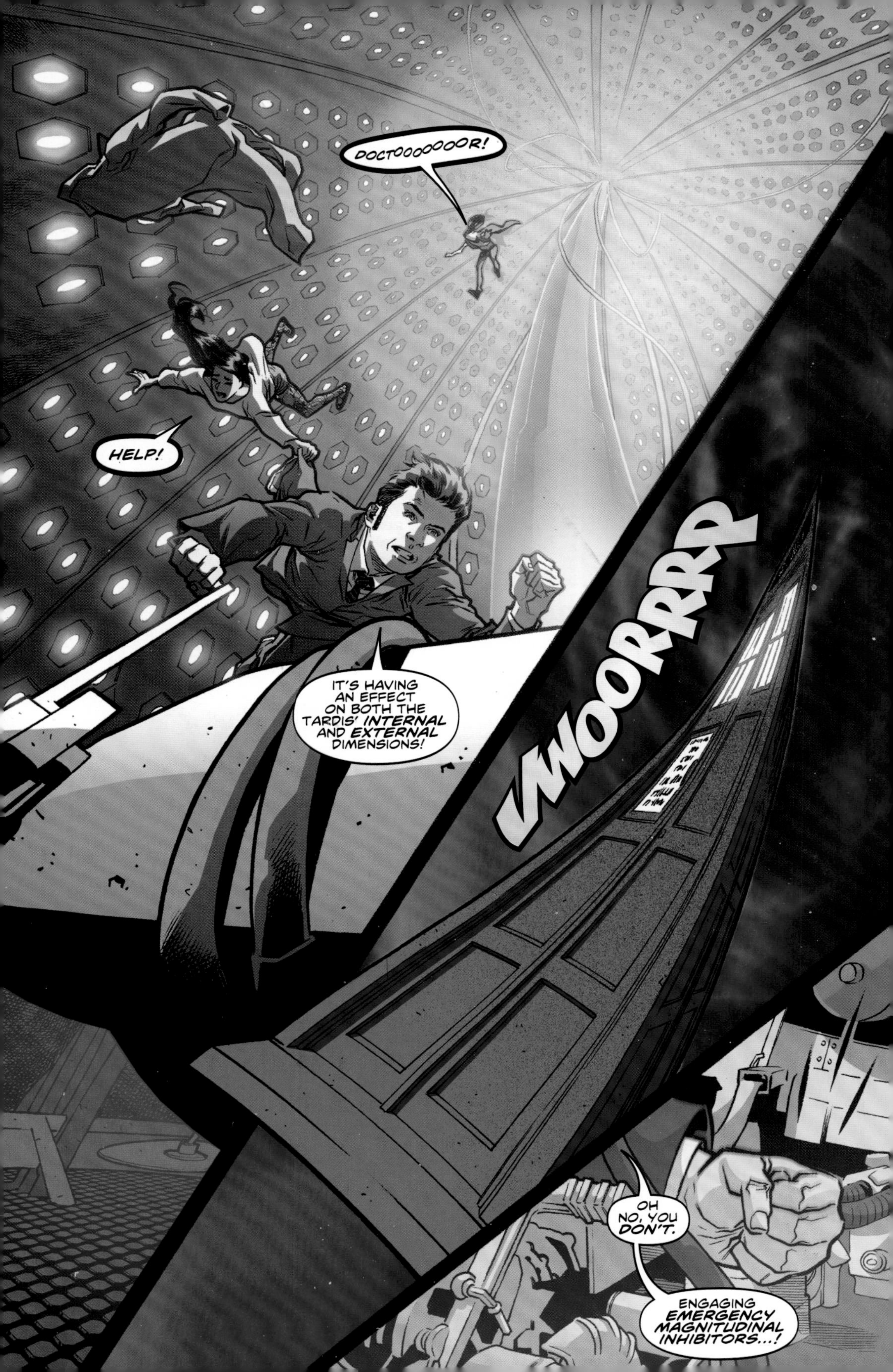
DOCTOOOOOOOR!
HELP!
IT'S HAVING AN EFFECT ON BOTH THE TARDIS' INTERNAL AND EXTERNAL DIMENSIONS!
VWOORRRP
OH NO, YOU DON'T.
ENGAGING EMERGENCY MAGNITUDINAL INHIBITORS...!

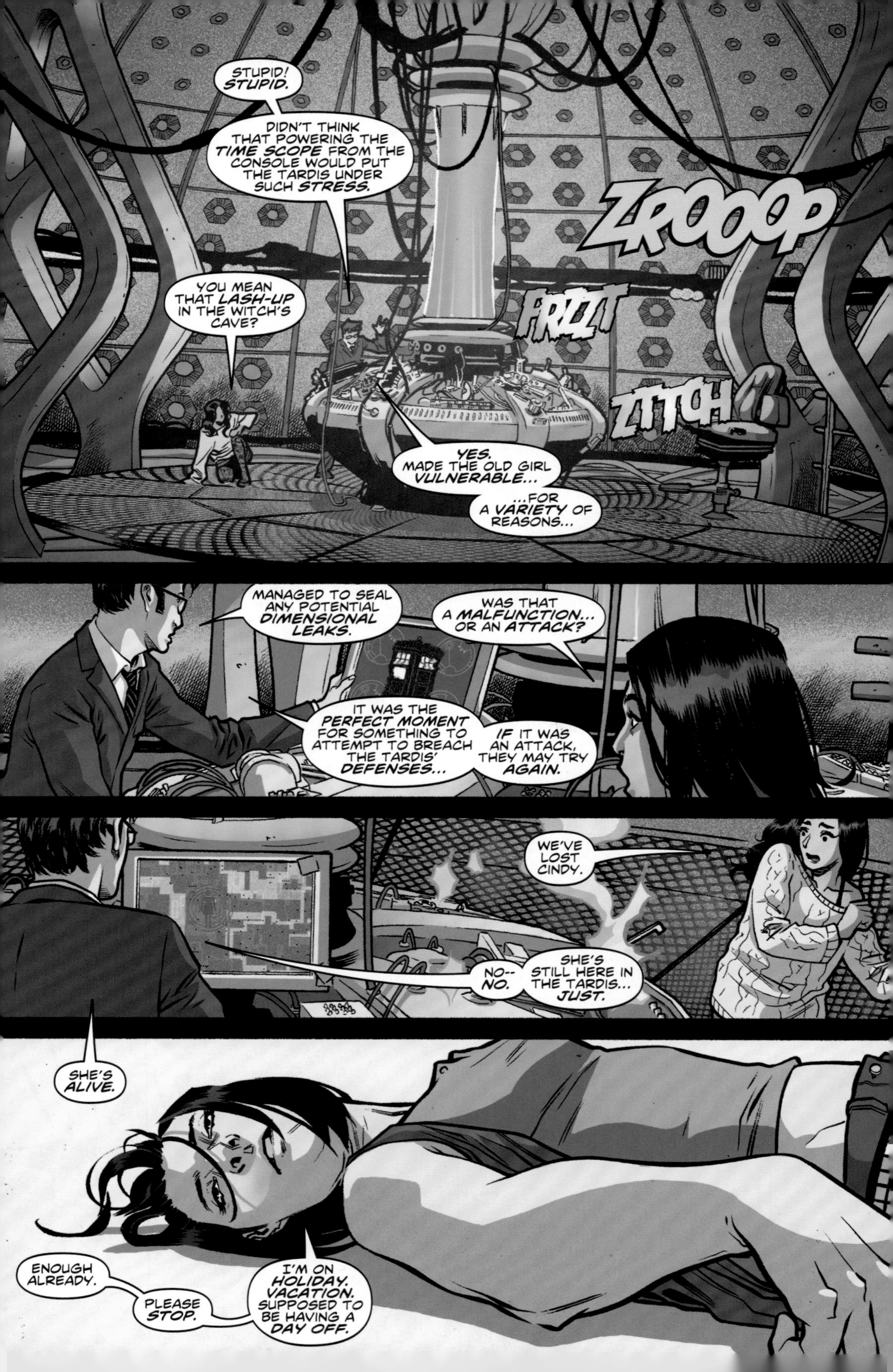
STUPID! STUPID.
DIDN'T THINK THAT POWERING THE TIME SCOPE FROM THE CONSOLE WOULD PUT THE TARDIS UNDER SUCH STRESS.
ZROOOP
YOU MEAN THAT LASH-UP IN THE WITCH'S CAVE?
FRZZT
ZTTCH
YES. MADE THE OLD GIRL VULNERABLE...
...FOR A VARIETY OF REASONS...
MANAGED TO SEAL ANY POTENTIAL DIMENSIONAL LEAKS.
WAS THAT A MALFUNCTION... OR AN ATTACK?
IT WAS THE PERFECT MOMENT FOR SOMETHING TO ATTEMPT TO BREACH THE TARDIS' DEFENSES...
IF IT WAS AN ATTACK, THEY MAY TRY AGAIN.
WE'VE LOST CINDY.
NO-- NO.
SHE'S STILL HERE IN THE TARDIS... JUST.
SHE'S ALIVE.
ENOUGH ALREADY.
PLEASE STOP.
I'M ON HOLIDAY. VACATION. SUPPOSED TO BE HAVING A DAY OFF.

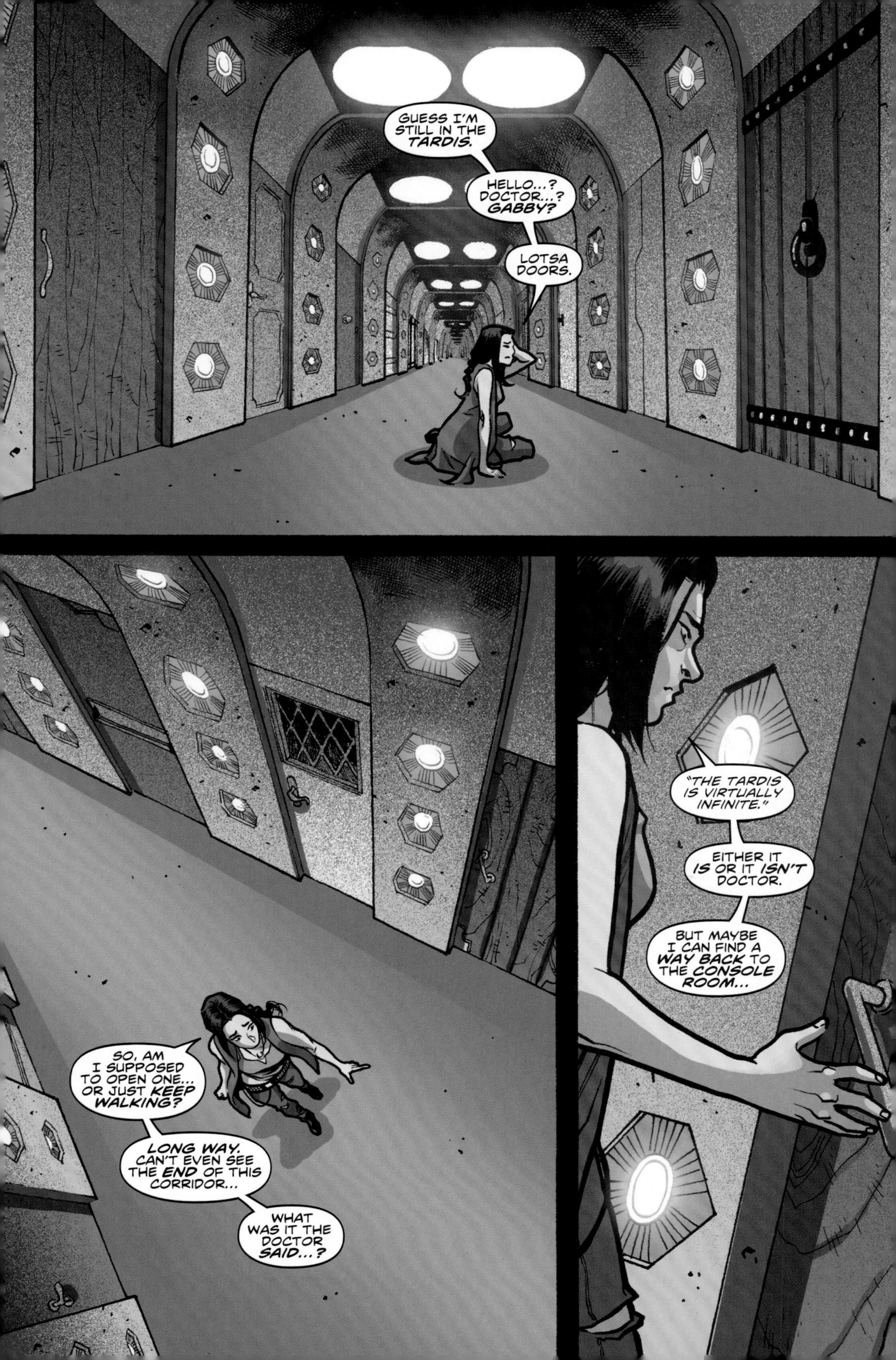
GUESS I'M STILL IN THE TARDIS.
HELLO...? DOCTOR...? GABBY?
LOTSA DOORS.
SO, AM I SUPPOSED TO OPEN ONE... OR JUST KEEP WALKING?
LONG WAY. CAN'T EVEN SEE THE END OF THIS CORRIDOR...
WHAT WAS IT THE DOCTOR SAID...?
"THE TARDIS IS VIRTUALLY INFINITE."
EITHER IT IS OR IT ISN'T DOCTOR.
BUT MAYBE I CAN FIND A WAY BACK TO THE CONSOLE ROOM...

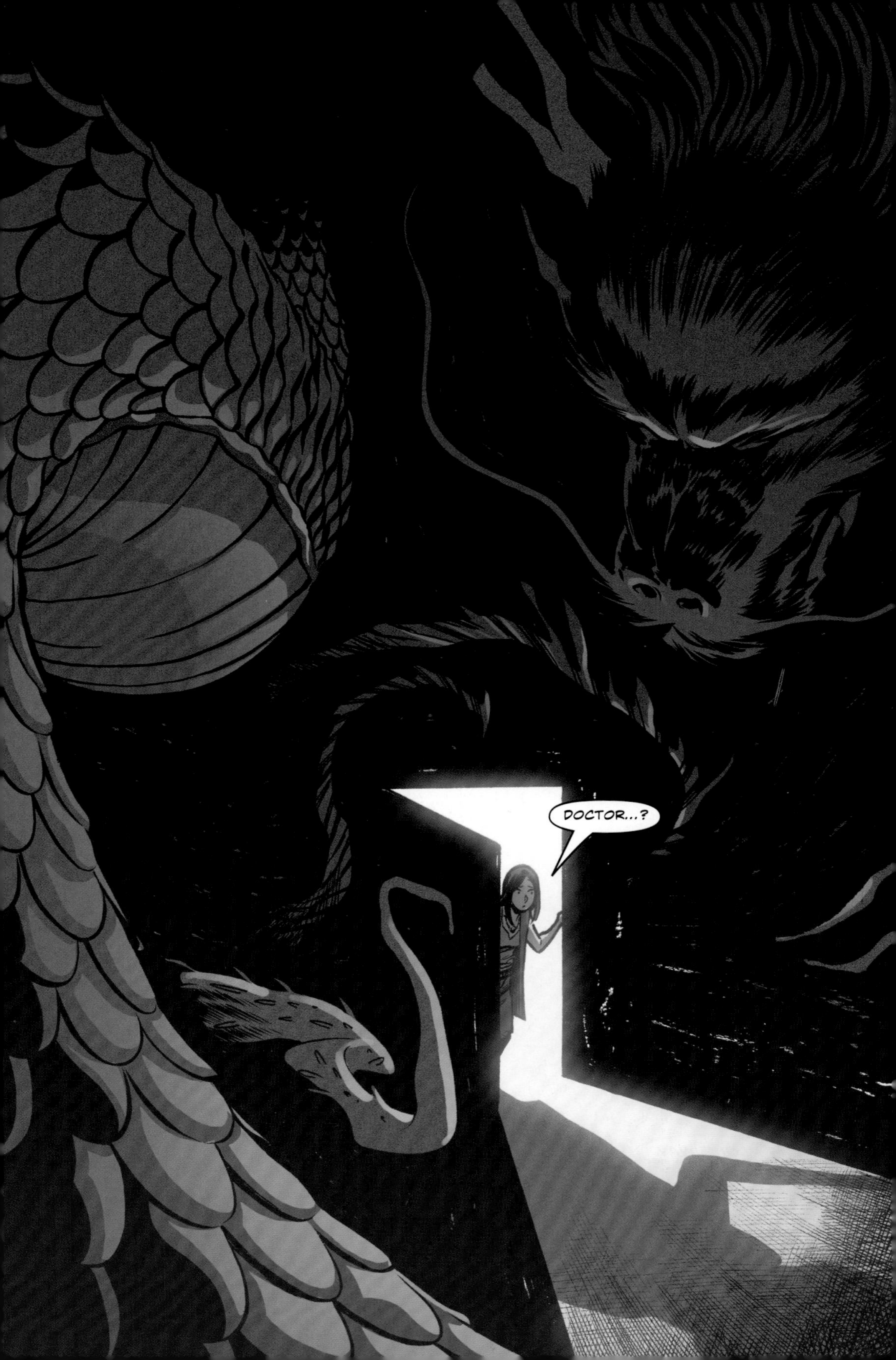
DOCTOR...?

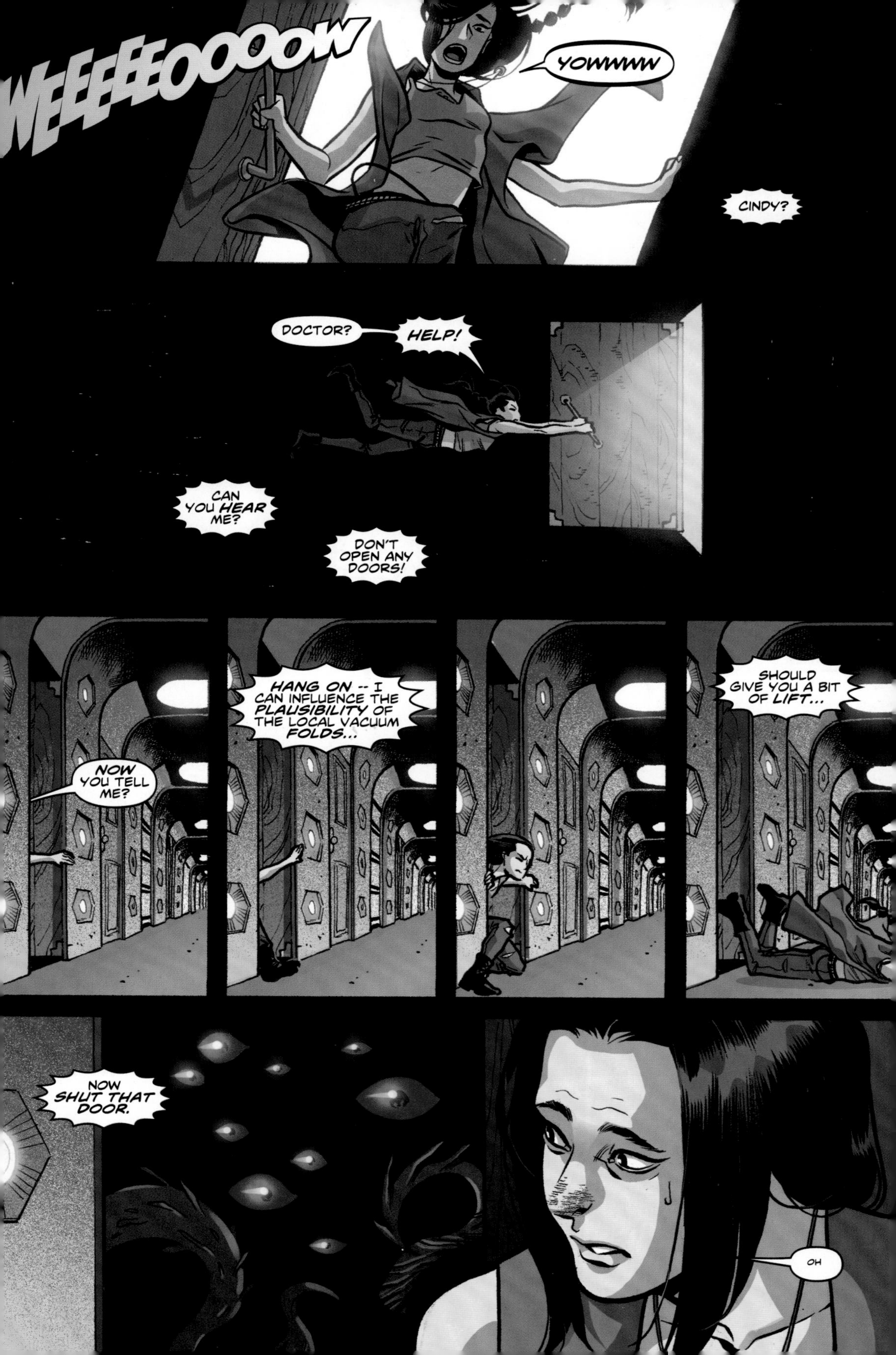
WEEEEEOOOOOW
YOWWWW
CINDY?
DOCTOR?
HELP!
CAN YOU HEAR ME?
DON'T OPEN ANY DOORS!
NOW YOU TELL ME?
HANG ON -- I CAN INFLUENCE THE PLAUSIBILITY OF THE LOCAL VACUUM FOLDS...
SHOULD GIVE YOU A BIT OF LIFT...
NOW SHUT THAT DOOR.
OH

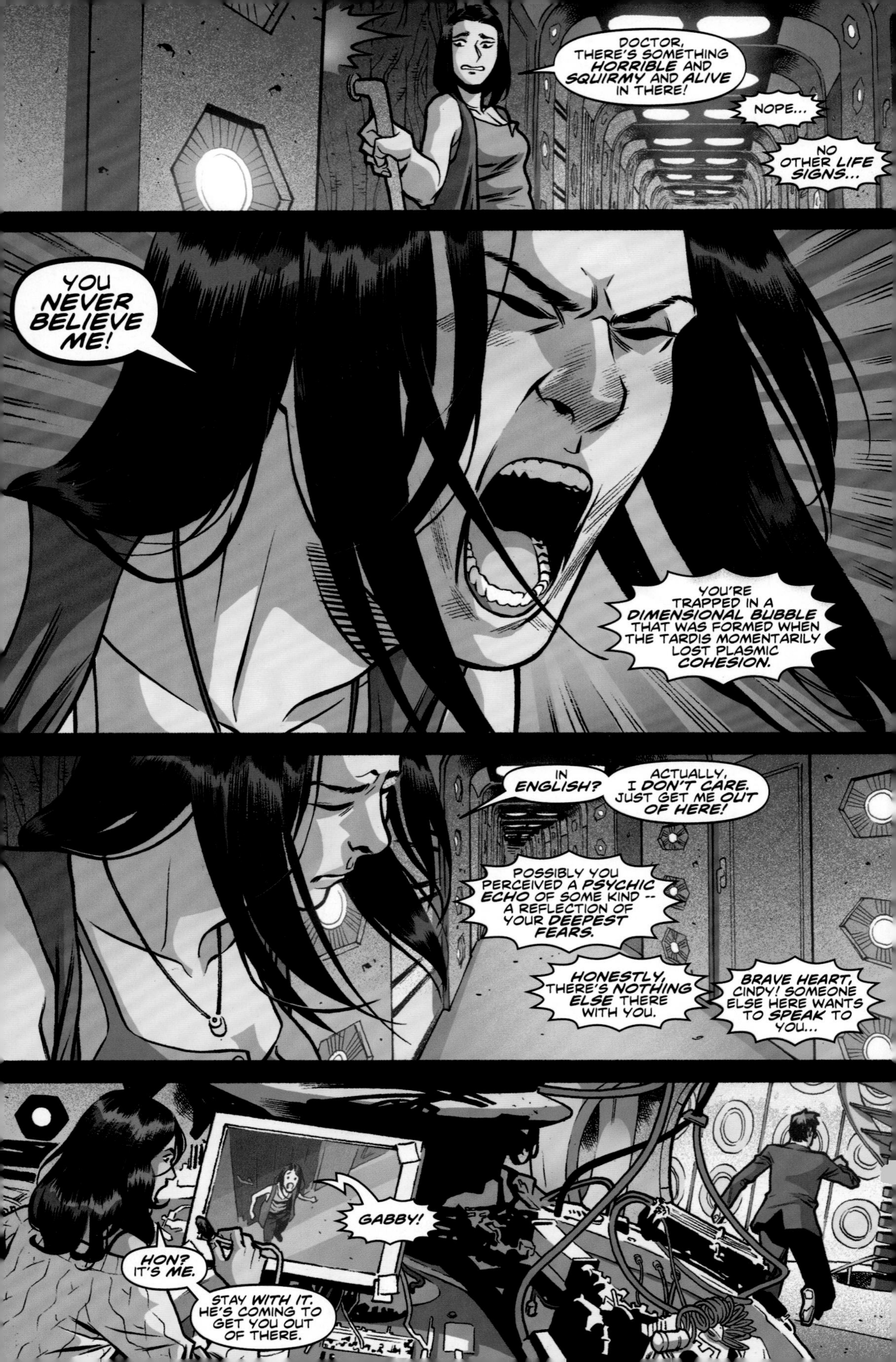

DOCTOR, THERE'S SOMETHING HORRIBLE AND SQUIRMY AND ALIVE IN THERE!
NOPE...
NO OTHER LIFE SIGNS...
YOU NEVER BELIEVE ME!
YOU'RE TRAPPED IN A DIMENSIONAL BUBBLE THAT WAS FORMED WHEN THE TARDIS MOMENTARILY LOST PLASMIC COHESION.
IN ENGLISH?
ACTUALLY, I DON'T CARE. JUST GET ME OUT OF HERE!
POSSIBLY YOU PERCEIVED A PSYCHIC ECHO OF SOME KIND -- A REFLECTION OF YOUR DEEPEST FEARS.
HONESTLY, THERE'S NOTHING ELSE THERE WITH YOU.
BRAVE HEART, CINDY! SOMEONE ELSE HERE WANTS TO SPEAK TO YOU...
GABBY!
HON? IT'S ME.
STAY WITH IT. HE'S COMING TO GET YOU OUT OF THERE.

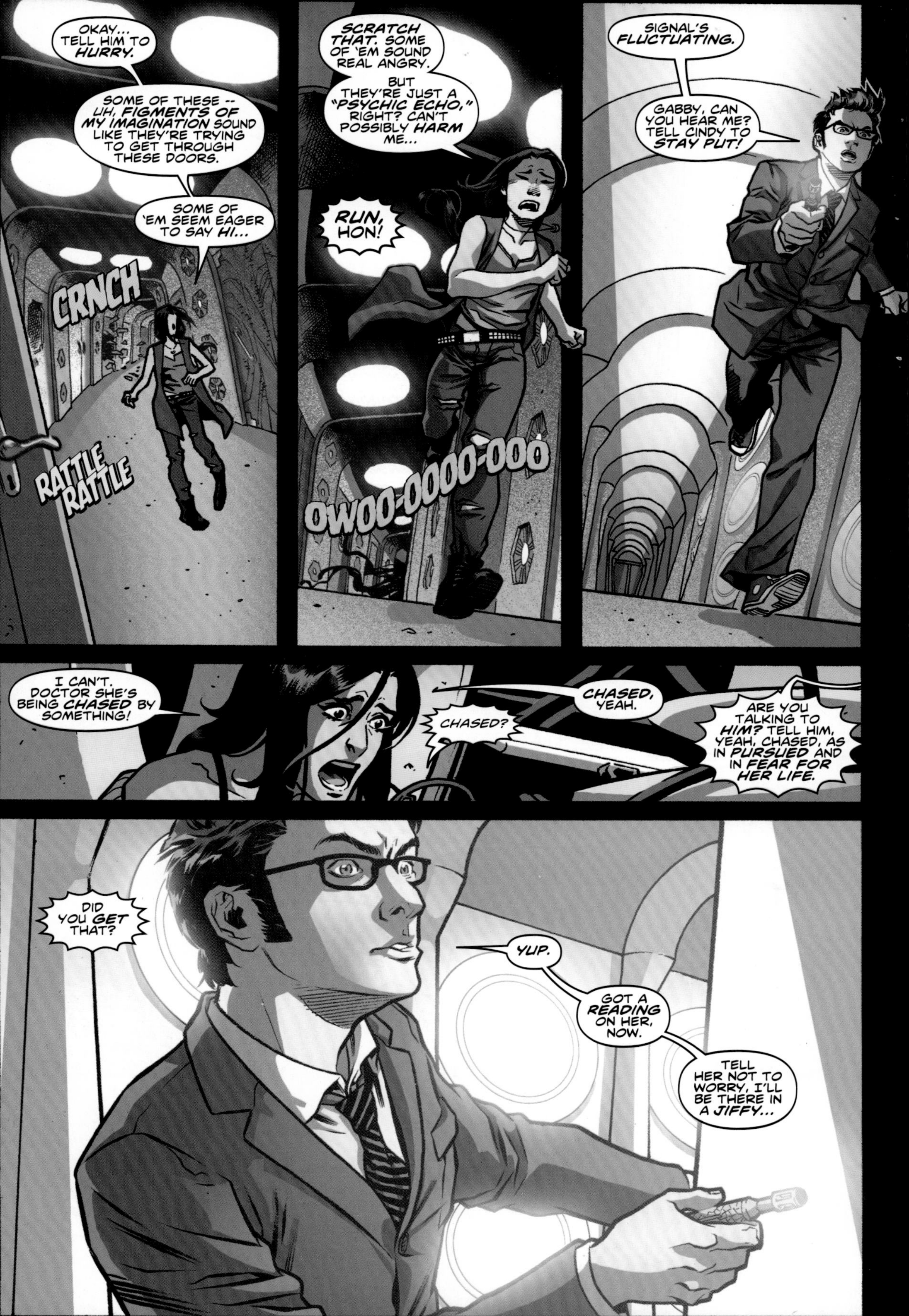
OKAY... TELL HIM TO HURRY.
SOME OF THESE -- UH, FIGMENTS OF MY IMAGINATION SOUND LIKE THEY'RE TRYING TO GET THROUGH THESE DOORS.
SOME OF 'EM SEEM EAGER TO SAY HI...
CRNCH
RATTLE RATTLE
SCRATCH THAT. SOME OF 'EM SOUND REAL ANGRY.
BUT THEY'RE JUST A "PSYCHIC ECHO," RIGHT? CAN'T POSSIBLY HARM ME...
RUN, HON!
OWOO-OOOO-OOO
OWOO-OOOO-OOO
SIGNAL'S FLUCTUATING.
GABBY, CAN YOU HEAR ME? TELL CINDY TO STAY PUT!
I CAN'T. DOCTOR SHE'S BEING CHASED BY SOMETHING!
CHASED?
CHASED, YEAH.
ARE YOU TALKING TO HIM? TELL HIM, YEAH, CHASED, AS IN PURSUED AND IN FEAR FOR HER LIFE.
DID YOU GET THAT?
YUP.
GOT A READING ON HER, NOW.
TELL HER NOT TO WORRY, I'LL BE THERE IN A JIFFY...

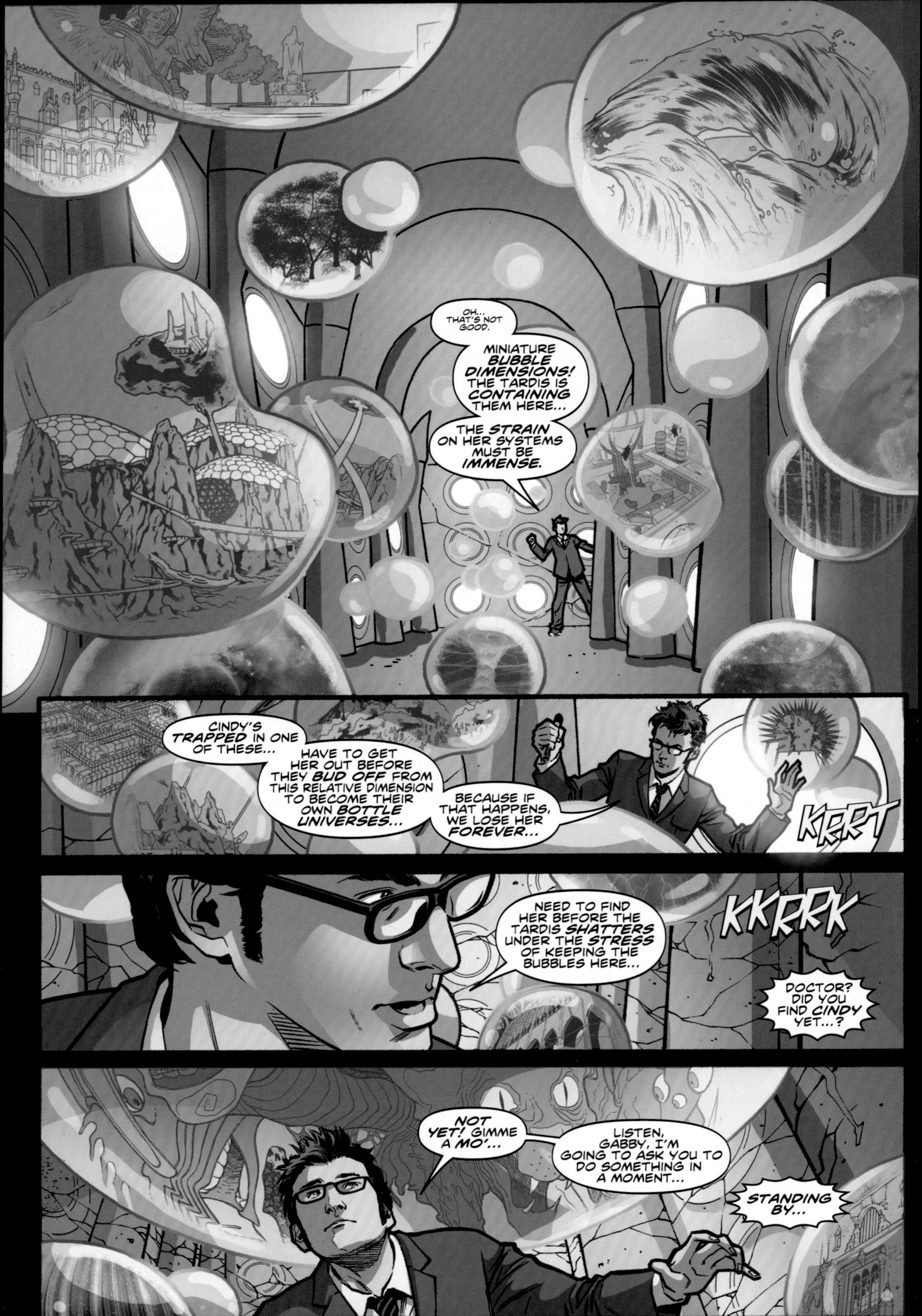
OH... THAT'S NOT GOOD.
MINIATURE BUBBLE DIMENSIONS! THE TARDIS IS CONTAINING THEM HERE...
THE STRAIN ON HER SYSTEMS MUST BE IMMENSE.
CINDY'S TRAPPED IN ONE OF THESE...
HAVE TO GET HER OUT BEFORE THEY BUD OFF FROM THIS RELATIVE DIMENSION TO BECOME THEIR OWN BOTTLE UNIVERSES...
BECAUSE IF THAT HAPPENS, WE LOSE HER FOREVER...
KRRT
KKRRK
NEED TO FIND HER BEFORE THE TARDIS SHATTERS UNDER THE STRESS OF KEEPING THE BUBBLES HERE...
DOCTOR? DID YOU FIND CINDY YET...?
NOT YET! GIMME A MO'...
LISTEN, GABBY, I'M GOING TO ASK YOU TO DO SOMETHING IN A MOMENT...
STANDING BY...

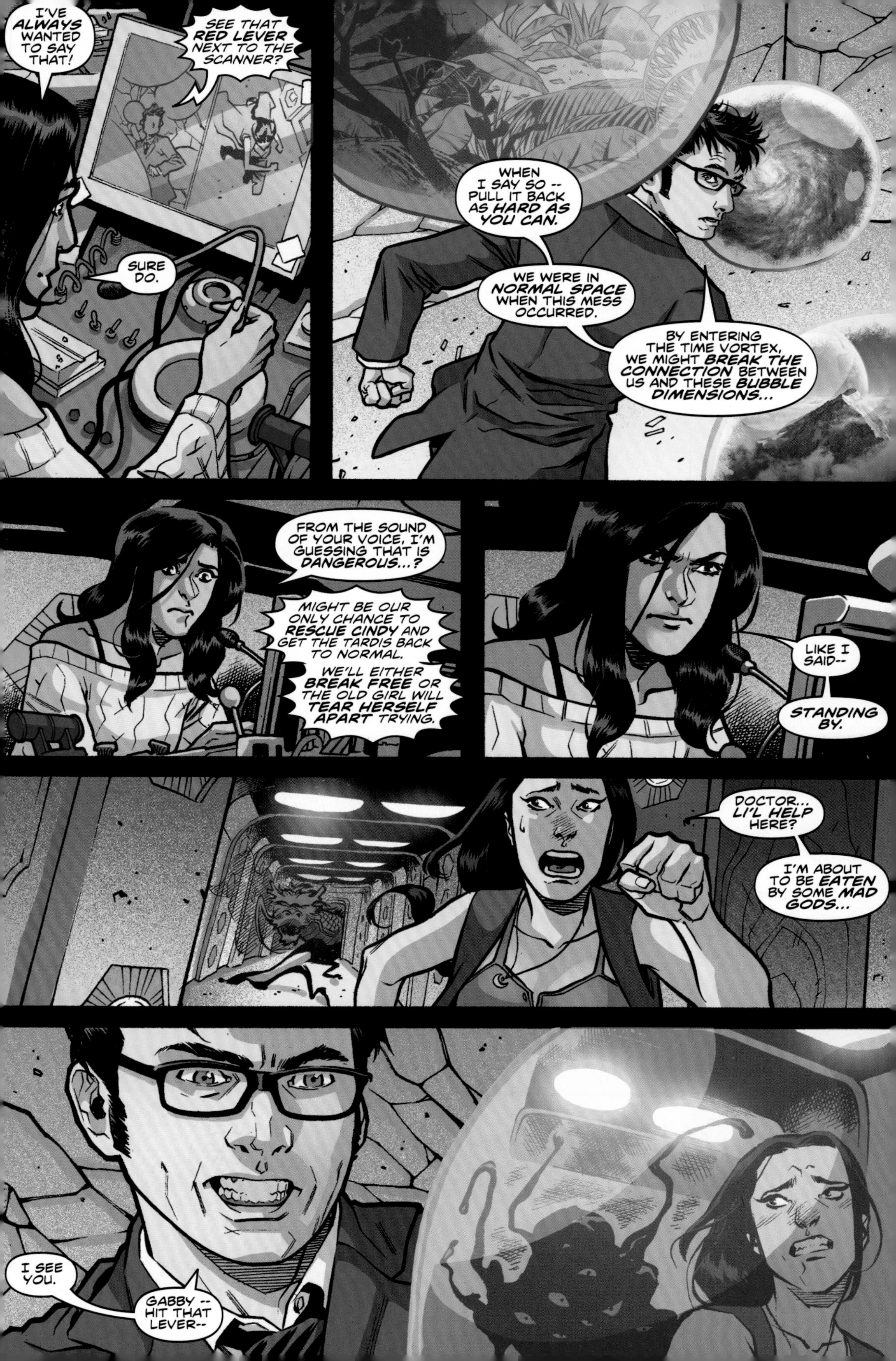

I'VE ALWAYS WANTED TO SAY THAT!
SEE THAT RED LEVER NEXT TO THE SCANNER?
SURE DO.
WHEN I SAY SO -- PULL IT BACK AS HARD AS YOU CAN.
WE WERE IN NORMAL SPACE WHEN THIS MESS OCCURRED.
BY ENTERING THE TIME VORTEX, WE MIGHT BREAK THE CONNECTION BETWEEN US AND THESE BUBBLE DIMENSIONS...
FROM THE SOUND OF YOUR VOICE, I'M GUESSING THAT IS DANGEROUS...?
MIGHT BE OUR ONLY CHANCE TO RESCUE CINDY AND GET THE TARDIS BACK TO NORMAL.
WE'LL EITHER BREAK FREE OR THE OLD GIRL WILL TEAR HERSELF APART TRYING.
LIKE I SAID--
STANDING BY.
DOCTOR... LI'L HELP HERE?
I'M ABOUT TO BE EATEN BY SOME MAD GODS...
I SEE YOU.
GABBY -- HIT THAT LEVER--

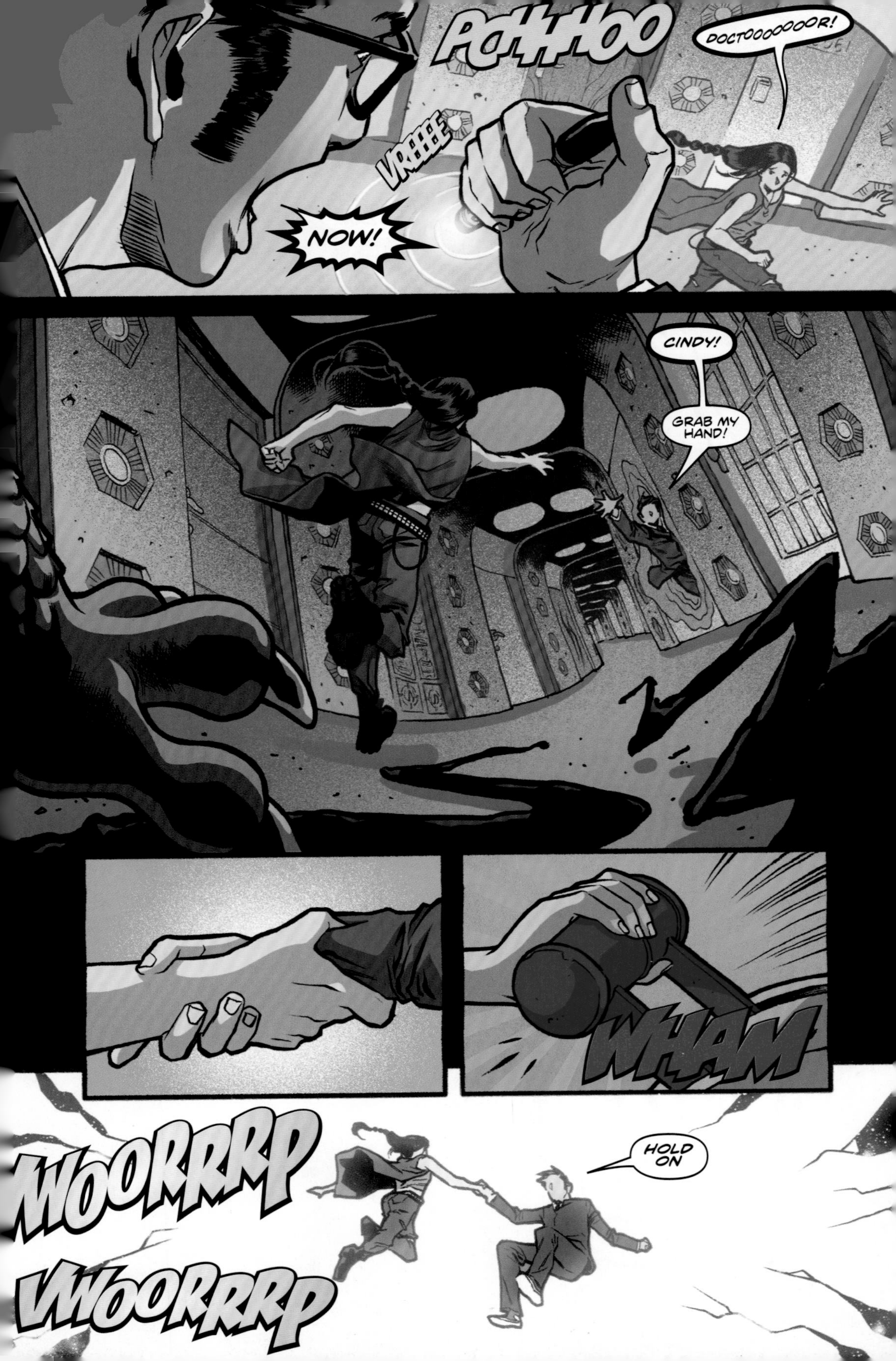
PCHHOO
DOCTOOOOOOOR!
VREEEE
NOW!
CINDY!
GRAB MY HAND!
WHAM
WOORRRP
VWOORRRP
HOLD ON

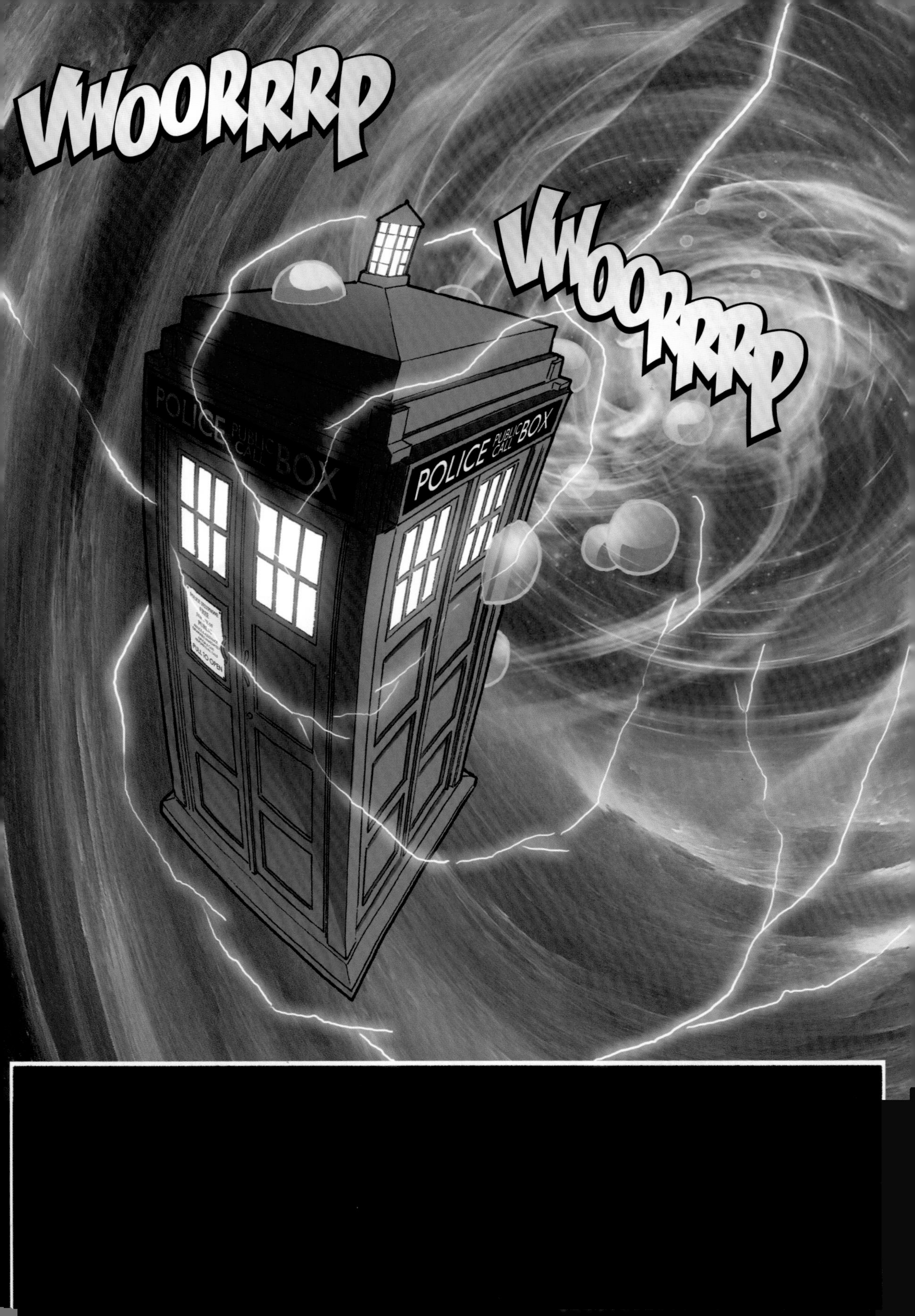
VWOORRRP
VWOORRRP
POLICE PUBLIC CALL BOX
POLICE PUBLIC CALL BOX
PULL TO OPEN

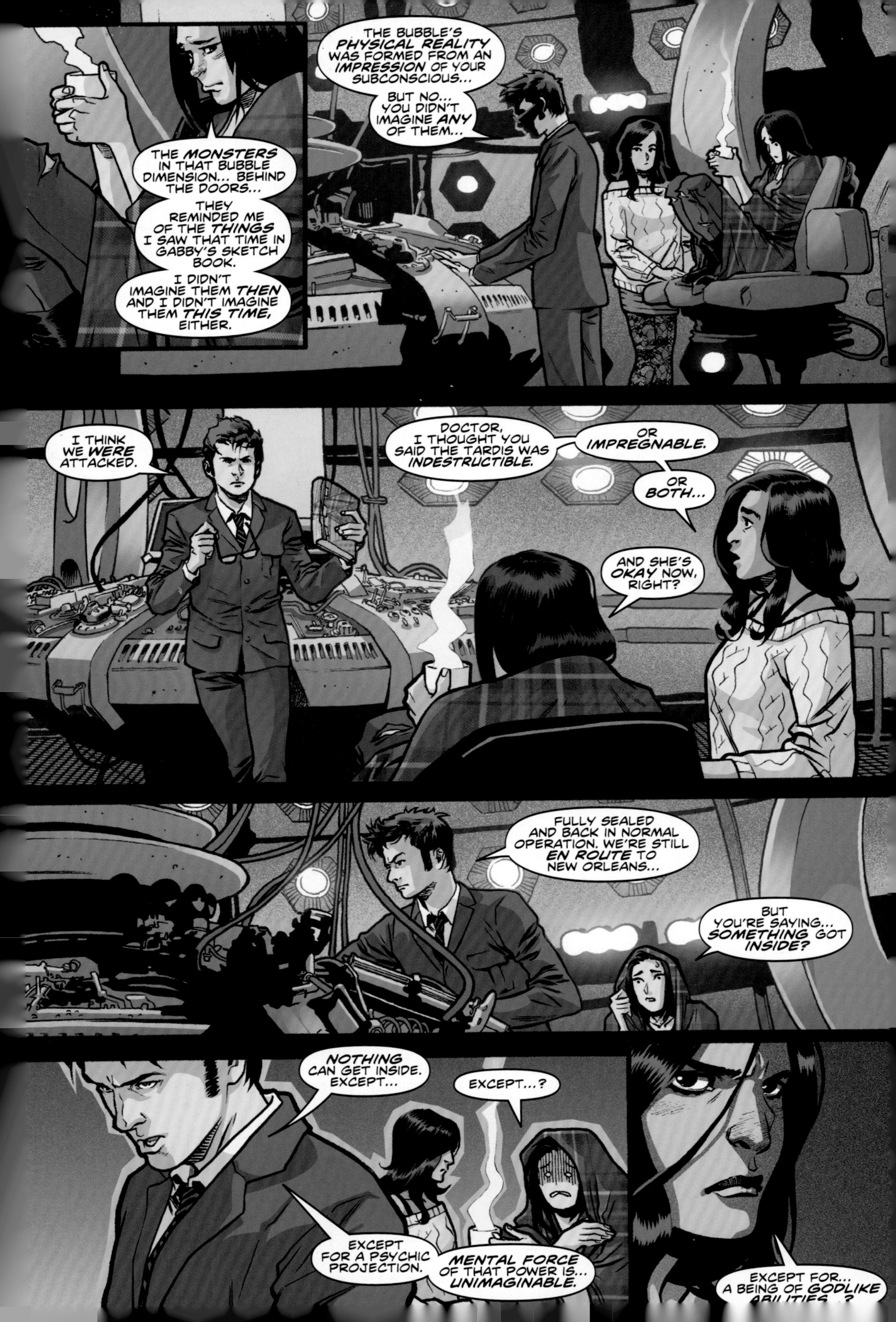
THE MONSTERS IN THAT BUBBLE DIMENSION... BEHIND THE DOORS...
THEY REMINDED ME OF THE THINGS I SAW THAT TIME IN GABBY'S SKETCH BOOK.
I DIDN'T IMAGINE THEM THEN AND I DIDN'T IMAGINE THEM THIS TIME, EITHER.
THE BUBBLE'S PHYSICAL REALITY WAS FORMED FROM AN IMPRESSION OF YOUR SUBCONSCIOUS...
BUT NO... YOU DIDN'T IMAGINE ANY OF THEM...
I THINK WE WERE ATTACKED.
DOCTOR, I THOUGHT YOU SAID THE TARDIS WAS INDESTRUCTIBLE.
OR IMPREGNABLE.
OR BOTH...
AND SHE'S OKAY NOW, RIGHT?
FULLY SEALED AND BACK IN NORMAL OPERATION. WE'RE STILL EN ROUTE TO NEW ORLEANS...
BUT YOU'RE SAYING... SOMETHING GOT INSIDE?
NOTHING CAN GET INSIDE. EXCEPT...
EXCEPT...?
EXCEPT FOR A PSYCHIC PROJECTION.
MENTAL FORCE OF THAT POWER IS... UNIMAGINABLE.
EXCEPT FOR... A BEING OF GODLIKE

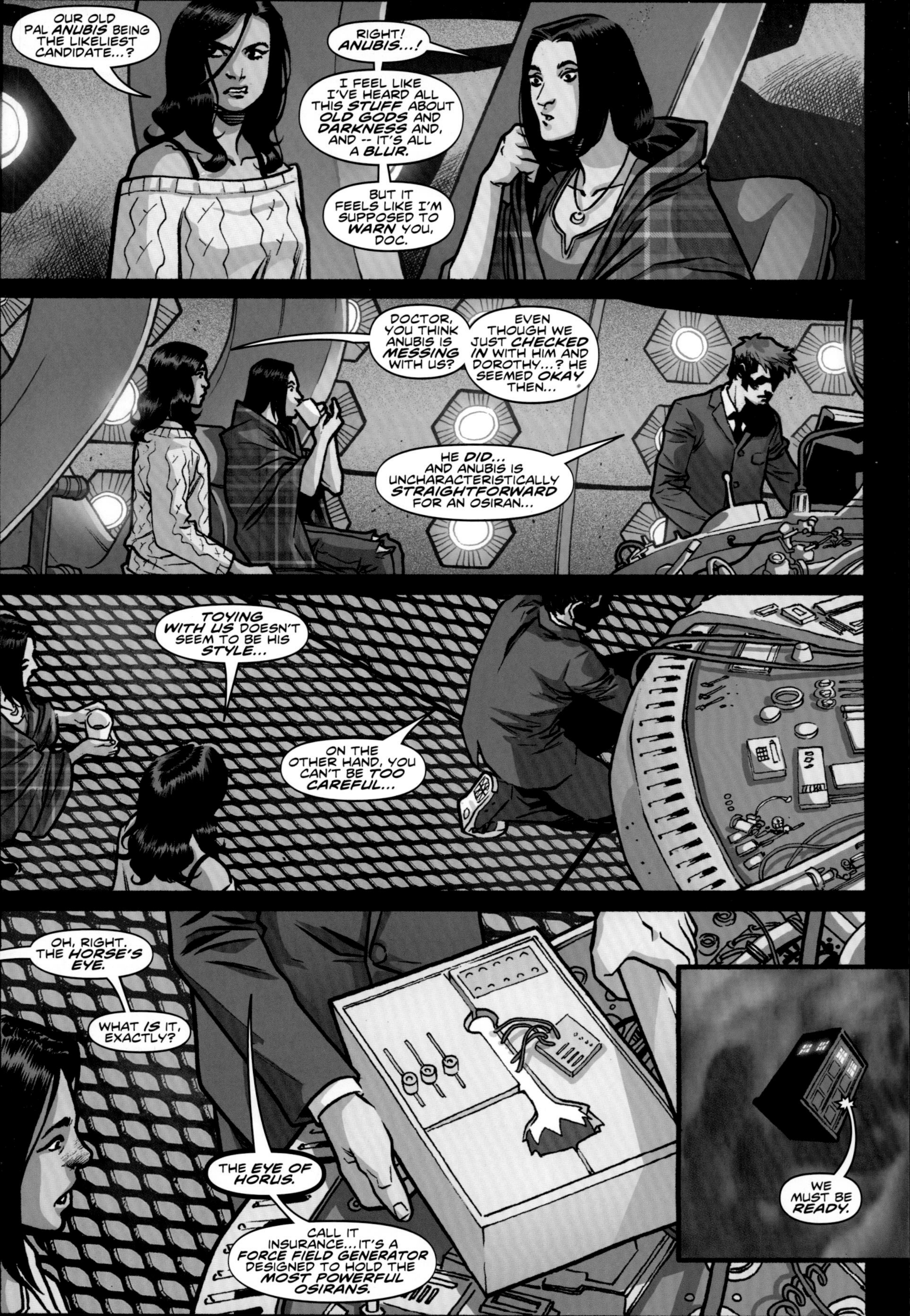
OUR OLD PAL ANUBIS BEING THE LIKELIEST CANDIDATE...?
RIGHT! ANUBIS...!
I FEEL LIKE I'VE HEARD ALL THIS STUFF ABOUT OLD GODS AND DARKNESS AND, AND -- IT'S ALL A BLUR.
BUT IT FEELS LIKE I'M SUPPOSED TO WARN YOU, DOC.
DOCTOR, YOU THINK ANUBIS IS MESSING WITH US?
EVEN THOUGH WE JUST CHECKED IN WITH HIM AND DOROTHY...? HE SEEMED OKAY THEN...
HE DID... AND ANUBIS IS UNCHARACTERISTICALLY STRAIGHTFORWARD FOR AN OSIRAN...
TOYING WITH US DOESN'T SEEM TO BE HIS STYLE...
ON THE OTHER HAND, YOU CAN'T BE TOO CAREFUL...
OH, RIGHT. THE HORSE'S EYE.
WHAT IS IT, EXACTLY?
THE EYE OF HORUS.
CALL IT INSURANCE...IT'S A FORCE FIELD GENERATOR DESIGNED TO HOLD THE MOST POWERFUL OSIRANS.
WE MUST BE READY.

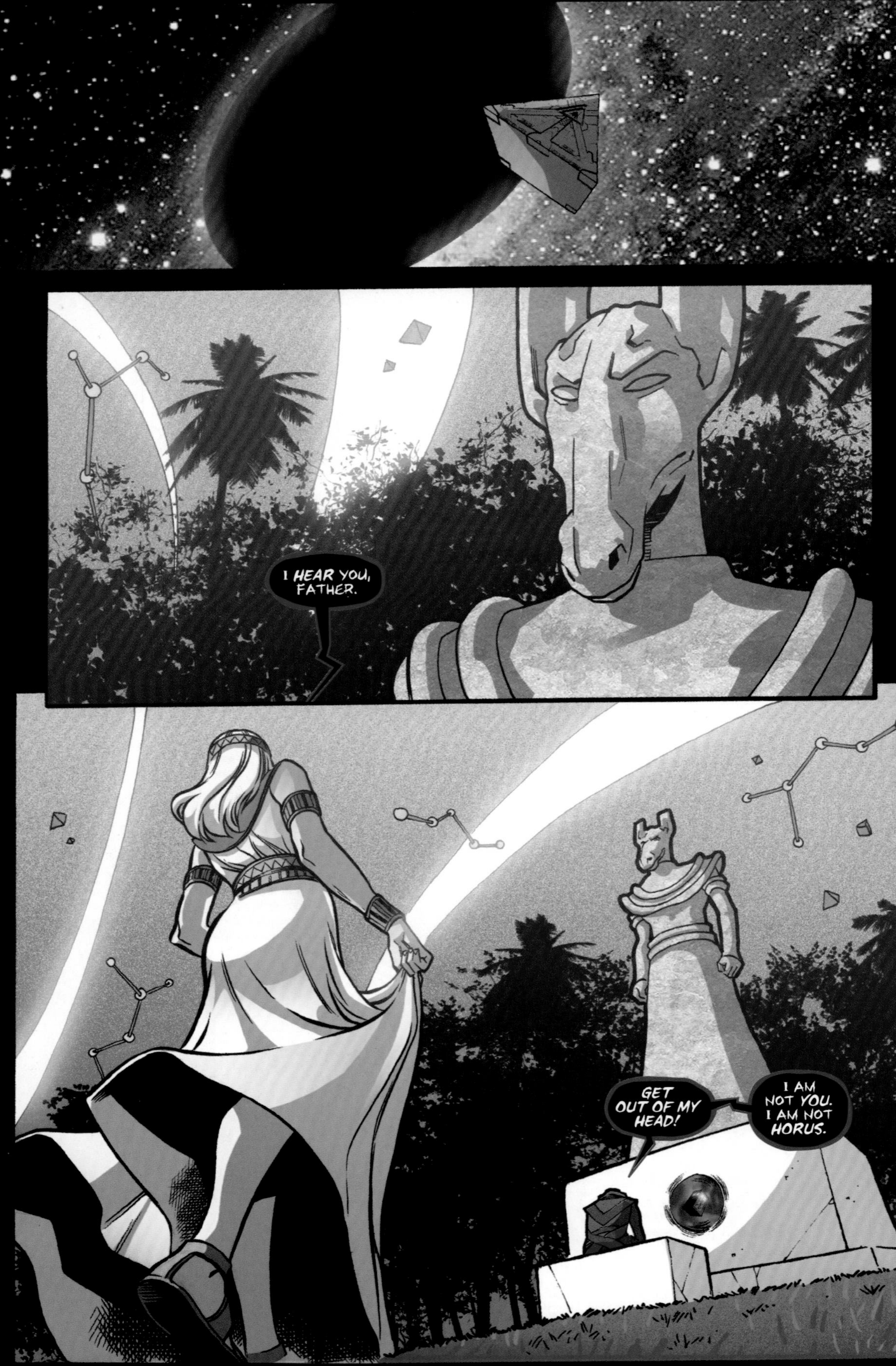
I HEAR YOU, FATHER.
GET OUT OF MY HEAD!
I AM NOT YOU. I AM NOT HORUS.

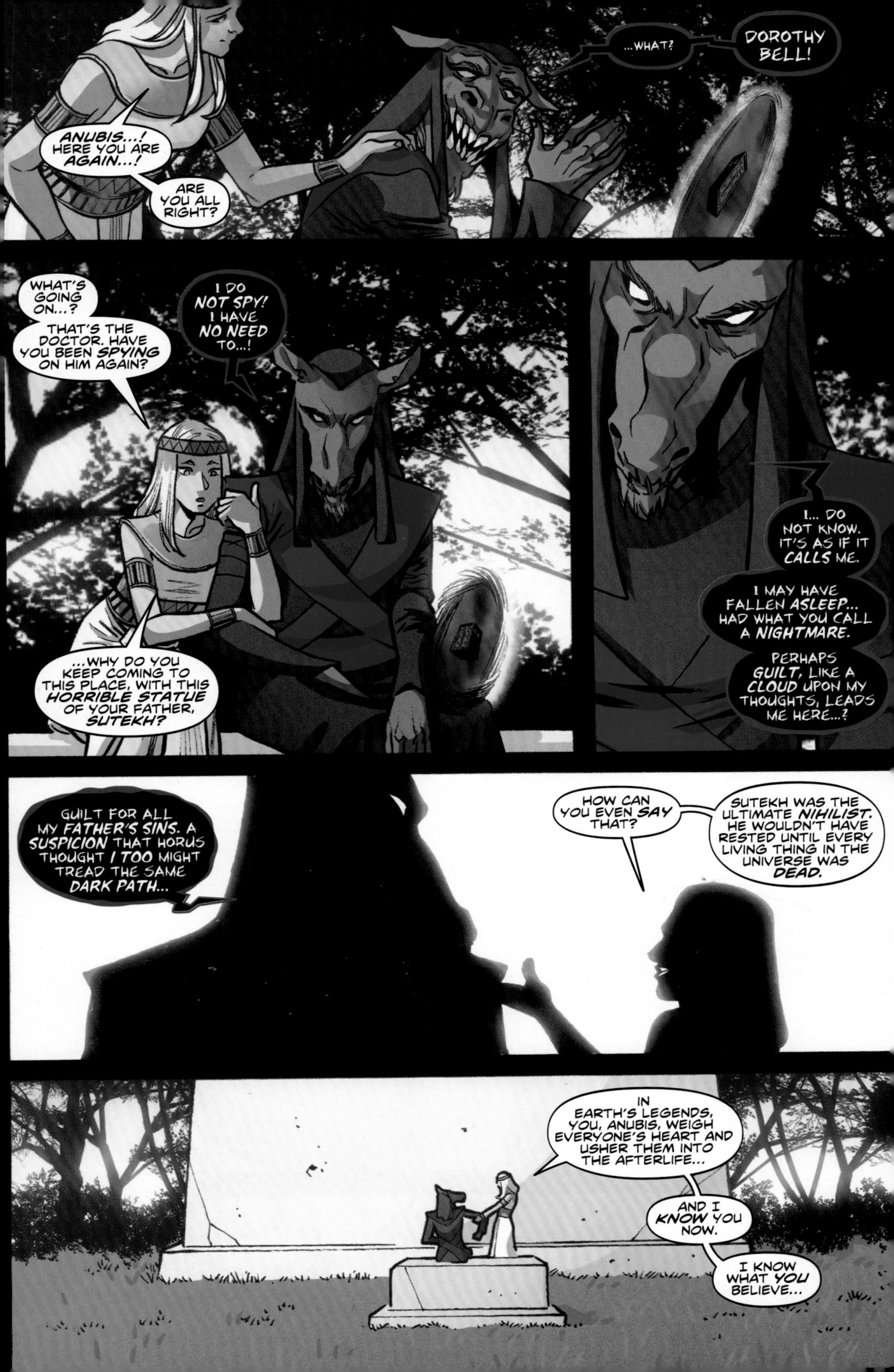

...WHAT?
DOROTHY BELL!
ANUBIS...! HERE YOU ARE AGAIN...!
ARE YOU ALL RIGHT?
WHAT'S GOING ON...?
THAT'S THE DOCTOR. HAVE YOU BEEN SPYING ON HIM AGAIN?
I DO NOT SPY! I HAVE NO NEED TO...!
...WHY DO YOU KEEP COMING TO THIS PLACE, WITH THIS HORRIBLE STATUE OF YOUR FATHER, SUTEKH?
I... DO NOT KNOW. IT'S AS IF IT CALLS ME.
I MAY HAVE FALLEN ASLEEP... HAD WHAT YOU CALL A NIGHTMARE.
PERHAPS GUILT, LIKE A CLOUD UPON MY THOUGHTS, LEADS ME HERE...?
GUILT FOR ALL MY FATHER'S SINS. A SUSPICION THAT HORUS THOUGHT I TOO MIGHT TREAD THE SAME DARK PATH...
HOW CAN YOU EVEN SAY THAT?
SUTEKH WAS THE ULTIMATE NIHILIST. HE WOULDN'T HAVE RESTED UNTIL EVERY LIVING THING IN THE UNIVERSE WAS DEAD.
IN EARTH'S LEGENDS, YOU, ANUBIS, WEIGH EVERYONE'S HEART AND USHER THEM INTO THE AFTERLIFE...
AND I KNOW YOU NOW.
I KNOW WHAT YOU BELIEVE...

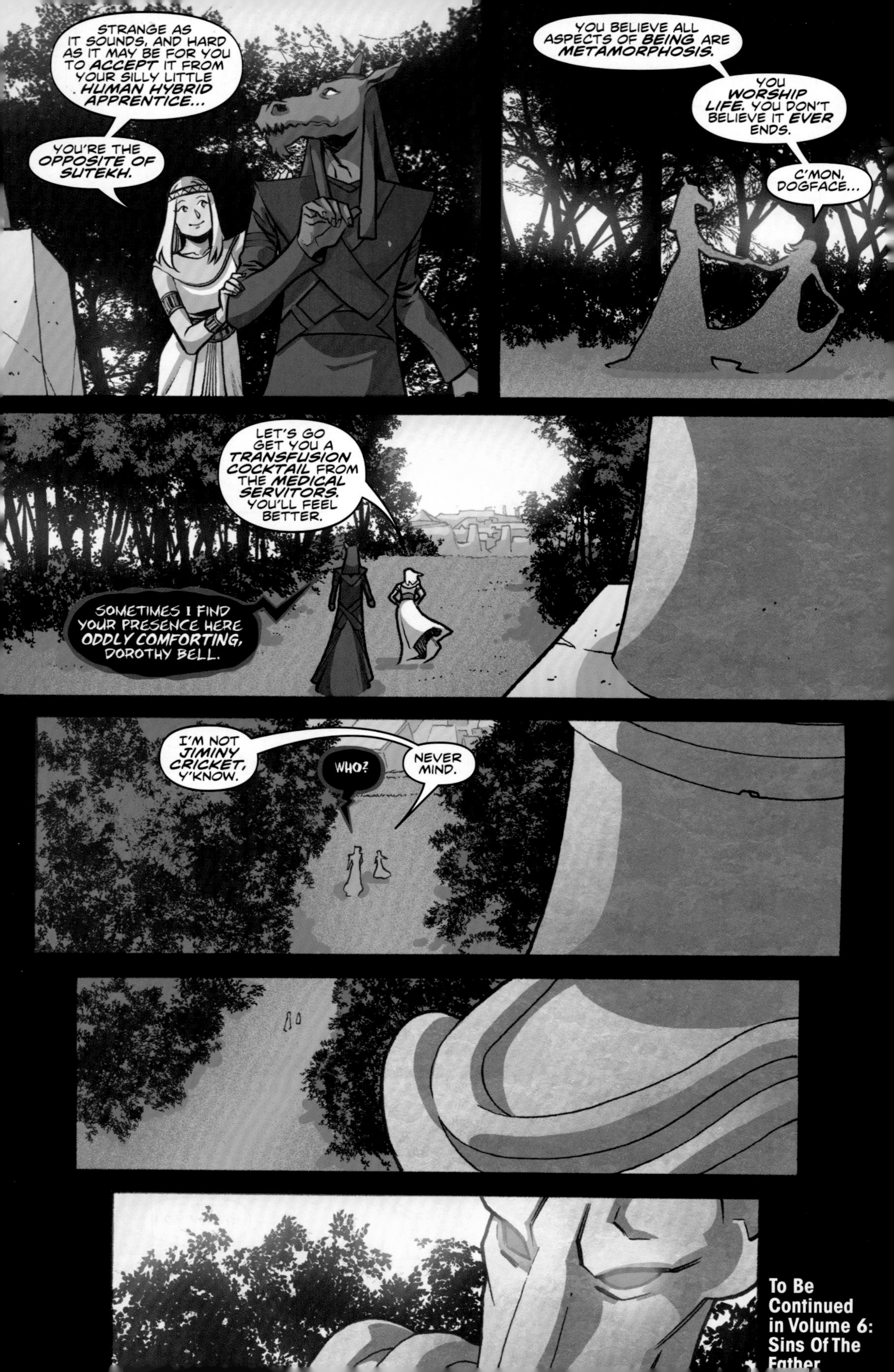
STRANGE AS IT SOUNDS, AND HARD AS IT MAY BE FOR YOU TO ACCEPT IT FROM YOUR SILLY LITTLE HUMAN HYBRID APPRENTICE...
YOU'RE THE OPPOSITE OF SUTEKH.
YOU BELIEVE ALL ASPECTS OF BEING ARE METAMORPHOSIS.
YOU WORSHIP LIFE. YOU DON'T BELIEVE IT EVER ENDS.
C'MON, DOGFACE...
LET'S GO GET YOU A TRANSFUSION COCKTAIL FROM THE MEDICAL SERVITORS. YOU'LL FEEL BETTER.
SOMETIMES I FIND YOUR PRESENCE HERE ODDLY COMFORTING, DOROTHY BELL.
I'M NOT JIMINY CRICKET, Y'KNOW.
WHO?
NEVER MIND.

To Be Continued in Volume 6: Sins Of The Father

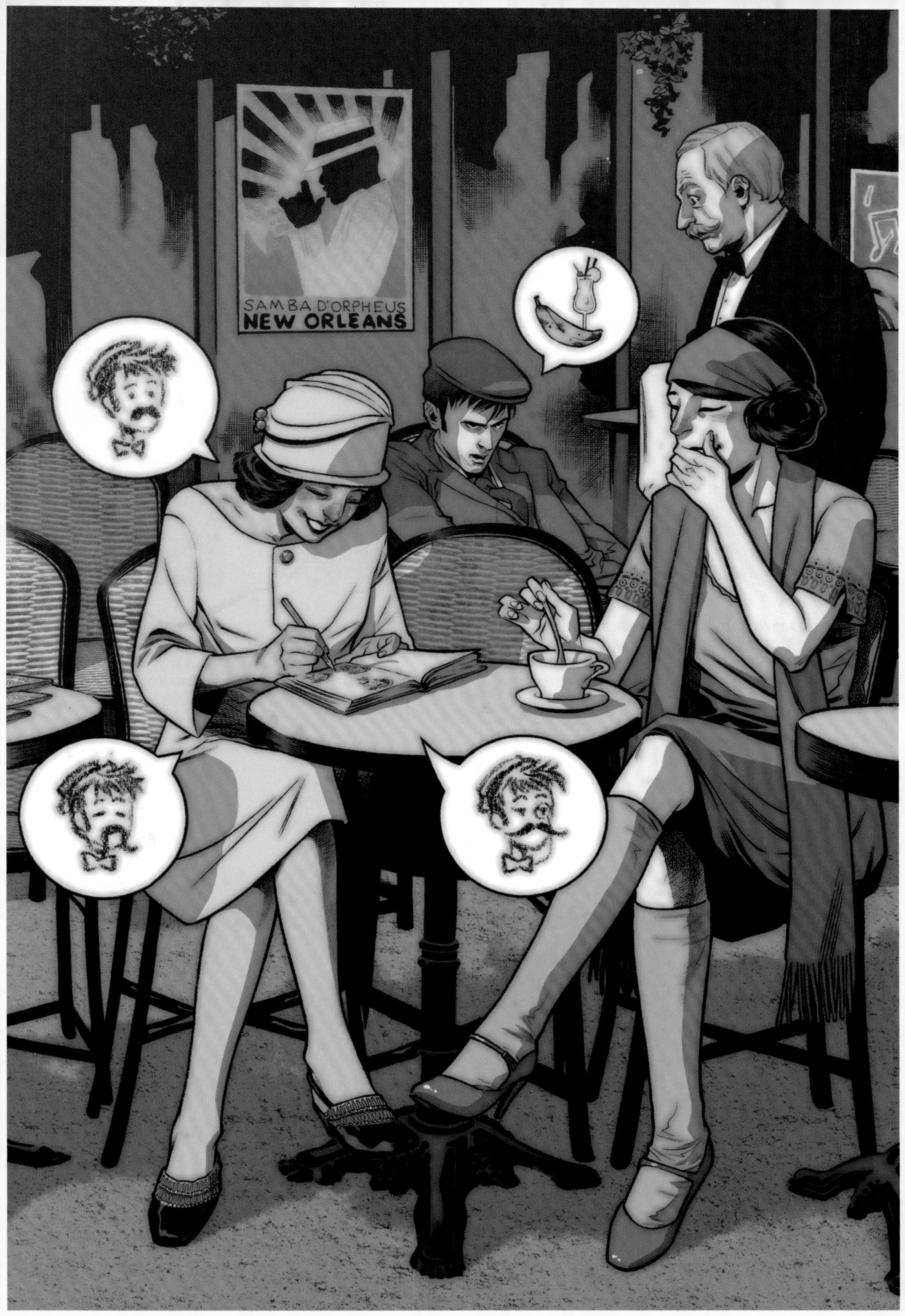
SAMBA D'ORPHEUS
NEW ORLEANS

FOLLOW YOUR FAVORITE INCARNATIONS ACROSS THESE FANTASTIC COLLECTIONS!

DOCTOR WHO: THE TWELFTH DOCTOR VOL. 1: TERRORFORMER

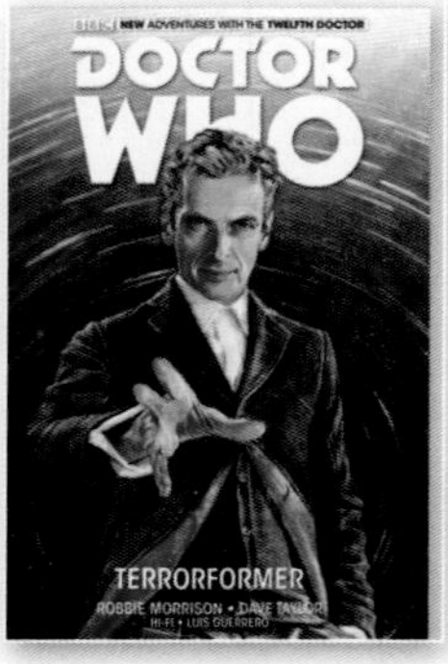
DOCTOR WHO
TERRORFORMER
ROBBIE MORRISON • DAVE TAYLOR

ISBN: 9781782761778
ON SALE NOW - $19.99 / $22.95 CAN / £10.99
(UK EDITION ISBN: 9781782763864)

DOCTOR WHO: THE TWELFTH DOCTOR VOL. 2: FRACTURES

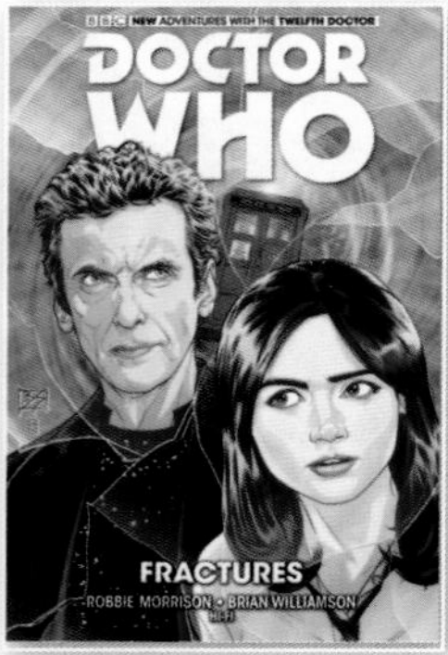
NEW ADVENTURES WITH THE TWELFTH DOCTOR
DOCTOR WHO
FRACTURES
ROBBIE MORRISON • BRIAN WILLIAMSON

ISBN: 9781782763017
ON SALE NOW - $19.99 / $25.99 CAN / £10.99
(UK EDITION ISBN: 9781782766599)

DOCTOR WHO: THE TWELFTH DOCTOR VOL. 3: HYPERION

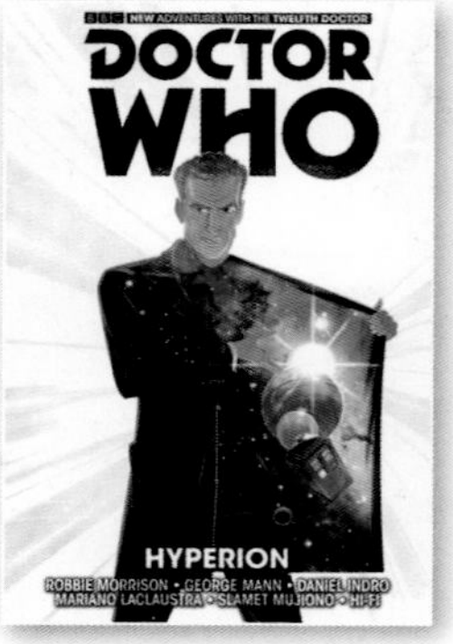
NEW ADVENTURES WITH THE TWELFTH DOCTOR
DOCTOR WHO
HYPERION
ROBBIE MORRISON • GEORGE MANN • DANIEL INDRO
MARIANO LACLAUSTRA • SLAMET MUJIONO • HI-FI

ISBN: 9781782767473
ON SALE NOW- $19.99 / $25.99 CAN / £10.99
(UK EDITION ISBN: 97817827674442)

DOCTOR WHO: THE TWELFTH DOCTOR VOL. 4: THE SCHOOL OF DEATH

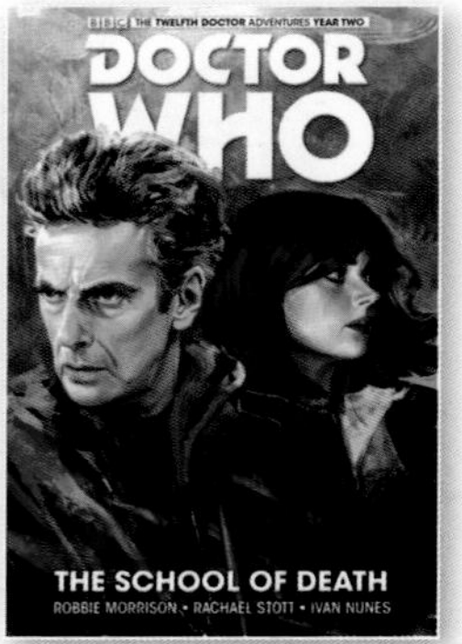
THE TWELFTH DOCTOR ADVENTURES YEAR TWO
DOCTOR WHO
THE SCHOOL OF DEATH
ROBBIE MORRISON • RACHAEL STOTT • IVAN NUNES

ISBN: 9781785851087
COMING SOON - $19.99 / $25.99 CAN / £10.99
(UK EDITION ISBN: 9781785851070)

DOCTOR WHO: THE ELEVENTH DOCTOR VOL. 1: AFTER LIFE

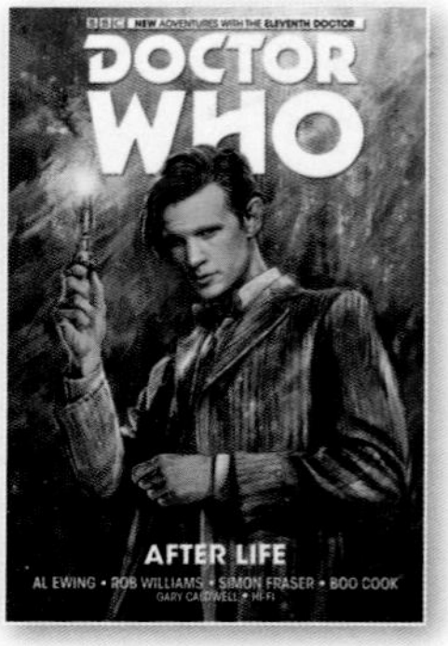
NEW ADVENTURES WITH THE ELEVENTH DOCTOR
DOCTOR WHO
AFTER LIFE
AL EWING • ROB WILLIAMS • SIMON FRASER • BOO COOK

ISBN: 9781782761747
ON SALE NOW - $19.99 / $22.95 CAN / £10.99
(UK EDITION ISBN: 9781782763857)

DOCTOR WHO: THE ELEVENTH DOCTOR VOL. 2: SERVE YOU

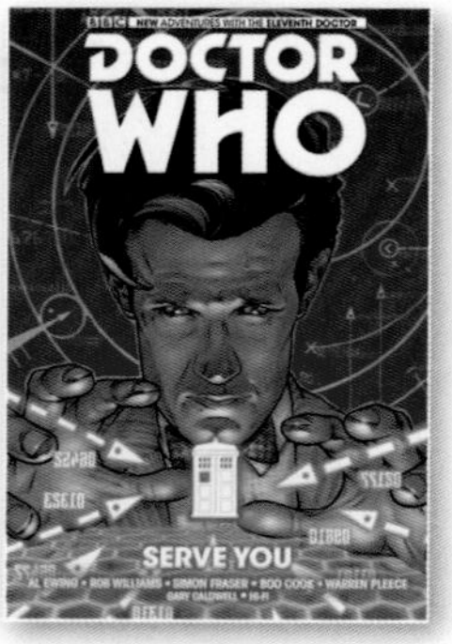
NEW ADVENTURES WITH THE ELEVENTH DOCTOR
DOCTOR WHO
SERVE YOU

ISBN: 9781782761754
ON SALE NOW - $19.99 / $25.99 CAN / £10.99
(UK EDITION ISBN: 9781782766582)

DOCTOR WHO: THE ELEVENTH DOCTOR VOL. 3: CONVERSION

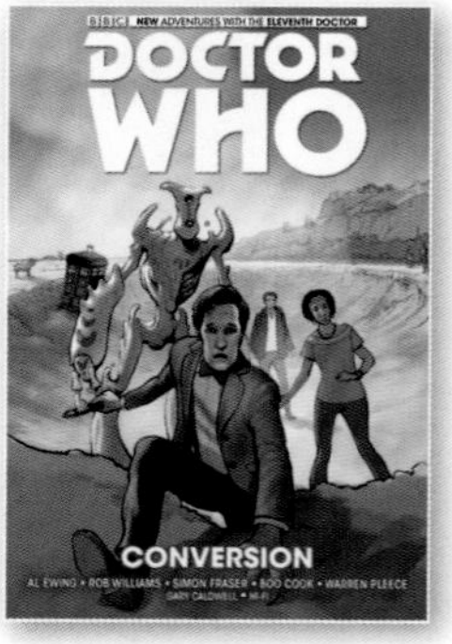
NEW ADVENTURES WITH THE ELEVENTH DOCTOR
DOCTOR WHO
CONVERSION

ISBN: 9781782763024
ON SALE NOW - $19.99 / $25.99 CAN / £10.99
(UK EDITION ISBN: 9781782767435)

DOCTOR WHO: THE ELEVENTH DOCTOR VOL. 4: THE THEN AND THE NOW

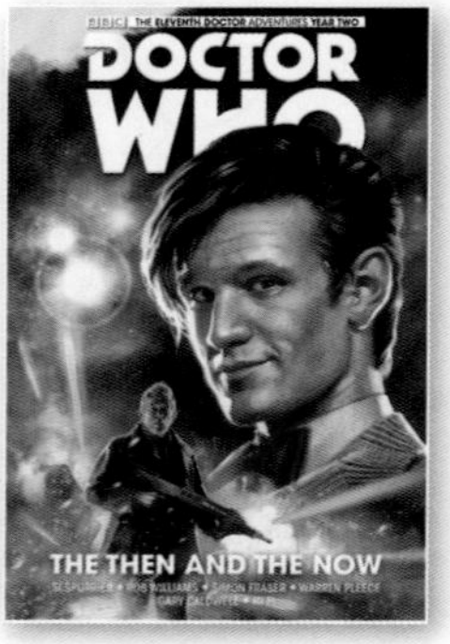
THE ELEVENTH DOCTOR ADVENTURES YEAR TWO
DOCTOR WHO
THE THEN AND THE NOW

ISBN: 9781782767466
ON SALE NOW - $19.99 / $25.99 CAN / £10.99
(UK EDITION ISBN: 9781722767428)

For information on how to subscribe to our great Doctor Who titles, or to purchase them digitally for your favorite device, visit:

WWW.TITAN-COMICS.COM

TITAN COMICS

COMPLETE YOUR COLLECTION!

DOCTOR WHO: THE TENTH DOCTOR VOL. 1: REVOLUTIONS OF TERROR

BBC NEW ADVENTURES WITH THE TENTH DOCTOR
DOCTOR WHO
REVOLUTIONS OF TERROR
NICK ABADZIS • ELENA CASAGRANDE • ARIANNA FLOREAN

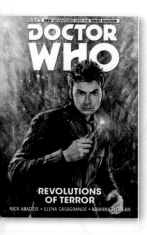

ISBN: 9781782761747
ON SALE NOW - $19.99 / $22.95 CAN / £10.99
(UK EDITION ISBN: 9781782763840)

DOCTOR WHO: THE TENTH DOCTOR VOL. 2: THE WEEPING ANGELS OF MONS

BBC NEW ADVENTURES WITH THE TENTH DOCTOR
DOCTOR WHO
THE WEEPING ANGELS OF MONS
ROBBIE MORRISON • DANIEL INDRO • ELENA CASAGRANDE
SLAMET MUJIONO • ARIANNA FLOREAN

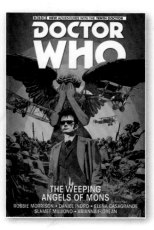

ISBN: 9781782761754
ON SALE NOW - $19.99 / $25.99 CAN / £10.99
(UK EDITION ISBN: 9781782766575)

DOCTOR WHO: THE TENTH DOCTOR VOL. 3: THE FOUNTAINS OF FOREVER

BBC NEW ADVENTURES WITH THE TENTH DOCTOR
DOCTOR WHO
THE FOUNTAINS OF FOREVER
NICK ABADZIS • ELENA CASAGRANDE
ELEONORA CARLINI • ARIANNA FLOREAN

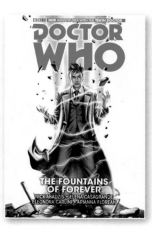

ISBN: 9781782763024
ON SALE NOW - $19.99 / $25.99 CAN / £10.99
(UK EDITION ISBN: 9781782767435)

DOCTOR WHO: THE TENTH DOCTOR VOL. 4: THE ENDLESS SONG

BBC THE TENTH DOCTOR ADVENTURES YEAR TWO
DOCTOR WHO
THE ENDLESS SONG
NICK ABADZIS • ELENA CASAGRANDE • ELEONORA CARLINI
ARIANNA FLOREAN • CLAUDIA SG IANNICELLO

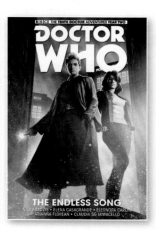

ISBN: 9781785854286
ON SALE NOW - $19.99 / $25.99 CAN / £10.99
(SC ISBN: 9781785853227)

DOCTOR WHO: THE NINTH DOCTOR VOL. 1: WEAPONS OF PAST DESTRUCTION

BBC NEW ADVENTURES WITH THE NINTH DOCTOR
DOCTOR WHO
WEAPONS OF PAST DESTRUCTION
CAVAN SCOTT • BLAIR SHEDD

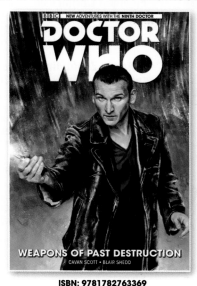

ISBN: 9781782763369
ON SALE NOW - $19.99 / $25.99 CAN / £10.99
(UK EDITION ISBN: 9781782761056)

DOCTOR WHO EVENT 2015 FOUR DOCTORS

BBC A DOCTOR WHO COMICS EVENT
DOCTOR WHO
PAUL CORNELL I NEIL EDWARDS
FOUR DOCTORS
WITH IVAN NUNES AND COMICRAFT

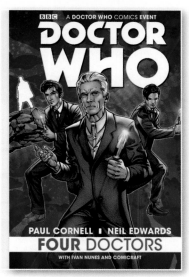

ISBN: 9781782765967
ON SALE NOW - $19.99 / $25.99 CAN / £10.99
(UK EDITION ISBN: 9781785851063)

AVAILABLE IN ALL GOOD COMIC STORES, BOOK STORES, AND DIGITAL PROVIDERS!

BBC

BIOGRAPHIES

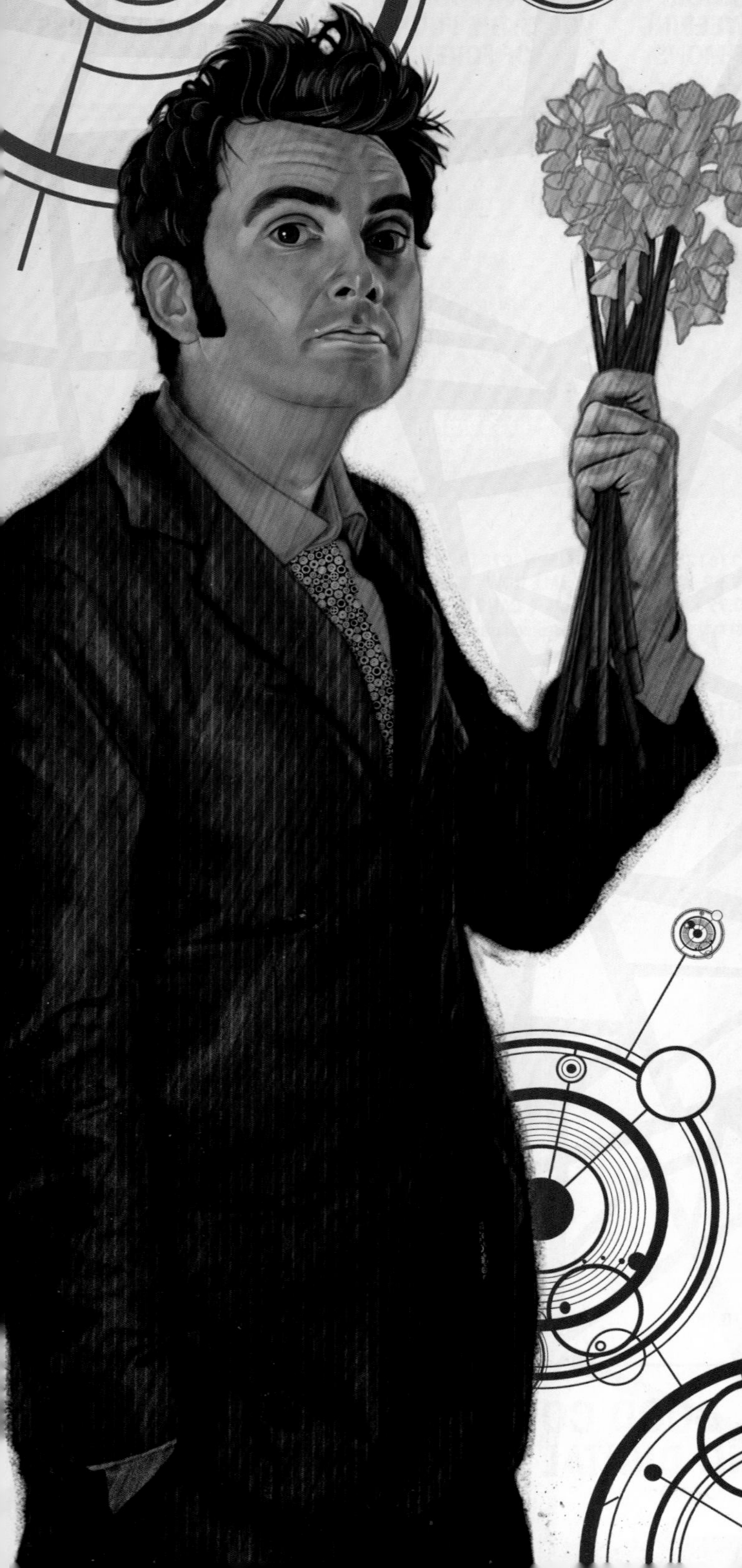

Nick Abadzis was born in Sweden to Greek and British parents and was brought up in England and Switzerland. He has been writing and drawing comics and graphic novels for over twenty-five years. His work has appeared in numerous books and periodicals around the world and he has been honored with various international storytelling awards, including an Eisner for his 2007 graphic novel, *Laika*. He lives in the USA with his wife and daughter.

Elena Casagrande has worked on titles as varied as *Hulk, Angel, Star Trek* and *The X-Files*. As well as drawing *Doctor Who*, she is best known for *Suicide Risk*, her creator-owned series with Mike Carey. She lives in Italy, where she works forty-eight hours a day and never sleeps.

Arianna Florean is Elena's preferred colorist, and has joined her on her many art adventures. A talented artist and cartoonist in her own right, Arianna lives and works in Rome, Italy, where she keeps pace with Elena without complaint.

Eleonora Carlini is an Italian artist on the rise, with her most recent high-profile appearance being in DC's *Batgirl*.

Iolanda Zanfardino is an Italian artist and newcomer to comics, and one who is going to go far.

Hi-Fi Colour Design was founded in 1998 by Brian and Kristy Miller and provides digital color for comic books, toys, video games, and animation, and tutorials on color through masterdigitalcolor.com.

Rodrigo Fernandes is a talented comic book colorist from Brazil.